Photography Performing Humor

Paulien Oltheten

La Défense, The Venturing Gaze
Selection of 3 video stills, total duration 42 min
2017 – 2018

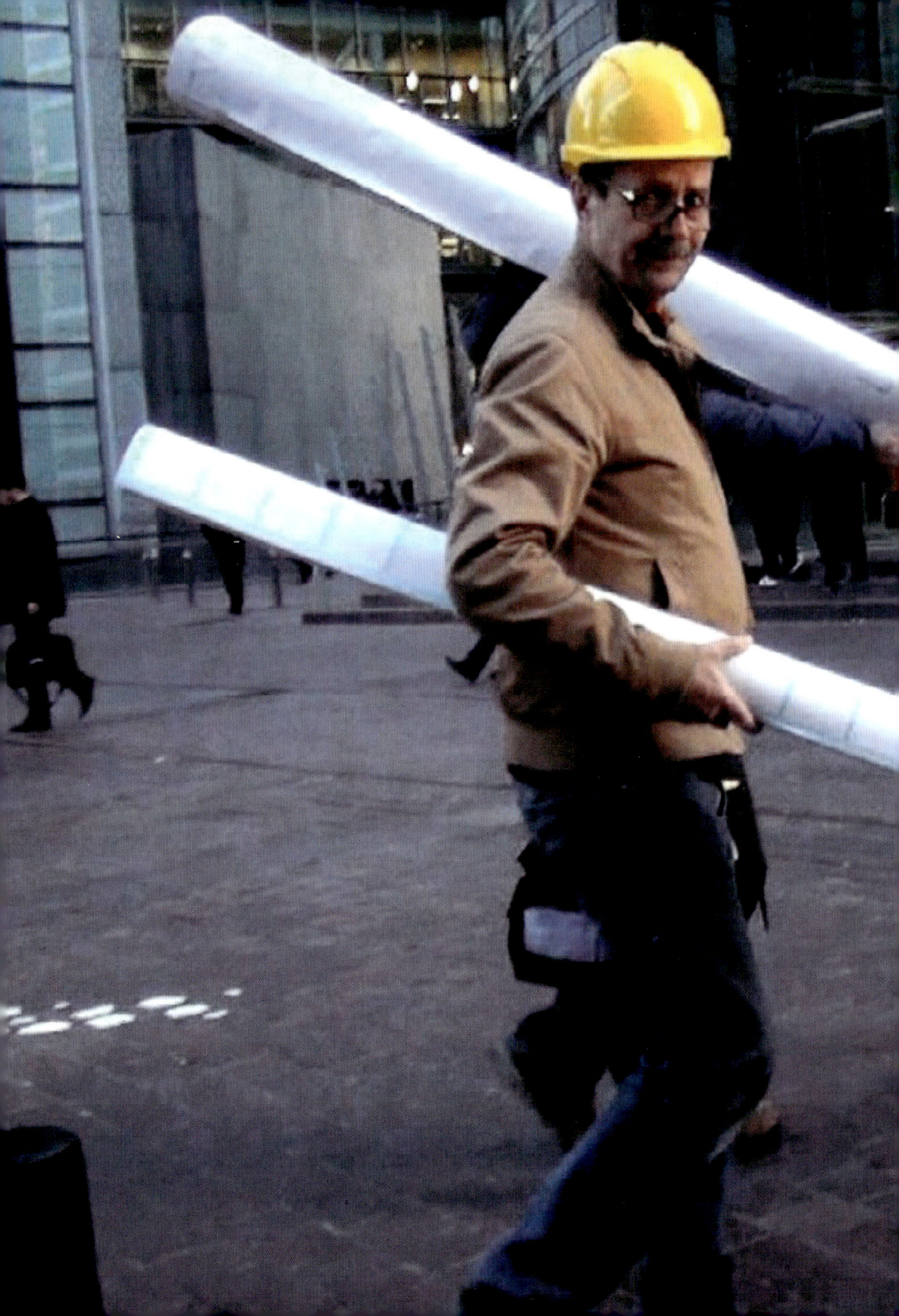

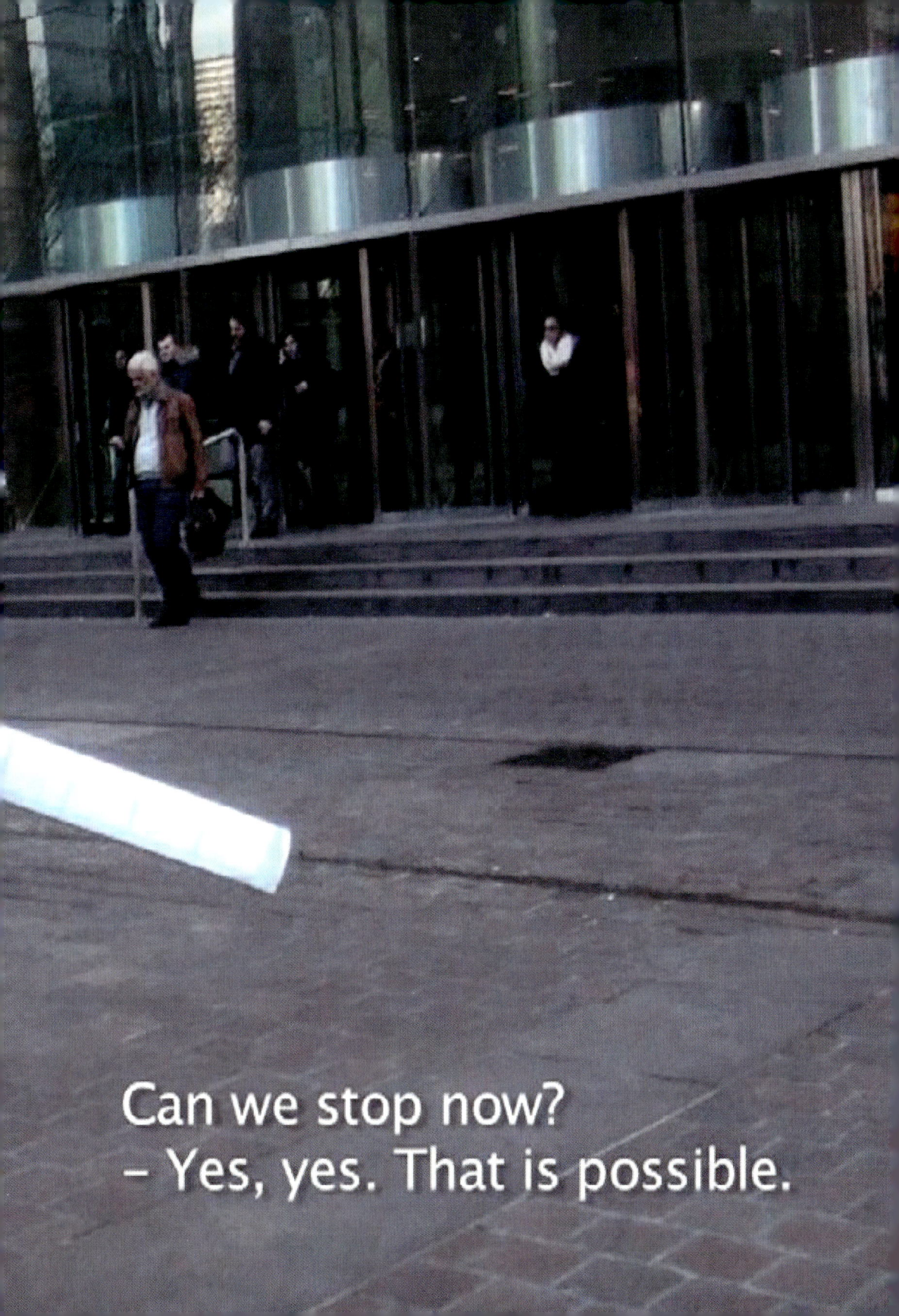

Can we stop now?
– Yes, yes. That is possible.

Okay like this?
Do you need more, or...

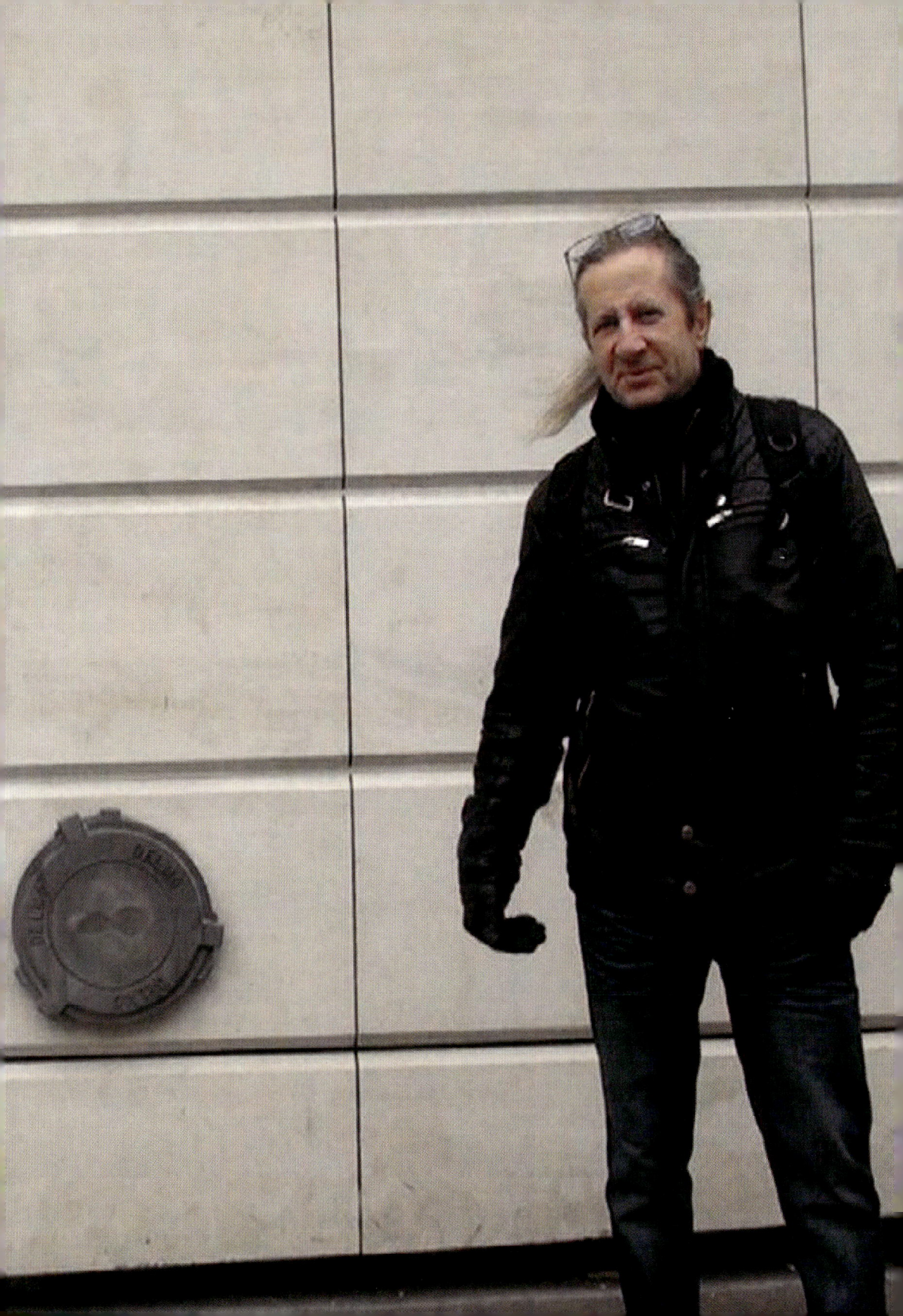

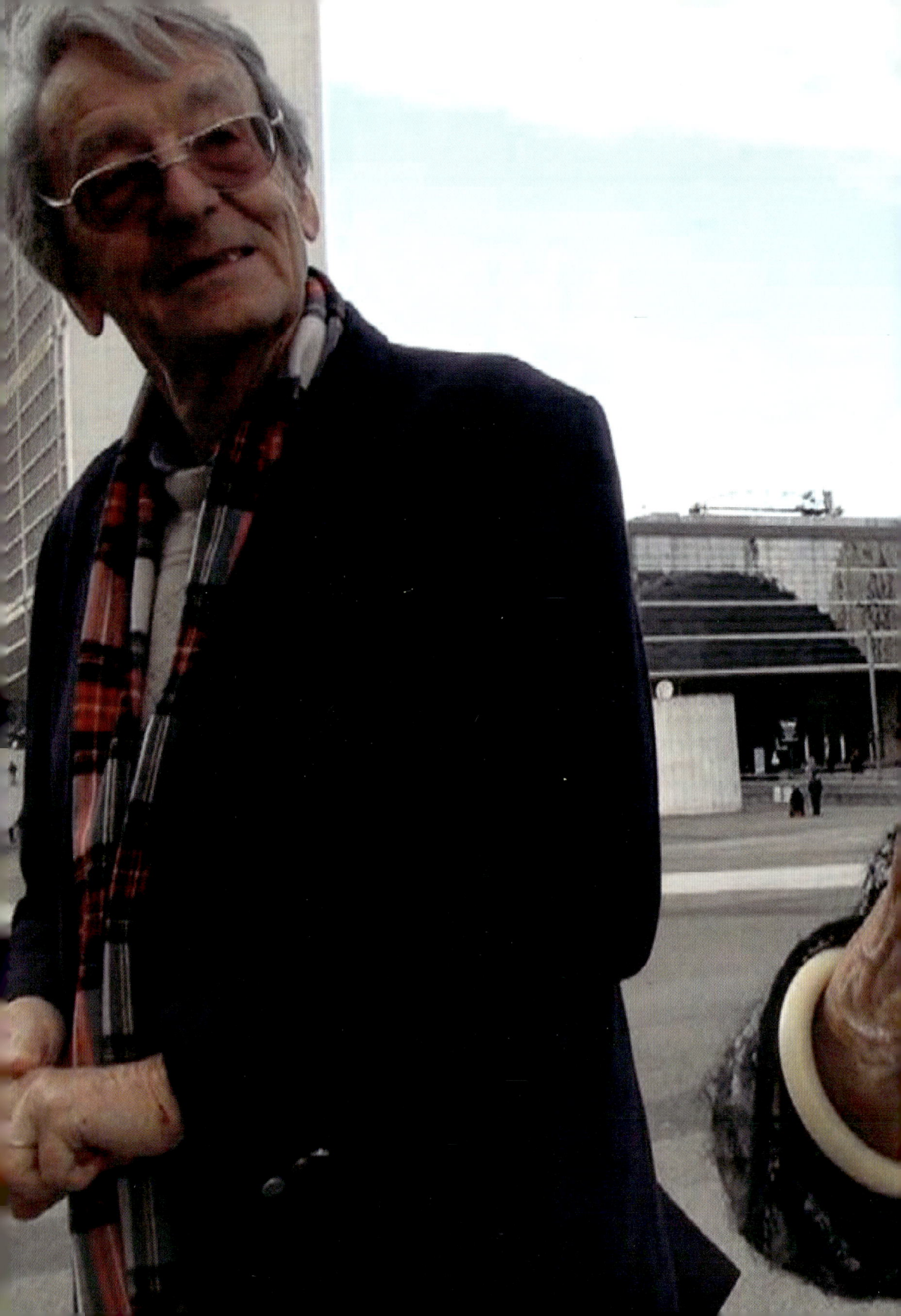

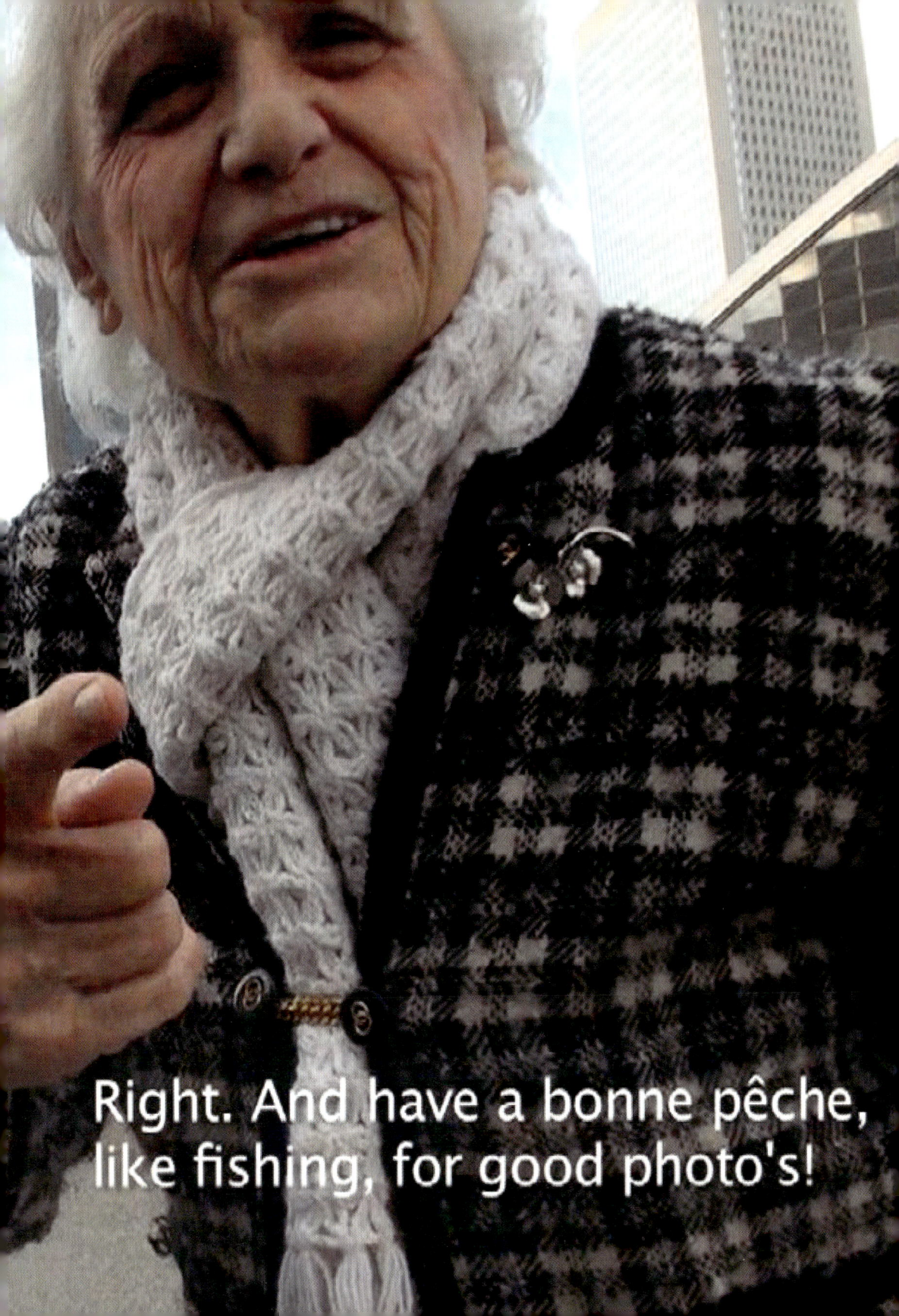

Right. And have a bonne pêche,
like fishing, for good photo's!

Thanks a lot!

To Luka and Jon

The Lieven Gevaert Series is a major series of substantial and innovative books on photography. Launched in 2004, the Series takes into account the ubiquitous presence of photography within modern culture and, in particular, the visual arts. At the forefront of contemporary thinking on photography, the books offer new insights on the position of the photographic medium within art historical, theoretical, social and institutional contexts.

The Series is produced by the Lieven Gevaert Research Centre for Photography, Art and Visual Culture (www.lievengevaertcentre.be) and covers four types of approaches: publication of outstanding monographic studies, proceedings of international conferences, book length projects with artists, translations and republications of classic material.

The Lieven Gevaert Series is published by Leuven University Press, and distributed in North America by Cornell University Press.

Photography Performing Humor

Edited by Mieke Bleyen and Liesbeth Decan

Leuven University Press

Contents

Part III
Photographic Wit in Conceptual Art

Acknowledgements

While it is certainly not uncommon to encounter friendship at university, rare is the opportunity to collaborate closely with someone with whom you have bonded for almost two decades of study and research (bachelor, master, PhD and post doc). We are grateful for this unique experience of complete trust, mutual respect and the untold rule that in times of need the other would always back you up, no matter what. However, as the list of authors suggests, this volume is hardly the project of two women alone. We are grateful for the shared enthusiasm, the keen insights and new perspectives offered by all authors and artists present in this volume and throughout the whole project.

We would like to extend special thanks to OPaK, the Research Platform for the Arts of LUCA School of Arts for granting us the research funds that enabled us to produce two exhibitions, a series of master seminars, a conference, and finally — the proceedings from the conference — this book. We are indebted to Sint-Lukasgalerie, LUCA School of Arts Brussels and Het Vlaams-Nederlands Huis de Buren for putting their spaces at our disposal, as well as to the Lieven Gevaert Leerstoel and the Lieven Gevaert Centre's research project Art Against the Grain of "Collective Sisyphus": The Case of Allan Sekula's Ship of Fools / The Dockers' Museum (2010-2013), funded by KU Leuven and the Research Foundation-Flanders (FWO), for additional funding.

We have been fortunate to be surrounded by a group of fantastic colleagues who have supported us especially during times of misfortune, such as when our conference needed to be postponed at the last minute due to terror attacks. A special word of gratitude goes to the staff and students of the photography department of LUCA School of Arts Brussels, who magically turned the photo studio into a real conference room, and the Cultural Studies team of KU Leuven.

We could never thank enough the two magnificent editors of the Lieven Gevaert Series, Hilde Van Gelder and Alexander Streitberger, who have been waving pillars of support for us, and the staff of Leuven University Press for engaging in a smooth publishing process.

Finally, we thank our close friends and our families.

Introduction

Mieke Bleyen & Liesbeth Decan

Our encounter with the silly, clumsy and at the same time smart photographic works made by Belgian Surrealist and Conceptual artists — Marcel Mariën and Jacques Lizène in particular — triggered us to study the relationship between humor, the medium of photography, and the aspect of performance, which eventually led to the current edited volume. (Bleyen, 2014; Decan, 2016) For these practices left us with a whole range of questions: where precisely do we locate the humor in these images, what is it in them that makes them "funny" and not for instance "uncanny"; to what extent does the humor in staged photographs differ from the humor in found situations such as in street photography and the decisive moment tradition; how does the performing body in the image affect the receiving body of the spectator; and how does the medium itself — photography — actively contribute to the joke work? How does the choice for the single image or the sequence play with the tension between duration (the building up of a joke) and the instantaneous (the joke hitting its target); what or who does the photograph invite us to laugh with/at; what or who is being torn down, elevated, or in a carnivalesque way turned upside down, and how does this relate to the politics of the image?

Looking for some answers in the existing literature, it quickly became clear that although humor is omnipresent in vernacular, professional as well as artistic photographic practices — Tower of Pisa jokes, humor in advertisement, and the photographic prank work of the historical avant-gardes here come easily to mind — the phenomenon has received little scholarly attention. More ink has been spilled in recent years on the subject in the visual arts. Jennifer Higgie's *The Artist's Joke* (2007), Sherrie Klein's *Art and Laughter* (2006), and Felicity Lunn's *When Humour becomes Painful* (2006) are but a few examples of a recent curatorial and scholarly interest in the use of humor in (especially modern and contemporary) works of art. These volumes and exhibition catalogues offer multiple inspiring case studies, quotes and artists' interviews. However, the theoretical or methodological implications of this new focus on the humorous remain sparse. Hence we were thrilled to read Louis Kaplan's *Photography and Humour* (2016), which offers the first and most welcome comprehensive study on humor in the field of photography research. Kaplan treats both photography and humor as firmly anchored in social practice and deliberately focuses on the manifold ways photographs make fun of the medium's key social functions. Covering a wide range of practices from photography's earliest days to the digital practices of today, he explores how humor destabilizes photography's role in identity formation and identification, in the building of social cohesion and being-togetherness, and, finally, how a darker, "morbid sense of humor" laughs in the face of photography's intimate relationship to death. (10)

We gladly follow in Kaplan's footsteps and are proud to include in this volume new material from his hand. We are also happy to complicate and enrich Kaplan's narrative, with its ambition to "constitute a canon of representative images," (9) by offering close readings of local photographic productions within European nations and regions that have remained until today less explored, especially in an international context. But more in general, our book has a slightly different accent, with its focus—as the title suggests—on the performative dimension within photographic humor. Our interest lies both in the performance done in front of the camera, often specifically created *for* the camera, and in the performative work done *by* the medium itself. In that sense, we are interested in how photography, defined by Sarah Kember and Joanna Zylinska as an "active practice of cutting through the flow of mediation," produces laughter and how—to borrow with Esther Leslie from Walter Benjamin—photography, due to its "shattering" qualities, turns into a privileged medium for eliciting humorous effects. (Kember and Zylinska, 2012: 72)

The focus on performativity, moreover, emphasizes the *affective* component of photography or its ability to touch, move and bring something about in the spectator. In that sense this volume attests to the larger affective turn in the humanities, (Cough and Halley 2007) which in recent years also started to resonate in photography research. Hence, after the much needed critical move towards "thinking photography" in the 1980s, (Burgin, 1982; Sekula, 1984; Tagg, 1988) the new Millennium started to shift the focus to that of "feeling photography," (Brown and Phu, 2014) inviting scholars to address the material, tactile, affective and performative qualities of photographs (see also Batchen, 2002; Edwards, 2001; Phu and Steer, 2009) and to readdress the ethical and ontological questions that were already raised in some of photography theory's foundational texts such as Sontag's *On Photography* (1977) and Barthes' *Camera Lucida* (1980). In line with these seminal texts, however, the focus has remained largely on photographic representations of suffering, trauma and loss. Given the fact that one of the central metaphors for the affective quality of the medium, Barthes' punctum, relates affect to being wounded, this comes of course as no surprise. By addressing humor and laughter, this volume resolutely chooses to elaborate a lighter, yet not always less serious side of photography and aims to map different strategies and practices.

As the opening lines of this text suggests, our motivation for tackling the question of humor originated from a practical need to deal with photographic corpuses that confronted us with the limitations of our own conceptual framework. This made us realize that dealing with humor is a tricky business, for one always faces the risk of either expelling oneself from the serious discipline of academic writing by tackling a subject seemingly too removed from the field of seriousness, or killing the artwork and the laughter it evokes by dragging it in the cold world of academic rigor and stiffness. Moreover, discussing photography from a "humor" perspective is almost an impossible undertaking. It is one thing to recognize a humorous photograph when you see it; it is another thing to formulate a (theoretical) argument around it. As we all know, to explain a joke is to ruin it and one could extend this more generally to the whole discipline of photography history and theory and the way it neutralizes much of the image's affective charge by turning an experience of punctum into studium, to refer once again to Barthes. Humor, experienced often fleetingly and in a bodily manner, presents itself as an obstacle to analysis, slipping through one's fingers the very moment one tries to capture it.

Does this problem leave us with nothing to write? Obviously, we think otherwise. Precisely because humor has this slippery or, to refer to the article by Martins & Corrigan, "fugitive" quality, it urges us to confront the rigidity of our existing disciplinary frameworks with their established sets of rules, procedures and forms of knowledge. As artist Lieven Segers, present in the artist's pages of this book, explored during his PhD research on humor in visual arts, entitled *The joke is on me* (2015), humor is often best tackled by not going straight at it, but by taking a detour. It is only by losing one's way and by looking obliquely that one may find an entrance to it. Dealing with humor thus necessarily entails a form of failure — something that in our present day and time, with its focus on winning and success, may seem a futile enterprise.

We found inspiration in and align ourselves to the project of Jack/Judith Halberstam's *The Queer Art of Failure* (2011), which argues that it is only by getting lost that new paths open themselves and alternative visions and futures can be imagined. As a believer in low theory and a rebel against disciplinary rigor, Halberstam builds his argument on the silly archives of amongst others animation movies, arguing that "under certain circumstances failing, losing, forgetting, unmaking, undoing, unbecoming, not knowing may in fact offer more creative, more cooperative, more surprising ways of being in the world." (2–3) The example of the stumbling man in Henri Bergson's famous *Laughter* essay demonstrates how falling (and failure) may very well be one of humor's primal scenes. (Bergson, 1900/2014) For many of the artists-photographers represented in this book, falling and failing precisely offer a valuable alternative for the formulas of success (economically, artistically and socio-politically) and often signal a form of resistance or even plain refusal to accommodate to the expectations of the art institution and its markets or to surrender to the socio-political status quo (for recent studies on photographic failure see Chéroux, 2003 and Maheu and Streitberger, 2017). Failure and silliness here become political statements, even at the risk of the "falling out" of art history altogether. This was the fate that largely befell some of the artists with whom this whole project started, including Jacques Lizène and Marcel Mariën—two artists whose deskilling practices debunked existing notions of authorship and mastery and who deliberately choose to excel in mediocrity instead. It is important not to frame this deliberate choice for mediocrity and failure as merely another form of success in an attempt to canonize that which wanted to escape the canonical framework from the beginning, but to preserve those artists' double position of simultaneously being apart from and part of the art world.

Like Halberstam's "silly archives," our attention for humor within art and photography thus unavoidably leads us to discover a different, what we have previously called "minor" photography history. This is a history that cannot exist apart from the "major," canonical stories of masters and masterpieces but is parasitically connected to it, at times resurfaces in it and yet at other moments goes completely underground. (Bleyen, 2012; 2014) This "minor" kind of art history and photography history is one that touches the uncomfortable and unstable surface where art meets its outside and can no longer be clearly distinguished from the sphere of the vernacular, kitsch, the silly or quirky.

The current volume is the result of a conference held in Brussels in April 2016 under difficult circumstances, not long after a terror attack had brought the city under what seemed like a military siege. A first attempt to organize it in November 2015 had to be cancelled due to an earlier attack in Paris with large safety repercussions in Brussels. It was a moment where the question of laughter seemed both out of touch with the gravity of the moment and simultaneously—with the earlier raid on Charlie Hebdo in mind—more necessary to be addressed than ever. We are grateful for all lecturers who came to participate despite the negative travel advices of that moment. We are also grateful for the long-distance Skype conversations with some of our overseas keynotes, which turned the conference into a success.

The Photography Performing Humor conference was part of a larger research project under the same title, which also included a year of collaborating with students (Masters in Photography and Cultural Studies), and an exhibition of the work of Jacques Lizène and Lieven Segers, held in LUCA School of Arts's gallery. From the beginning, the project was conceived as having both a theoretical and practice-based component. Reading seminars were followed by workshops, and photographers and artists were invited to "perform" as keynotes during the conference. This double approach also resonates throughout this book, the theoretical contributions of which are literally enveloped by artist's pages. The book opens with work from Dutch photographer Paulien Oltheten, who has a keen eye for the small and, once noticed, often comic public performances in daily life. In recent years she has turned her photographic experiences into performance lectures in which she narrates and reenacts some of the peculiar gestures captured on camera. In the photo-video-essay *La Défense, the Venturing Gaze*, Oltheten's camera registers the daily patterns, routines and singular forms of human behaviour that she came to observe within the Parisian business district. The selection of videostills present in this volume, highlights the performative practice of taking photographic images itself.[1] A shutter is opened, the world opens itself to us. The illusion of the fourth wall—granting the viewer a sense of immediate optical, disembodied mastery of the world—is crushed. Instead, the photographic event or the encounter between photographer, photographed subject and spectator, mediated through the camera and the printed page, now takes center stage, albeit as a slightly absurd non-event.

The photographic event and its relation to humor is also the central focus of the first part of our volume. In the opening essay, Esther Leslie, departing from Walter Benjamin, draws a parallel between laughter and photography by describing them both as "shattered articulation," as interruptions of the flow of things—of speech, of time, of space, of action. Photography, the medium of mechanical reproduction, altered and shattered traditional ways of envisioning and relating to the world by showing worlds within worlds and discovering previously unperceived or "subperceived" facets within our humanly experienced world (Benjamin's optical unconscious). Leslie covers a wide range of photographic practices, from the stiff and absurd staging in early portrait photography, Karl Blossfeldt's secret plant worlds, and the visual fakery of ectoplasm to the ultimate serious image of the atomic bomb. Linking these diverse practices and making use of Benjamin's notion of "diabolical laughter," she suggests that photography as shattered articulation might equally lead to the absurd and humorous, and the utterly disruptive. But what ultimately is at stake for Benjamin, and remains highly relevant for our increasingly self-enclosing selfie-culture driving on algorithms is the question of what should happen with the shattered fragments, how and whether they still could be reorganized, reshuffled and thereby playfully lead to the imagination of a different world.

The second text, by Katarzyna Ruchel-Stockmans, suggests that for many artists working in very restricted and harsh conditions, such as Poland in the 1970s and 1980s, failure and falling can precisely provide the necessary room to maneuver and play. In line with Kaplan's "morbid sense of humor," this essay reflects on the way photography is able to elicit convulsive laughter through its intricate relationship with death. Taking a detour through an animated story on falling, Ruchel-Stockmans discusses the mediumspecificity of photographic humor while focusing on the motive of the fall within humor theory and an interesting group of orchestrated falls within Polish photographic practice. The essay distinguishes between two types of laughter that might occur when facing a falling person: the laughter of superiority versus the laughter that connects the fall of the other to our own fragile bodies leading us to imagine our own death. Ruchel-Stockmans follows Leszek Kolakowksi, for whom only this second sort of laughter could be considered humor, here defined as that rare ability to laugh with oneself. Humor within this definition requires a form of splitting up or doubling of the self, and a watching yourself as if from a distance, which is at work in the Polish performances of falling in front of the camera.

The third text, written by Ann Kristin Krahn, even more explicitly discusses the figure of the double as a witty tool for self-criticism by focusing on the role of the photographer's shadow in the work of Lee Friedlander. Deliberately inserting his shadow in his photographic work, Friedlander turns what was once considered exemplary of photographic failure within vernacular photography into an ally to perform medium-specific jokes. His shadow self-portraits, pointing as indexical figures both at the presence and absence of the photographer, allow Friedlander to see and capture himself as other. They also invite the spectator to step into the photographer's shoes and become complicit in his sometimes voyeuristic and violent photographic act troubling all too easy identifications in the process.

The last contribution to the first section, "Performing the Performance Documentation" by Kevin Atherton, plays with the problematic role of photographic documentation within the history of performance art. The text serves as a solidification of a lecture-performance done during our conference (2016). Atherton discussed a performance held in 1978 in the Whitechapel Art Gallery in which the photographing of the audience witnessing the performance turned out to be the performance itself and a fictive re-enactment of that same performance in 2015. Atherton's text brings a minute report of every act and gesture, reconstructing the slowly built-up group portrait of the performance audience and parodying the reliability of both the photographic archive and the lecture format. His reflections end with the affective afterlife of his performance, namely his experience of failure when large parts of the audience did not seem to have got the joke and did not see the parody work, believing every word of his exposition instead.

The second part brings together three texts that discuss practices of photographic trickery and montage as critical tools for examining photography's popular social functions. In "Ghost Just for Laughs," Louis Kaplan elaborates on the heated and often hilarious 19th century debates surrounding the widely popular practice of spirit photography, focusing on the infamous trial of spirit photographer William Mumler and the debunking strategies used in the testimony of P.T. Barnum. Kaplan traces a long tradition of arch-debunkers, from Barnum over Houdini to recent television shows repudiating so-called manifestations of the paranormal. What all these arch-debunkers — often stage magicians or illusionists — have in common is a shared project of bringing the so-called magical and mystical back to the earthy realm of magic or material tricks and mechanical procedures, often by using iconoclast humorous gestures. Discussing two images featuring the then recently deceased Abraham Lincoln, Kaplan demonstrates how the Janus face of spirit photography, hovering between the supernatural and the mechanical, between a pious faith system and entertainment, between the magical and magic, functioned in practice.

Hilde D'haeyere's text, "Comedy Performs Photography," discusses how the increasing importance of photography in nearly every facet of interbellum culture is reflected in and commented upon by its younger sister-art, cinema. She elaborates on a group of silent slapstick comedies in which photography, as a quickly evolving technology, a mass medium present in press and nearly every important social institution, and a changing profession increasingly also welcoming women, becomes the subject of merriment and ridicule. D'haeyere's text was originally brought as a lecture-performance that played with the tension of a classic lecture format and the screening of gags from silent slapstick comedy, in this volume present as a pair of film frames. During her presentation, D'haeyere was assisted by a *lafograph*, which was installed right in front of her, facing the audience. This peculiar instrument was originally invented in 1928 by P. K. Thomajan to capture and graphically register the laugh reactions of an audience to a movie. (D'haeyere, 2011: 33) By using this "comedy barometer," which — slapstick-wise — often got stuck, D'haeyere was able to track, measure and evaluate the laugh reactions to the screened film fragments and thus test these comedies' vitality for a 21st century audience.

The final contribution to this section, co-written by Susana Martins and Anna Corrigan, explores the *Sueños* (Dreams), a series of witty photomontages made between 1948 and 1951 by German-Argentinian artist Grete Stern for a juvenile feminine magazine. Serving as illustrations to a psychoanalytic column analyzing dreams of female readers, these photomontages humorously subvert and play with the expectations and images of femininity within Argentinian society. In line with Surrealist tradition, they complicate and often ridicule the rather conservative textual components of the magazine and column. Through a play of at times violent juxtaposition, these photomontages make fun of the dominant images of femininity during the high days of Peronism. Parasitically operating within a magazine that sells the dream of consumerism and promotes the ideal of female domesticity, the *Sueños* create a space for reflection, imagining alternative visions of womanhood in the process.

The third and last section of this volume focuses on one of the art "movements" that by a wider audience has perhaps been most associated with the intellectual seriousness and gravity of the contemporary art world: conceptual art. Yet, in recent years we have started to see cracks in the façade of earnestness of conceptual art as more and more authors have started to address its joke and parody work. One of the authors who started readdressing conceptual art through a humor lens, Heather Diack, opens this section with a series of reflections on the role of the "straight face" or deadpan aesthetics within conceptualism. Diack discusses how similar this is to classic comedy situations where the "straight man" serves as the necessary counterpart to the clown, conceptual art's deadpan, expressionless tone is a prerequisite for its often all too banal or even absurd content. She brings new readings of some key works of early conceptual artists such as Douglas Huebler, Bruce Nauman and Fred Lonidier, arguing that humor may very well have been the cornerstone of conceptual art's critical project. Moreover, photography, as a vernacular, ready-to-use medium that served conceptual artists to break with the artistic tradition while equally enabling them to reconnect to the world, seems to be the movements' privileged means to bring this critical performance about.

In the same vein, Johan Pas' article, "No Photographs Allowed," outlines the productive relationship between photography, humor and the printed or photocopied page within Belgian conceptual art. Pas' essay starts with Marcel Broodthaers' witty commentaries on the exhibition catalogue and the artists' book format but also includes printed work from artists such as Jef Geys, group CAP, Jacques Charlier and Leo Copers. Pas discusses the strategies of parody, persiflage, irony and anachronism present in this corpus with strong resonances of Belgian's Surrealist artistic legacy, focusing more specifically on the playful interactions between the photographic image and the written word within the intermedial and performative book medium.

The last essay in this volume, written by Sandra Križić Roban, explores "Elements of Humor in Proto- and Conceptual Photography in Croatia" and further addresses the importance of horizontal art histories for our better understanding of photography within conceptual art, as an international phenomenon with local specificities. The text also demonstrates that humor, although a universally shared aspect of humanity, is strongly culturally embedded. Within the specific artistic and socio-political context of Croatia in the 1960s and 1970s, the artistic choice for humor as social commentary was not without possible repercussions and a radical move in itself. Križić Roban brings to our attention a fascinating body of the purposely boring, small or ridiculous performative gestures by the proto-conceptual Gorgona group that remained within the private sphere and deliberately in the shadow of the official art circuit. She demonstrates how, in line with Gorgona's radical stance, later Croatian conceptual artists such as Goran Trbuljak and Mladen Stilinović critically made use of humor and parody as tools to question the role of the artist within society and the political and social norms of that period.

Our book closes with two artists' contributions. The first artists' pages are designed by Lieven Segers, who through every stage of the project has been our partner in crime. He ran a workshop with MA Photography students, resulting in the one-day showcase entitled *Green, Yellow and Black* (LUCA School of Arts, March 13, 2015); in the *Petit Maître liégeois meets Bassie Lebon* exhibition his work dialogued with that of Jacques Lizène (Sint-Lukasgalerie, Brussels, October 30, 2015 – November 28, 2015); he spoke at our conference and now is present in this volume. Within his varied practice as artist, curator and teacher, humor is a recurrent strategy to address uncomfortable or unintelligible situations. He compares it to "a sauce that is poured on the darker sides of the human condition, which makes it simultaneously more tasteful and then unexpectedly highlights its sharpness." The mask-like collage faces present in this volume first figured within a sculptural set-up in Segers' exhibition *Niets aan de hand, niets in de mouw, niets tegen de muur* (Nothing wrong, nothing in the sleeve, nothing against the wall) (Base Alpha Gallery, Antwerp, 2017). There, they were attached to white plinths, turning these funny shapes into crawling and swaying bodies. The faces are the visual translations of Segers' *Sharing is Caring* project, in which he invited people he met in bars to share their drunken thoughts with him by texting him during the night. The intoxicated messages were interpreted by the artist and transformed into portraits, made by a collage of cut-outs from make-up advertisements, photographs of body painted figures and medical images. Partly hidden behind a layer of black paint, these deformed, cubist faces come across as masks that celebrate the non-hierarchical being together in difference during those early, intoxicated morning hours.

We close our volume with a playful wink at contemporary selfie-culture by means of a small excerpt from the ongoing *Trying to Look Like a Building* series by the German performance artist David Helbich. What started more or less as a joke in front of the Guggenheim in 2015 while on a trip to New York, and was shared on the social media platforms Instagram and Facebook, turned out to be the beginning of a new selfie genre: the performative selfie in front of an architectural landmark. The series, although one of the more frivolous performative gestures by Helbich, connects to his wider practice of performances in urban contexts that also include witty variants to the guided tour format, and the wider known project *Belgian Solutions,* which operates both on the web and in printed form. In this project, "not every solution is an answer to a problem," and humor takes the role of social anthropology as described by David Critchley in *On Humour,* turning the familiar into the strange. (65) Helbich's photographic images bring the perspective of the expat living in Brussels and seeing the poetics and absurdity of the daily bricolage logic that is ubiquitous in Belgian urban life. Specifically for this book, Helbich went to one of the weirdest symbols of this strange nation without a proper sense of nationality, the Atomium. With his blown-up cheek — trying to look like an atom — our volume closes while touching upon a range of questions that other authors and volumes will hopefully further explore. Giving its focus on artistic examples, this volume does not enter the immensely fascinating world of contemporary vernacular photography, with all its circulating memes and snapchat fun and misery. It will — we hope — extend the "silly archive" of photography and open the sometimes too serious history, theory and practice of photography to more humorous alternatives.

Note

1. To see Oltheten's "live video essay" of La Défense (45 min), consult https://vimeo.com/284821161

Bibliography

Roland Barthes, *Camera Lucida. Reflections on Photography*, Richard Howard (transl.) (New York: Hill and Wang, 1980/1981).

Henri Bergson, "Laughter. An Essay on the Meaning of the Comic," in *Henri Bergson. Key Writings,* eds Keith Ansell Pearson and John Ó Maoilearca, Bloomsbury Revelations (London – New Delhi – New York – Sydney: Bloomsbury, 1900/2014), 465–479.

Mieke Bleyen (ed.), *Minor Photography. Connecting Deleuze and Guattari to Photography Theory*, Lieven Gevaert Series, vol. 13 (Leuven: Leuven University Press, 2012).

Mieke Bleyen, *Minor Aesthetics. The Photographic Work of Marcel Mariën*, Lieven Gevaert Series, vol. 17 (Leuven: Leuven University Press, 2014).

Elspeth H Brown and Thy Phu (eds), *Feeling Photography* (Durham: Duke University Press, 2014).

Victor Burgin (ed.), *Thinking Photography* (London and Basingstoke: Palgrave Macmillan, 1982).

Clément Chéroux, *Fautographie: Petite histoire de l'erreur photographique* (Crisnée: Editions Yellow Now, 2003).

Simon Critchley, *On Humour* (Routledge, 2002).

Patricia Ticineto Cough and Jean Halley (eds), *The Affective Turn. Theorizing the Social* (Durham: Duke University Press, 2007).

Liesbeth Decan, *Conceptual, Surrealist, Pictorial: Photo-based Art in Belgium (1960s-early 1990s)*, Lieven Gevaert Series, vol. 22 (Leuven: University Press, 2016).

Hilde D'haeyere, *Dislexicon* (Ghent: KASK School of Arts, University College Ghent, 2011).

Elizabeth Edwards, *Raw Histories. Photographs, Anthropology and Museums* (Oxford – New York: Berg, 2001).

Judith Halberstam, *The Queer Art of Failure*, a John Hope Franklin Center Book (Durham: Duke University Press, 2012).

Jennifer Higgie, *The Artist's Joke,* Documents of Contemporary Art (London: Whitechapel Gallery – The MIT Press, 2007).

Louis Kaplan, *Photography and Humour*, Exposure (London: Reaktion Books, 2017).

Sarah Kember and Joanna Zylinska, *Life after New Media. Mediation as a Vital Process* (Cambridge, Mas. – London: The MIT Press, 2012).

Sheri Klein, *Art & Laugher* (London – New York: I.B.Tauris, 2007).

Felicity Lunn (ed.), *When Humour becomes Painful* (Zurich: JRP/Ringier, 2005).

François Maheu and Alexander Streitberger (eds), *L'expérience de l'erreur en photographie/The Experience of Error in Photography*, special issue of *Image [&] Narrative*, Vol. 18, No.4 (2017): http://www.imageand-narrative.be/index.php/imagenarrative/issue/view/94

Dominic Molon and Michael Rooks, *Situation Comedy: Humor In Recent Art* (New York: Indepedent Curators International, 2005).

Thy Phu and Linda M. Steer (eds), *Affecting Photographies*, special issue of *Photography & Culture*, Vol. 2, No.3 (November 2009).

Allan Sekula, *Photography Against The Grain: Essays and Photo Works, 1973–1983* (Halifax: Press of the Nova Scotia College of Art and Design, 1984).

Susan Sontag, *On Photography* (New York: Picador, 1977/2001).

John Tagg, *The Burden Of Representation: Essays on Photographies and Histories* (University of Minnesota Press, 1988).

Part I

Finding Humor in the Photographic Event

Photography and Laughter's Shattered Articulation

Esther Leslie

"Shattered articulation"—that is how Walter Benjamin describes laughter. (Benjamin, 1999: 325) Laughter by this definition is not inarticulate; rather it performs the breaking up of articulation into parts, which might render it non-functional, or might just lay out its pieces, in order to better understand its inner workings. Laughter is "shattered articulation." Laughter is an interruption to the flow of speech: words can no longer pass out through the mouth, perhaps even new thoughts can't be gathered, when the peal of laughter interferes with their formation. Laughter breaks up the flow. Laughter is just the cackle, the snigger, the roar, the scream of mirth cutting across anything else. Laughter shatters articulation, and that includes the coherent articulation of the body, as laughter forces the limbs, the diaphragm, facial muscles, the mouth, the neck to contort spasmodically, the larynx and epiglottis to contract, the breathing pattern to be interrupted, as the body collapses in laughter, twists and deforms itself. Self-control is lost. Everything is in uproar. If the body is excessively stirred into action, it might be said that there is also, simultaneously, a dissociation; conscience and sentiment are stilled, permitting detachment from engagement in the world, in process, from emotional involvement. This is what lies behind Henri Bergson's observation that in the comic, which always has a certain brutality about it, there is "something like a momentary anaesthesia of the heart." (Bergson, 1980: 64) The heart stops. The heart stops responding to sentiment. The laughing person disengages from caring. Perhaps even disengages for a moment from being alive, at least figuratively. The laughing type is a thing, beside the self.

If language, thought and the body are disarticulated, or interrupted and disrupted, in laughter, the photograph too might be seen as a disarticulation or interruption of time, of action, of space. The photograph shatters. It shatters the coherence of events, the flow of time. It displaces space, transporting an event from one place to another. It meddles with scale and coordinates. This at least is how Walter Benjamin characterizes it, allowing a link to be drawn between laughter and mechanical reproduction. Just as Brecht's *Gestus* interrupts the course of time, just as the gag breaks the flow of things, the photograph holds up and disorders the flow of time and the consistency of space. Photography shatters. Its mode of mechanical reproduction, of dislodging the image from time and space, its severing of originality and undermining of artistry, produces, Benjamin states, "a tremendous shattering of tradition." (Benjamin, 1969: 221–222) And it shatters the coherence, the assumed, conventional consistency of the world. Audiences penetrate the secrets contained even in very ordinary reality, once it has been fractured into shards. The world seen through glass in photography is as if of glass, shatterable. In being smashed, once having passed through the glass of the camera, it releases meaning for us. The broken parts of a recorded actuality are combined into new chains, or left fractured, a handful of scraps of the world.

Laughter shatters. Photography shatters. Does the shattered articulation of photography bring it close to the shattered articulation of laughter, or humor? Is there something humorous about breaking the normal course of things or bodies and holding them up as images? Is there an inherent humor to freeze-framing, a practice that, while a matter of historically necessary image capture time, is inherent to all photography. Interrupting the flow of time, holding it up, startles, and disaggregates a view as well as a viewer. Is there an intrinsic humor to this? Photography and humor alike depend on time, or on timing. The joke's punchline and the shutter must be detonated at just the right moment, producing a heightened instant. Freud observes that, in some circumstances, when humor is related to the tensions incumbent on repression, laughter comes as "a surplus of energy which has to be discharged." Photography might also be conceived of as a buildup of tension to a specific point when it is discharged—the button pressed, the shutter triggered. (Freud, 1976: 766) All photographs are freeze-framed, except for the most blurry perhaps, which stretch time across the photograph. In its freezing of a frame of the world, the photograph captures that which is momentary and, in some circumstances, what is caught is something that cannot normally be seen under the usual conditions of perception: the splashed corona of a milk drop, horses' legs as they gallop, the crystal formations of a snowflake, a fly on a single sugar crystal, the proleg of a caterpillar. All this is a seeing beneath seeing, facilitated in the shattering of unaided vision by the camera. Through the practice of freezing time and excerpting space in the photograph there can arise a humor, though, that may be a black, mordant one, as terrifying as it is amusing, provocative of a shattering of self and world, to which sometimes the only response is a kind of demonic laughter.

Of course, the shattered articulation that is the photograph in a more obvious sense deals not with the shattered articulation that is laughter. The photograph deals with smiles, or at least it came to deal with smiles historically. To be before the camera required, in time, as the medium settled into the world as a familiar, if not a friend, the adoption of a particular look: a smile. Smiles are the polite capturing of laughs, holding them in abeyance. Laughs, by contrast, sometimes shoot out involuntarily. Eyes closed, teeth exposed, crease-filled, the laughing face may not be a perfectly photogenic one. Smiles in photography have a history and they have evolved. (Jeeves, 2013) The smile, controlled, neat, comes at a certain point as a historical achievement of photography, once the snapshot is prevalent and the smile need not be a rictus grin. The smile is slowly cultivated as an attitude before the camera, but it is only allowed in certain circumstances, when neutrality or gravitas is not required. The selfie pout has come into being historically. It requires no smile and certainly no laugh. Is it impossible to smile at oneself? At least in the early days, around 2013, when the word was named the Oxford English Dictionary's "Word of the Year," the smile was banished from the selfie trend for reasons, presumably, to do with the management of an image that requires a certain kind of self-control, an exuding of "coolness." The smile cracks the face, smashing efforts at perfection. The smile hints at a possibility of inter-subjective exchange — and it thins the lips and smudges the contours of the cheekbones, which disturbs current beauty predilections. But selfies have their own history of repertoire of stances: the duck face, the sparrow face, the fish gape, which returns the teeth to the image, in that controlled way that the smile sometimes allowed. These ritualized poses are meant to work as self-approved self-advertising, but they function too as absurdities, cartoon-like transmogrifications of the human — young women and girls for the most part — into animalized forms. Here we see women as hybrids, cartoonic, caricatures. These photographic absurdities may in some circumstances, such as an academic conference on photography, draw out a knowing smile or a burst of laughter. Much as they repress the smile or confine it to a performed, pre-scripted gesture, they evoke in others the opposite response: an involuntary sneery smile, a snort of superiority, a plosive "pah" with its flash of teeth and tonsils.

If we read these images as absurd, if they have a humor about them, intended or not, then they join those other absurd poses that have appeared before the camera, more or less stiffly, since its earliest days. Benjamin writes in his *Small History of Photography* about the contents of the albums that began to arrive in the 19th century in bourgeois parlors:

Photography Performing Humor

They preferred to site themselves in frosty spots of the apartments, on console tables or Gueridons in the reception room: leather tomes with forbidding metal hasps und gilt edged pages, each a finger thick, on which are scattered clownishly posed or corsetted figures—Uncle Alex and Aunt Riekchen, little Trudy when she was small, daddy in his first term at university—and finally, in order to compound the shame, we too; as parlour Tyroleans, yodelling, brandishing our hats in front of painted snow, or as dapper sailors, leaning on a polished stanchion, one leg weight bearing, one free, as is only proper. The accessories in such portraits, with their pedestals, balustrades and tiny oval tables, recall now the time when, because of the long exposure times, the models needed to have a support, so they might remain fixed in place. If in the early days one made do with "head rests" or "knee clamps," soon after there followed "further accessories, such as appeared in famous paintings, and therefore were perceived as 'artistic.' At first it was columns and curtains." The more capable men turned against all this flimflam as early as the 1860s. For example, a English trade gazette noted: "In painted pictures the column is shown with some chance of possibility, but the way in which it has been used in photography is ridiculously absurd, it generally being placed on a carpet. Now everybody must be open to the conviction that marble or stone pillars are not built on carpets for a foundation." (Benjamin, 2015: 75–76)

Those early photos often required a serious look on the sitter's face, though smiles and other grimaces appeared, induced for the machine and for analysis, and even occasioned by the machine, as in the induced electric convulsions, apparent in the original form of an illustration from Charles Darwin's *The Expression of the Emotions in Man and Animals*, from 1872. (Fig. 1.1) Titled *Expression Plate III, Fig. 6*, the images stemmed from the collection of Benjamin Amand Duchenne, promulgator of electrodiagnosis, electrotherapy and electrical stimulation for the purpose of inducing facial expressions for photographs. The originals show the stimulation machinery that Darwin's reproductions erased.

Photography, from the start, is bound up with fakery, and this often appears as absurd, not least because it is often obvious. In addition, the serious look on the sitter's face in the early days of portrait photography, before smiling was elicited, the frozen gait, the silly props—columns, sailor's hat, tropical fern—are all laughable. The studio illusions are ridiculous. The costumes are ludicrous. There seems to be something stupid about early photography. These are people, but they look like things, just as much a prop as the lifeless objects surrounding them. People looking out from the ever more distant time of the photograph look out of place, perhaps always looked out of place, except they were in place, right in the place where photography caught them and forced them to hold still. It is just the case that this place was a godforsaken one, presided over, according to Benjamin "by the increasing degeneration of an imperialist bourgeoisie." (Benjamin, 2015: 81) Or at least this is how it all becomes socially legible for Benjamin, especially perhaps as his epoch, the decades he lived through of the 1920s and 1930s, witnessed a certain freeing up of photography, a more or less cultivated casualness before the camera. These are the days when the smile becomes a fixture in portrait photography. Walter Benjamin traces a history of gazes into and out of the photograph. The shy averted eyes of the early days, unconfident looks, faces held still anxiously, are replaced by "that 'looking at *you*' of animals, people or babies, which mixes in such a tainted way with the buyer." (Benjamin, 2015: 69) Here comes the smile, the appeal, which makes the photograph a human analog of something Marx and Engels discovered in the middle of the 19th century in Francis Bacon's bourgeois materialism from some 350 years before: "Matter, surrounded by a sensuous poetic glamor, seems to attract man's whole entity with winning smiles." (Engels, 2008: 11)

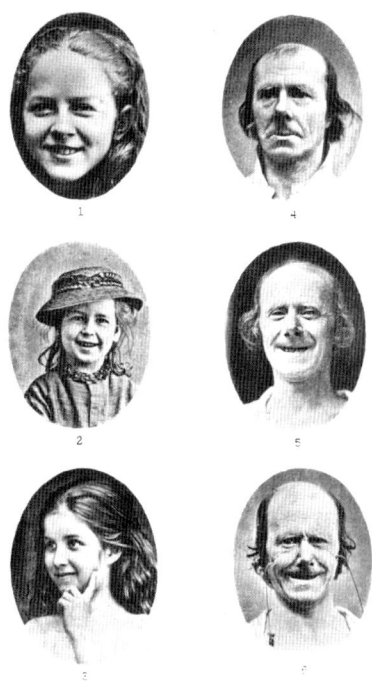

Figure 1.1

Illustration from Charles Darwin's *The Expression of the Emotions in Man and Animals*, 1872 (Titled Expression Plate III, Fig. 6, the images stemmed from the collection of Benjamin Amand Duchenne.)

Photography as a new material in the world, and photographed bodies and things as new substances in the world, beam out at their viewers, capture their gazes, and indulge them with smiles. This new photographic being entices all and everything to become part of its milieu. Now the whole world is smiling under photographic lights. Photography exists to capture and hold for posterity good humor, positive moods. At the same time, as portrait photography comes to establish the subject as attractive, presenting the self as friendly, approachable and appealing—a mission which has only increased, as the calling card becomes the LinkedIn or Facebook profile image—another branch of photography takes another tack, moving behind the smile, inside the body, inside nature and far from the scene of human politeness. This photography is engaged in making visible the previously unseen for the purposes of knowledge or for scientific ends. However much it pushes inside or away from the surface of civilization, it also finds itself trapped in it, to absurd or surreal effect.

Benjamin identifies such pushing of photography into farcicality in the botanical photography of Karl Blossfeldt. Here, in images of fronds, calyxes, blossoms, buds, he finds what he calls an "optical unconscious," something that might be located as rendering a realm of puns, jokes, confusions, and affinities.

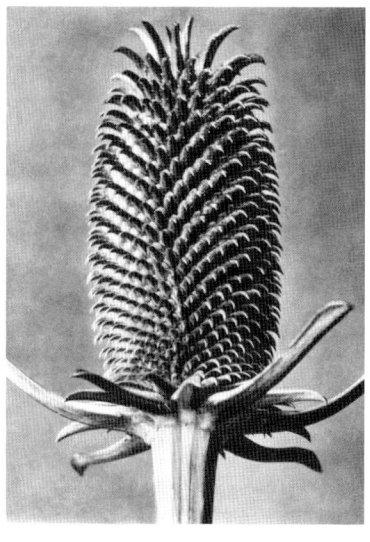

Figure 1.2

Karl Blossfeldt, from *Urformen der Kunst* (Berlin: Ernst Wasmuth, 1928).

> One learns of this optical-unconscious only through photography, just as the instinctual-unconscious is discovered in psychoanalysis. The composition of structures, cellular tissue, all that stuff with which technology, medicine reckons to deal, is primarily more related to the camera than the atmospheric landscape or the soulful portrait. But at the same time, photography discloses in this material physiognomic aspects, image worlds, which inhabit the smallest things, interpretable and latent enough to have found a bolthole in daydreams. But now, as they have become enlarged and articulable, they make manifest how the difference between technology and magic is a thoroughly historical variable. In this way, in his astonishing photographs of plants, Blossfeldt brought out the most ancient column forms in horsetail, a bishop's crozier in an ostrich fern, totem poles in tenfold enlargements of horse chestnut and maple shoots, gothic tracery in the Indian teasel. (Benjamin, 2015: 68)

Blossfeldt's close-ups of plants, their buds, blossoms, stems, and leaves, are presented in as precise a detail as his long-exposure and printing up times would allow. (Fig. 1.2) This was an art of detail—for Blossfeldt nominated areas of the negative for enlargement, blasting into visibility one minor part, perhaps the tip of a shoot or the joining point of two twigs. This fragment might be enlarged up to forty-five-fold. Sometimes Blossfeldt cut into the plants that he wished to portray, opening up their seed sacs or stripping back sepals to reveal their contents. Under his hand and lens, the plant becomes a construction and a revelation. Benjamin proposes in his short review on the work that such photographic techniques as close-up and magnification can make even the most familiar, the most natural, reveal itself to be transformed and transformable—that is to say, it is shown as historical. Inside nature, behind its surfaces, in the magnification of its scale, is to be found portions of our world, our human world, appropriated, seemingly, by plants. At least, that is what the camera would have us believe. It shatters what we thought we knew to be there. It recomposes it in ways that are recognizable, but implausible. Elsewhere Benjamin points out that Blossfeldt's photographic images allow exploration in an estranged, though once familiar, landscape: "We observers, though, wander beneath these giant plants like Lilliputians." (Benjamin, 2015: 126) The image is aggrandized. Benjamin notes, in *New Things about Flowers*, that:

> These photographs disclose within plant existence a whole unsuspected treasury of analogies and forms. Only photography is able to do this. For it requires a powerful magnification before these forms can cast off the veil which our inertia has thrown over them. (Benjamin, 2015: 124)

Photography releases reserves of analogies through its capacities to magnify. Within a form, there are other forms that can be brought out by the technical capacity of the camera. The camera donates life, to the extent that our liveliness dissipates, and so, through its machinery, revives our capacity to see. But what we see is something ridiculous—the plant as twisting body, architectural details, ritual objects. Analogy is the mode of Surrealism. Its energies come from incongruity. Benjamin understood this photographic analogizing as deriving from a longer tradition than that of his contemporaneous Surrealists. This tradition of making dreamy analogies, of seeking correspondences went back further to Charles Baudelaire's poetics, wherein things, words, selves, everything loosens up, encouraged by intoxication, and partakes of realms of possibility, connection and alteration: "Nature is a temple where living pillars/Let sometimes emerge confused words;/Man crosses it through forests of symbols/Which watch him with intimate eyes." (Baudelaire, 1974)

For Walter Benjamin, the play with correspondence and analogy is carried out masterfully by the 19th century caricaturist J.J. Grandville. Benjamin regarded the caricaturist and comic writer Grandville as an onlooker to the occurrence of commodity fetishism and an antecedent to the appearance of animation. In Grandville's sketches forms transpose, collapse into each other, and merge. Grandville drew lampoons of the excessive vitality of these new worldlings named commodities, and he depicted the apparent conquests of fleeting fashion over unending nature: flowers flaneuring in furs and jewels, a cast-iron balcony around the planet Saturn, impeccably placed for night-time gadding, and the wheel of fashion, a diagram of fashion's interminable and conformist push, its machine-driven ahumanism that would like to present itself as the most natural rhythm in the world. Grandville imagines the plant world—as well as the animal world—in the guise of the human world. Grandville, according to Benjamin, is also the progenitor of advertising, that high art of commodity fetishism. "Grandville's works are the sibylline books of publicité. Everything that with him has its preliminary form as a joke, or satire, attains its true unfolding as advertisement." (Benjamin, 1999: 172) Benjamin notes of Grandville that he mastered the basic form of the advertisement—graphic sadism. Karl Blossfeldt, by contrast, uses another principle of advertisement, "magnification of the plant world to gigantic proportions," a process which Benjamin sees as "gently healing the wounds which caricature inflicted on it." (Benjamin, 2015: 124) The image as wound, a violation of nature distorted with a human face in Grandville. The image as healing, in Karl Blossfeldt, not by the restitution of normal, unimpeded vision, but rather by re-adapting the distorting eye of advertising—repeating the spell—and incorporating advertising's extraordinary vision into its own. This allows audiences to re-see the distortions of advertising gaze in the realm of nature. Repeating the spell that enlarges objects, Karl Blossfeldt's photography incorporates advertising's flawed vision into its own. A world of giant foliage, of supersized vegetables and monster flowers might be yet a charming playground for future people, who are better suited to a world in which endless re-discovery is the norm. Gigantic nature is a counter-image to the gigantic commodity. In the modern metropolis, the "threatening and alluring face" of myth gleamed, notes Benjamin in *One Way Street.* (Benjamin, 2004: 476) Characters from new capitalist myths beamed down from hoardings on street walls that advertised "toothpaste for giants." (Benjamin, 2004: 476) The advertisement is one method whereby the commodity infiltrates the dream-world of the consumer. It blurs over the commodity character of things. But then and there, here and now, such a vision charms us into buying. It should be noted how often the joke is used to clinch the sale in advertising.

In his riposte to Henri Bergson's ideas on laughter, Wyndham Lewis derives the root of the Comic in another kind of muddling of things and humans. It is not, he notes in "The Meaning of the Wild Body," (1927) only comic to observe a person behaving like a thing—Bergson's theory of humor asserts laughter results from witnessing mechanical aspects grafted onto the living, such that a person gives the impression of being a thing (Bergson, 1980: 97)—rather the root of the Comic, for Lewis, "is to be sought in the sensations resulting from the observations of a thing behaving like a person." If this is the case, then all humans are comic, for each is a physical thing, a body, which assumes to act as a person. The world is absurd, and so are all those in it, according to Lewis.

> To bring vividly to our mind what we mean by 'absurd,' let us turn to the plant, and enquire how the plant could be absurd. Suppose you came upon an orchid or a cabbage reading

Flaubert's *Salammbô* or Plutarch's *Moralia*, you would be very much surprised. But if you found a man or a woman reading it, you would not be surprised. Now in one sense you ought to be just as much surprised at finding a man occupied in this way as if you had found an orchid or a cabbage, or a tom-cat, to include the animal world. There is the same physical anomaly. It is just as absurd externally, that is what I mean. — The deepest root of the Comic is to be sought in this anomaly. (Lewis, 1982: 158–9)

Lewis asserts that the most ridiculous aspect of it all is that a person is deluded enough to assume that they are a person. Matter behaving in an intelligent way strikes Lewis as ludicrous. Perhaps Lewis disassociates matter and mind excessively, such that he is unable to conceive of a dialectical overcoming of dualism. The notion of plants acting as humans — and thereby exposing the absurdities of our own existence — however, gives another steer for the interpretation of Grandville's images of humanoid plant life. The flaneuring plants remind us that we too are hunks of meat and bags of gas, who only dress ourselves up and pretend to be elsewhere.

Made explicit in photography is a shattering of nature's apparent laws, or a demonstration of the quest to establish new ones. The break in the law has something funny about it, and, as Benjamin notes: "The cracking open of natural teleology proceeds in accordance with the plan of humor." (Benjamin, 1999: 635) Photography, like laughter, shatters world and self, interrupts the flow of things, reimages matter, makes it smile and dance, and it breaks up the world. Photography discovers, or projects, worlds within worlds, forms within form, evokes new nature, different nature, otherness. What might a few absurd frames from the history of photography demonstrate about shattering, about calling forth childish or even satanic laughter, demonic forces, the "derisive laughter of hell," (Benjamin, 1999: 325) even, as Benjamin terms it, drawing on Charles Baudelaire's notion of laughter as hellish: "The comic element is a damnable thing, and one of diabolical origin." (Benjamin, 1999: 285) Of course it is none the less human for that: "Laughter is satanic; it is thus profoundly human." (Benjamin, 1999: 325) Laughter revels in incongruity. Laughter associates and disassociates. In what ways might photography's access to the anatural align it with that which is not human, or with the human in the guise of the thing, or the thing masquerading as human?

At a certain historical point, as shown from the appearance of Eadweard Muybridge's serial photography of the 1880s onwards, photography is presented as that which is able to extend human sight mechanically. This machinic vision occludes the eye's. Viewers are able to see the moment a person takes a stride, or a milk drop hits a surface. In photography, a snow crystal is arrested in its melting. Behind, inside, underneath the world of appearance is found another realm, new vistas, impossibilities made possible. The development of rapid shutter technology, the invention of cinema, the improvement of flash technology—all this made it possible to capture movement as more than just a blur. Unseen movements are within the grasp of recording. The dream worlds of photography, which are sometimes false ones, certainly not magical, but of cognitive interest, also emerge. Such as the photography of ectoplasm, not a freeze-framed moment of photography, but an apparent freezing of a moment, in order to bring the unseen into vision. Ectoplasm, through Charles Richet's experiments in psychic phenomena and through F. W. H. Myers, who used the word ectoplasm in his *Human Personality and its Survival of Bodily Death*, (1903) became the name for a substance or spiritual energy which is exteriorized by mediums when they are in a state of trance. Ectoplasm is presented as "a viscous substance...from which spirits make themselves visible forms...alive, sensitive to touch and light...cold to the touch, slightly luminous and having a characteristic smell." (Warner, 2006: 290) It gathered on the body or face of a medium, who had the capacity to call it into the world. The findings of a French physician and ectoplasm researcher Dr. Gustave Geley were reported in Guy Christian Barnard's study *The Supernormal: A Critical Introduction to Psychic Science*. Amongst ectoplasm's characteristics were the fact that it was usually white, sometimes opaque, sometimes incandescent. (Barnard, 1933: 88) It seemed soft and a bit elastic when it spread; hard, knotty or fibrous when it formed strings. Sometimes it seemed like a spider's web fluttering over the hand. The substance was mobile. At any moment, so the doctor reported from the experience of a medium, it might evolve, rise, fall, wander over the medium, her shoulders, her breast, her knees, with a creeping motion that recalls that of a reptile. The same witness warned that any touch will resonate painfully on the medium who is touched by it. If the touch is ever so slightly harsh or prolonged, the medium evinces pain compared to that which a shock to the quick would produce. After making its appearance, ectoplasm was re-absorbed into the medium's body. It came to be known in the world largely through its photographic capture. The photographing of the moment is said to record it, but is also the agent that destroys it. Ectoplasm photography is a variety of spirit photography in which something more material than "aura" is captured. Albert von Schrenck-Notzing researched and publicized the existence of ectoplasm and, in 1923, published the book *Phenomena of Materialisation* with photographic illustrations of the medium he studied, Eva Carrière, between the years 1909 and 1913. (Fig. 1.3) (Schrenk-Notzing, 1923)

Albert von Schrenck-Notzing believed that ectoplasm could become the basis for a thought-ography or ideoplasty, whereby the medium could project images from her mind onto the surface of the ectoplasm. The photographic results seem fairly clearly to anyone's eyes to be cut-outs of faces and other photographic images from illustrated magazines glued onto the cheesecloth and gauze that purports to be ectoplasm. There is a double photography at work: The photographs of the mass media—of Woodrow Wilson, King Ferdinand of Bulgaria, Raymond Poincaré, and the actress Mona Delza—and the constructed photograph of the séance situation. These "ideoplasts," or projections of the mind of the medium, are the capacity of photography to invent a world, and even to invent a world that is only visible

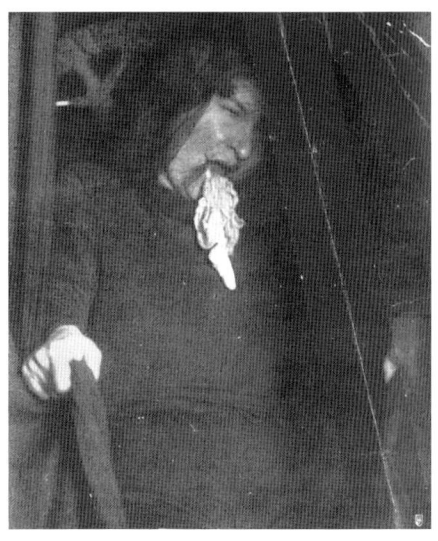

Figure 1.3

Eva Carrière, born Marthe Béraud, exuding ectoplasm, ca. 1910, photograph published in Albert von Schrenck-Notzing, *Phenomena of Materialisation*, 1923.

through its vectors. Thomas Glendenning Hamilton was a photographer who is believed to have grafted cut outs from magazines onto the scene he photographed. His photograph of the medium Mary Ann Marshall is apparently tissue paper with a stuck-on cut out of Arthur Conan Doyle's head from a newspaper.[1]

Ectoplasmic photographs were clearly faked, but there was a desire on the part of various credulous people to believe in the process, to believe that what was shown in the photograph was something beckoning from another side, a dark side, not normally exposed to photographic illumination. The body of the medium, exuding ectoplasm, is a chemical agent, a reactor, a set of processes, a site of unconscious, involuntary and frankly absurd productivity. Its normal processing is interrupted by something that cannot be controlled, even if it can be captured by another chemical system, that of photography. Through photography, a body—most often a female body—is captured oozing something. This ectoplasm is, according to the narratives, a material shot out painfully from the medium's body. Sometimes a spasming body is caught by the camera, frozen in a tortured pose. Inner bodily excretions are forced out to produce an image for the camera. Could this be seen as an analog of the photographic procedure itself, whereby photography captures bodily states, or states of nature, that are hitherto unknown, unpredictable, unconscious, unseeable, except for in their mediation? Once they are seen, these registrations, though, appear more akin to a dream vision, relating to the fantastical, the absurd, the something beneath the surface, not that which reflects immediately on the glossy surface of photographic papers. They capture an "optical unconscious," seemingly.

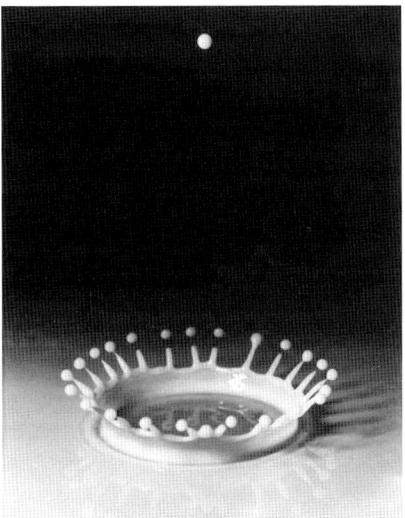

Figure 1.4

Harold Eugene Edgerton, *Milk Drop Coronet*, 1936.

What other impossible, undetected matter of nature might find only photographic form in the coming years? What collapses of machine and human vision might poke around the other side of nature and find something possible that appears absurd. Harold Edgerton perfected the electronic flash and used this blitz of light to freeze time into space, to make an image of a micro-moment. Time's interruption by light was an effect he had noticed accidentally while working under stroboscopic conditions at the factory of General Electric in Schenectady, New York, in the 1920s. From the 1930s onwards, he used his techniques and devices of arresting time to capture the crown-like shapes of a milk drop as it hit a surface, (Fig. 1.4) or the steady progress amidst chaos of a bullet as it tore through a card or an apple. There is much that happens sub-perceptually in the world. There are worlds existing within worlds, things yet to be seen or discovered. New technologies can bring those new worlds to light, in order to be glimpsed through the machinery.

In the few years after World War II, Harold Edgerton took photographs of atomic bomb explosions during test detonations. He invented a special camera called the "rapatronic"—Rapid Action Electronic—for the purpose of capturing in severe outlines the growing blaze of the nuclear fireball in the initial splinters of a second after release. Edgerton's camera, with its non-mechanical, near instantaneous polarizing shutter, took photographs seven miles away from the blast one ten millionth of a second after ignition with an exposure time of ten nanoseconds. (Fig. 1.5) (Elkins, 2004: 74–81) The fireball was, within that chip of time, massive in diameter and it exuded the heat of several suns. Its blinding light was captured in a sequence of images. The viewer learns that the first micro-moments of an atomic

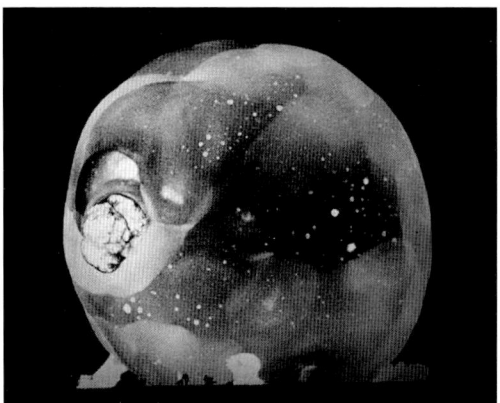

Figure 1.5

Harold Eugene Edgerton,
*Rapatronic photograph of
an atomic blast*, 1952.

explosion produce weird irregular baubles, mottled by variations in the
density of the bomb's casing and augmented by protuberances caused
by the swift vaporization of the wire support cables. The atomic explosion turns time and matter inside out. The rabbit was pulled from
the hat—impossibilities appear on the photograph. In photographing
the atomic explosion, Edgerton produced an exaggeration, an amplifi-
cation, a hyperbole of a tiny moment.

The above examples of photography are just a few of the many
possible ways in which the interposing of a lens, a glass, mediates the
recompositions of nature, including in its form as human body. The
human body, its eye, its gaze, or what we might call the human senso-
rium, is subjected to such reorderings through technological development. A defamiliarization is at work. In these examples, the absurdity
of human life and of the matter that composes all of us and everything
else is foregrounded. The photographs chosen here are absurdities, in
various ways. In one example, fakery highlights the promise of photography to reveal the hitherto unrevealable, as it undermines it. The results are ludicrous, but the gesture has a truth to it—even as fakery,
photography will show us what hope it is invented for, to see an image from beneath the surface, an unseen, an unknown, a perspective
from another place. In another example, parts of the world, plants, are
dragged from the realm of the familiar to the realm of the unfamiliar,
displaced into the subperceptual world, when they are magnified into
image. These "new" plants throw into relief all our fragments of culture,
our buildings, our clothes, our props and make us wonder if it is only
we who have purpose in the world, or only we who are vain enough
to need a world of possessions. These photographs enable a different
reconciliation between nature and culture to coalesce. These reconcil-
iations have a humor about them, perhaps a humor that recuperates,
in the sense understood by the Situationists, as photographic humor

is so frequently mobilized by advertising. In yet another example, the world is shattered or contorted in the image, just as it is by the force of the thing, the nuclear event, imaged. Through this distortion, those unrealistic chunks of the real, hitherto unseen, now visible, yet still obscure, an analysis of those shattered parts becomes possible, in order to open the way to a reconfiguration of our world, as it is blasted into change, at least in thought. This is a photograph of terror, the smallest atomic portion of nature made fatal, but it is also madly absurd—that these weird shapes can be forced into the world through energy, these explosions, deadly mockeries of our own explosive, ejaculative laughter. But if nature can be so remade, so tempted into energetic release, might it be tempted otherwise to deploy that power against death? At its most extreme, the image of shattered nature—if not the shattered nature itself—might be recombined into something new, and something that exceeds the image space. It plays out something that can be achieved socially, through revolution, a world of play, a *Spielraum*, a play space, room for maneuver, to be gained. (Benjamin, 1996: 117)

In the present, photography extends vision further into realms that have not been seen before, most dramatically when scanning tunneling microscopy composite greyish images from the smallest parts of nature, from the nanoscale. Scientific photography uses digital compositing not only to extend vision through magnification, but rather to work on and over time. Such photography explores processes, gathering up time on one photographic image, in a manner not unlike Etienne-Jules Marey and his chronophotographs of a bird's beating wing and the like, (Braun, 1994: 32) in order to show neural networks or language pathways in the brain or the passage of planets over the course of a year. These are images that are facilitated by digital technologies. An image note for a photograph in the Wellcome Trust image banks, titled *The Placenta Rainbow*, gives an indication of the typical amount of disarticulation at work in the process of representing the sight seen. The photograph highlights differences in mouse placental development that can result from manipulation of the mother's immune system:

Imaging technique: Confocal microscopy

A type of light microscopy that uses visible light (usually in the form of one or more lasers) to illuminate part of the object being viewed. Out-of-focus light above and below the point of focus is filtered out and eliminated from the final image. Thin optical slices through an object can be stacked on top of one another to produce a digital 3D reconstruction.[2]

What remains as image is a careful reconstruction, in which disarticulated, or shattered, parts are rearticulated digitally into an esthetically pleasing and scientifically significant whole, whose layering, whose duration over time, are not apparent. The results are designed to be eye-catching, and so, in this case, the coloration of the materials is to serve a scientific and an esthetic end. The colorings emphasize the curiosity factor, which brings the image into the realm of the Surreal or bizarre.

But most photographic imagery that circulates nowadays is not in the service of science or even esthetics. It is banal, transitory, slipping past the eye. And what is important about it may be less what it shows than that we look at it, that we are known to be consumers of it, for this relationship between looker and looked at is what is key, and is able to be monetized. From the perspective of the present, the smile that found its way into photography in time, the laugh that photography elicits, the signs of emotional state that might flicker across a face, are becoming operative in new ways. The smile came into being historically as a gesture produced for the machine, but its eye was perceived as dead. But that is the case no longer, now that cameras have "smile detection" technology: "The software looks for the open eyes and upturned mouth associated with a smile once it identifies a face or faces on the screen. Many cameras allow users to differentiate between small smiles and big grins so that the camera knows exactly what to look for."[3] This is just another step along the way of intelligent imaging systems. Computing systems are developing affectively through machine-learning algorithms that can detect laughs, smiles, as well as all the negative emotions, and adjust or adapt their functioning accordingly. Emotions communicate with the machine. One of the many projects happening under this guise turns the gaze of the human into an active element, providing data, in an infernal and diabolical loop that represents a hellish development in digital bio-political management, with obvious commercial and political uses. Research into Smile Tracking was active at MIT in 2014 and 2015, as part of the Affective Computing grouping:

SmileTracker

SmileTracker is a system designed to capture naturally occurring instances of positive emotion during the course of normal interaction with a computer. A facial expression recognition algorithm is applied to images captured with the user's webcam. When the user smiles, both a photo and a screenshot are recorded and saved to the user's profile for later review. Based on positive psychology research, we hypothesize that the act of reviewing content that led to smiles will improve positive affect, and consequently, overall wellbeing.[4]

In this communication, it is not apparent that the photographic system is working to extract meaning from stance, attitude, small gestures. It happens somewhere else, as the human—become thing—is a resource of data. It is absurd to see, be photographed, as you work or consume, and to not know that you are emanating value for others—emotional states, sentiment analytics. What might shatter this tight communication, in which one inanimate thing assumes the ability to interpret the other animate one, and in interpreting it subtract its animation as data inputs? How might it be disarticulated? Is there any *Spielraum* left, any room for maneuver or is the circuit of gazes—the machine's to our one—too tightly drawn for anything to interrupt or break the rules? The laugh is operationalized. The photographic machine plays its role in this. What new gestures might we work on to confound the machine, and for our own amusement, just for the humor of it?

Notes

1. See Clément Chéroux, *The Perfect Medium: Photography and the Occult* (London: Yale University Press, 2005).

2. See Suchita Nadkarni, "The Placenta Rainbow," Welcome Image Awards 2017, http://www.wellcomeimageawards.org/2017/the-placenta-rainbow (accessed October 4, 2017).

3. Smile Detection, http://smiledett.blogspot.co.uk/ (accessed October 4, 2017).

4. SmileTracker, MIT Media Lab, https://www.media.mit.edu/projects/smiletracker/overview/ (accessed October 4, 2017).

Bibliography

Guy Christian Barnard, *The Supernormal: A Critical Introduction to Psychic Science* (London: Rider & Co., 1933).

Charles Baudelaire, *Selected Poems of Charles Baudelaire,* translated by Geoffrey Wagner (New York: Grove Press, 1974).

Walter Benjamin, *Illuminations* (New York: Schocken, 1969).

Walter Benjamin, *Selected Writings, Vol. 3* (Cambridge, MA.: Harvard University Press, 1996).

Walter Benjamin, *The Arcades Project* (Cambridge, MA.: Harvard University Press, 1999).

Walter Benjamin, *Selected Writings, Vol. 1* (Cambridge, MA.: Harvard University Press, 2004).

Henri Bergson, *Laughter* (Baltimore: The Johns Hopkins University Press, 1980).

Marta Braun, *Picturing Time: The Work of Etienne-Jules Marey (1830–1904)* (Chicago: University of Chicago Press, 1994).

James Elkins, "Harold's Edgerton's Rapatronic Photographs of Atomic Tests," *History of Photography,* 28, 1 (2004): 74–81.

Friedrich Engels, *Socialism: Utopian and Scientific* (New York: Cosimo, 2008).

Sigmund Freud, *The Interpretation of Dreams,* trans. J. Strachey (London: Penguin, 1976).

Nicholas Jeeves, "The Serious and the Smirk" (2013), http://www.nicholasjeeves.com/The-Serious-and-the-Smirk (accessed October 4, 2017).

Wyndham Lewis, *The Complete Wild Body* (Santa Barbara: Black Sparrow Press, 1982).

Frederic William Henry Myers, *Human Personality and its Survival of Bodily Death* (London: Longmans, 1903).

Baron von Schrenck-Notzing, *Phenomena of Materialisation, A Contribution to the Investigation of Mediumistic Teleplastics,* translated by E. E. Fournier d'Albe (London: E. P. Dutton, 1923).

Marina Warner, Phantasmagoria: Spirit Visions, Metaphors, and Media Into the Twenty-first century (Oxford: Oxford University Press, 2006).

Falling as Art: On Orchestrated Accidents in Photographic Practice in Poland

Katarzyna Ruchel-Stockmans

Tomek Bagiński's animation *Fallen Art* (*Sztuka spadania*) (2004) shows an entirely improbable—at once amusing and despicable—scenario. In a beguilingly natural scenery fabricated by the CGI technology, a group of soldiers is coerced to commit suicidal jumps purely for the sake of creating a mesmerizing and lively dance on screen.[1] Through the transformation of the still into the moving image, photography of the just dead is reanimated in cinema. This could be an exquisite illustration of the Barthesian distinction between photography and film—between the immobility of death snapshots and the captivating movement of cinema—be it for one incongruous detail: the dead have to be produced especially for the photographic images. Photography is here linked with a darker kind of humor, the one which is signaled by convulsive laughter. Leaving behind its benign and jovial varieties, dark comedy touches on incomprehension, revulsion, and even dying. There are few attempts at investigating that risky terrain of photographic practices. This chapter takes as its point of departure Bagiński's short film in order to revisit the particular motive for the fall in the photographic work from 1970s and 1980s Poland. Humor in this approach aligns itself with the act of falling which is inextricably intertwined with the operations of the photofilmic apparatus. Several theorists of humor provide clues for an understanding of the fall as the central motive of dark comedy. Staging and repeating an accidental fall, the artist engages with the contradictory condition of human existence. Through this extensive excursus into theory, Bagiński's animation is revealed as a multiple repetition of that humoresque performance of falling. But it also becomes a vehicle to revisit a number of works of art by Paweł Kwiek, Andrzej Lachowicz, Zbyszko Trzeciakowski and Kultura Zrzuty, in which photography can be said to perform the darker sort of humor.

Fallen Art: Animating the Dead

Bagiński's grotesque fable is located in a remote military base inhabited by a peculiar army unit led by a fatigued general hidden in a dark and decrepit cinema. After being awarded a medal and convivially patted on the shoulder, a soldier is pushed off a makeshift wooden tower. On the ground, an absent-minded medic-photographer awaits his death and takes a top-down photograph of his protracted body. The Polaroid snapshot is then brought to a darkened cinema room where it is passed on to a slumbering general who feeds it into a giant motion picture machine. The machine lights up and begins the process of montage, in which the still photographs are re-animated on screen. The effect of the photo-filmic projector is mesmerizing: the mortified figure from the photograph comes to life in cinematic image. The many similar dead soldiers appear as one moving body dancing to gripping Romanian music. Remarkably, they are not the only ones who convulsively dance, as their every movement is imitated by the lone spectator in the cinema, the suddenly energetic general. At odds with his heavy build, the general effortlessly follows the demanding dancing routine as long as the projection goes on, but as the film abruptly ends returns to the vegetative state. Yet the end of the projection is a new beginning — he sends a signal to the officer who dutifully helps another docile soldier to fall from the tower, so that a new photograph of a dead body can be fed into the machine. A seemingly perpetual life and death cycle continues and the dance performance returns on screen.

The animated world shown in *Fallen Art* is a closed circuit of action and reaction, as if it was a giant production machine. What it produces is a vibrant moving image, perhaps an anachronistically clad vision of the animation's own origin. Within that system nobody seems to mind that it also, repeatedly, produces death in the process. Men die literally for and in front of the camera. They become part of the all-encompassing apparatus, in which the photographic camera and the projector-cinematographer require operators and human fodder as their material. The surprising aspect of the animation seems to lie in that incongruity: a simple set of rules is applied in an all too rational and methodical way.

There are many ways in which this short animation can be perceived as humorous. First, there are the outspoken characters that are grotesque caricatures of themselves. The blocky officer Al shows tender affection for the coy and meager soldiers whom he pushes off the tower. The absent-minded doctor-photographer Dietrich behaves like the romantic-visionary artist who inhabits the upper regions of his thoughts and is eternally dissatisfied with the photographs he creates. The overweight, hunchbacked general A, the one who orchestrates the whole cinematic factory, shows true emotional rapture when seeing a new photograph of a dead soldier. He is the creator but also, strangely, the only consumer of the collectively produced work of art. Finally, there is the puzzling little frog, which assists the peculiar procedure of deadly falls. What binds these distinct characters together to an overall comic effect is the apparently ridiculous and macabre activity they all solemnly commit to perform and, more so, to repeat it endlessly. The central moment in this collective manufacture is the deadly fall.

This vision of a depraved fancy could be read as an ironic take on the Polish heroic-martyrological complex.[2] Similarly to other satires exposing the irrationality of militarism, *Fallen Art* could be seen to ridicule blind obedience, patriarchy and the readiness to kill or die on command.[3] The film remains ambiguous in terms of historical references. It is for the viewer to decide whether to read it as a political critique or a wink at the erotic charge of militarism.[4] As promising as these interpretative tropes might be, I propose to see the animation in a different context. The Polish title of the animation, *Sztuka Spadania*, hints at a mock vision of art production whereas the English translation into *Fallen Art* suggests a derailed form of artistic practice. In the former, falling is elevated to art as it becomes part of artistic endeavor. In the latter, art is fallen and thus sinks to a base, vile, and despicable state. When read as a defiant proposal for envisioning the essence of the photo-filmic art process, this title invites the viewer to approach the image of the fall, of photography, film and repetition in a new way. Strikingly, Bagiński seems to irreverently reshuffle some of the well-known tropes in photography and media theory. The deadly fall performed for the camera becomes a necessary sacrifice assuring that art can become alive. Horrifying in its inhumane logic, it triggers uncomfortable laughter.

Humor versus Gravity

The theme of photography performing humor provokes a number of questions. In what sense can humor be performed by photography? Does somebody perform a humorous act in front of the camera? Or perhaps it is the photographic apparatus itself that is an agent in staging a comedy? In the first case, the camera is used consciously by an operator — or a monteur — in order to create an opportunity to laugh. In the second, the humorous moment happens without anybody's intentional doings. The first modality seems to have an obvious, because intentional, comic dimension. Think of gags, jokes, slapstick comedy, unexpected juxtapositions in photomontage. The second is more elusive. Glenn Hartz and Ralph Hunt introduced the distinction between advertent (our first case) and inadvertent humor (our second case).

The advertent humor is more prone to becoming an object of analysis. The inadvertent one is more difficult to tackle. Hartz and Hunt even find it somehow ethically repugnant. An example they give is ominous for this analysis: inadvertent humor occurs in a situation when a person slips and falls while walking down a pavement. Others see this unfortunate accident and burst out laughing. For Hartz and Hunt, this means laughing at the perpetrator, which is, least to say, problematic. The advertent humor, on the other hand, means laughing with the perpetrator—laughing with the comedian who cracks a joke, for example. (Hartz and Hunt, 1991)

The phrase "photography performing humor" shifts the performative agency from the comedian or camera operator towards photography itself. I take this phrase to indicate that what is sought is something akin to inadvertent humor, although in what follows I also challenge the distinction between the inadvertent and advertent humor mentioned above. In order to arrive at a better understanding of these categories with respect to the humorous performativity of photography, it is first necessary to interrogate the notion of humor itself.[5]

Numerous theories of humor focused either on its objects (what is funny?) on the attitudes it favors (does it stem from an acceptance of the given situation or its critique?) or effects it has on a person (is it beneficial or harmful for the people's well-being?). One thing the various theories of humor want to avoid at all costs, argues Henri Bergson, is to codify and entrench the lively phenomenon in rigid categories and concepts. (Bergson, 2005: 8–9) For him laughter is like a living organism, a creature which remains unpredictable and capricious. But is it always desirable to let the creature alive?

Humor has often been treated with suspicion or overtly criticized for seemingly the same reasons it was praised in the first place. Following the early advice of Hobbes, one should be wary of a humorous attitude, as it implies we laugh at our fellows. (Hobbes, 1991: 43) Laughing means looking down at other people, and this position of superiority can be boiled down to a man feeling superior over "nature." A human subject perceives herself as something different from the crude and thoughtless creatures. In his celebrated essay on laughter, Charles Baudelaire describes a typical circumstance which most people find funny: a man tripping and falling on ice or a pavement. (Baudelaire, 2008 (1855): 21) An inadvertent fall, as a spectacular failure, is an exemplary situation that triggers laughter. From the ancient philosophers to slapstick comedy and animation, an inadvertent fall remains funny even if repeated ad infinitum. Many of the theorists of laughter return to that model situation of falling in spite of the critiques it has received.[6]

Henri Bergson analyses it in the perspective of the object of laughter and comes to the conclusion that what is funny in a man stumbling and falling is the perceived automatism, or mechanical aspect, of a living being. The unfortunate man fails to notice a puddle or a banana peel; continues to walk, but abruptly stumbles and falls to the ground. It is as if his body was unable to catch up with his intentions. Others see this incongruity between the body and the spirit and burst out laughing. Moreover, for Bergson it is crucial that a group of people finds this incident funny. Humor implies a common understanding of what is accepted and experienced as amusing. Laughter is collective, even when that common dimension is only imagined or assumed. In other words, I can laugh when I'm alone, but still I imagine, or sense, being part of a community of like-minded people. (Bergson, 2005: 11) These two characteristics: something mechanic encrusted on the living and the community aspect of laughter will inform my subsequent analysis.

Consider again the critiques of the superiority theory of humor, namely the fact that comedy of that sort must imply making fun of other people. Laughing "at" is exclusive, as those who are the object of laughter are excluded from the community.[7] Following a clue provided by the philosopher Leszek Kołakowski, laughing at others, although a common affect, is not yet humor. While many people might be all too eager to make fun at others, humor is that rare ability to laugh at oneself. (Kołakowski, 2009) Without naming it such, Baudelaire also distinguishes that precious self-critical attitude which for him characterizes a philosopher. That attitude requires a splitting or a doubling of the self and looking at oneself as if from outside. It encompasses a realization of one's own inferiority, fragility and, ultimately, finality. A wise man can laugh only with trembling, says Baudelaire. The merry feeling is always tinged with horror — it is therefore always a mixed and conflicting affect. In the most gripping passages of the essay Baudelaire describes true laughter as violent. (Baudelaire, 2008 (1855): 26)

This idea has often been misunderstood or simplified. Charles Baudelaire demonstrates that the elevated position from which a subject laughs is actually based on a false perception of superiority. The subject who laughs considers himself better than the one who inadvertently falls to the ground. Yet, this situation can easily be reversed and the laughing subject can become the object of laughter. For Baudelaire this duality of man is the symptom of him being stranded between the inferior matter (or thoughtless nature) and the immaterial absolute (or the elevated spirit). Yet it is important to note that this dualism is something he puts into question. As Debarati Sanyal demonstrates, Baudelaire's theory of laughter is a continuous unraveling of the apparent oppositions between matter and spirit, self and other, object (falling) and subject (laughing at falling). (Sanyal, 2006: 44–50)

For Baudelaire, laughter is thus inevitably concatenated with finality and death. This however is a challenging point in the understanding of dark humor. The comic moment that occurs when one realizes one's own finitude does not entail a pathetic reversal of tragedy. In other words, it is not simply a way of reconciling oneself with death. Laughing at somebody falling does not, or should not, result in an acceptance of the fact that "we will all die." Rather, as Alenka Zupančič argues, it is a confrontation with and a realization of a "hole" in that finitude itself. In Zupančič' words, "'man,' a human being, interests comedy at the very point where the human coincides with the inhuman; where the inhuman 'falls' into the human (into man), where the infinite falls into the finite, where the Essence falls into appearance and the necessary into the contingent." (Zupančič, 2008: 48–49) Note how the initial comic situation of a man falling on a pavement migrates to a metaphor and becomes a figure of thought aimed at a better understanding of the human condition. In this abstracting operation, it is no longer the initial physical fall of somebody that is at stake here. "Falling" takes place in between the seemingly oppositional categories of finitude and infinity. If we think about the human in terms of oppositions (finite versus infinite, dead matter versus lively spirit, intelligent man versus instinct-driven animal, organism versus machine), then the reflection on dark humor guides us towards complicating these binary categories. Following this path, it is necessary to confront a paradox. Zupančič resorts to the visual representation of the Moebius strip. When walking on one "side" of the strip, one is compelled to discover the other side. But continuing on the strip will inevitably result in going to the "other" side or, rather, the other side is already part of this side. Laughing at a man falling surprisingly brings with it a discovery of that paradoxical character of human being, where the finite uncomfortably meets the infinite, the organic and lively turns out, at the same time, to be brute, animalistic or mechanic.

Let us return to Baudelaire and his idea of doubling necessary for reflexive laughter. The individual, who is able to look at herself as if from outside, as oneself and other at the same time, is a true philosopher. Her task, which for Baudelaire is akin to that of the artist, is to reenact that inadvertent fall for the public. It is in the repetition of the accidental falling that the spectators follow the path from the false sense of superiority to the self-reflexive realization of their own contradictory nature. Ultimately, the opposition between the advertent and the inadvertent fall also becomes unraveled.

Recourse to the mechanic or seemingly automated aspect of the fall brings back the question of photography. Although absent from the aforementioned theories of humor, photography enters this discussion through a back door.

From Death Snapshots to Laughter Machines

Photography is not often approached from the humorous side,[8] and yet it seems to have at least two things in common with the notion of humor sketched above. First, photography effectuates that doubling of the self which is the condition of self-reflexive laughter. Roland Barthes noted that quality of the medium when he announced that "the photograph is the advent of myself as other." (Barthes, 1982: 12) A close resemblance of oneself, the photograph is an imitation of that self, forcing the sitter to confront herself in the picture. In some circumstances, seeing a photograph of oneself from a moment which cannot be recalled from memory can result in a sensation of meeting one's double. (Webb, 2008: 70)

Second, photography has long been seen as having a pronounced relationship with death. Repeatedly, cameras were used to capture that elusive transition from life to death. Throughout history, Malkowski argued, "image-makers sought to freeze the 'moment' of (violent) death in a photograph or contain it within a strip of film." (Malkowski, 2017: 24) In the theoretical contributions of, among others, Barthes and Christian Metz, photography is the emblem of death, especially when seen in contrast to the moving, and thus animated, image on film. Metz associated photographic authority with its immobility and silence, which for him are two objective aspects and symbols of death. (Metz, 1985) And according to Barthes, a photograph is "this image which produces Death while trying to preserve life." (Barthes, 1982: 92) There is, therefore, something deeply ambiguous in the relationship a photograph has with life and death. Seemingly capturing the appearance of somebody and preserving it for the future, it, for Barthes, effectuates the opposite. By freezing a fleeting moment in life it inevitably becomes a reminder of death.

What characterizes these thinkers of photography is the solemnity and seriousness of their approach towards the subject of death. This approach is so entrenched in academia that it seems improbable to change its register from serious to humorous. Humor is conspicuously absent from academic research on death. This lack is due, as Jack Halberstam argues, to the fear of not being taken seriously as a historian, academic, or theorist.[9] More than that, humor is a risky subject, because it is often expected that its analysis and interpretation should equally be humorous. A comic situation easily induces indignation or embarrassment instead of laughter. Meandering through these contradictions, Bagiński's animation facilitates a methodological leap in photography performing humor. Revisiting visual tropes from contemporary art and photography through the lens of the theoretical insights on falling, this animated fable becomes a vehicle in thinking about humor in photography.

Jump, Die, Repeat

In Tomek Bagiński's animation one can find many of the building blocks of the theory of humor on the one hand and of photo-filmic media and death on the other, yet their role or significance is inverted. The death caused by a fall is a necessary element of the creative process. The morbid cruelty of the scenario resembles Shirley Jackson's short story *The Lottery*, where the peaceful little community of villagers commits a yearly ritual of stoning of one villager selected in a lottery. One can also think of Jonathan Swift's pamphlet in which child consumption is proposed as a solution to famine. *Fallen Art* could also be read as a solution for all the war-thirsty militaries, who would be sent to an island where war would be a game soldiers play among themselves. Yet what distinguishes Bagiński's animation from these literary examples is the role of the photo-filmic apparatus. The animation is built on a repetition of the fall, but also repeats other images and image operations known from history. Bagiński's soldiers leap into certain death in order for their protracted bodies to be photographed. In their falling, there is a mean echo of the most famous war photograph, namely the *Falling Soldier*. In 1936, Robert Capa captures the moment a bullet reaches a loyalist soldier in Franco's Spain. On the photograph, the soldier is frozen eternally in the instant before falling completely to the ground. Strangely perhaps, the visual reportage in the magazine VU from that year shows not just one but two photographs with similar moments just before the death. (van den Berghe, 2011: 50–51) History repeats itself, and dead soldiers keep falling. The biographer of Capa Richard Whelan mentions that early commentators even saw in these two photographs two consecutive moments in the death of the same soldier. (Whelan, 2006) Later it was demonstrated that they only resemble each other, but are in fact two different persons. It seems quite odd that Capa made two very similar photographs of dying — and falling — soldiers. A well-known controversy around the photographs focuses on the possible staging of the whole scene, which, as some investigations show, could (partly) be correct. One plausible explanation is that the photographs were made in a posed photo session, during which the soldiers were unexpectedly gunned by a sniper. The photographs therefore show the real death of the soldiers, which is more or less accidentally captured by Capa.[10] The dramatic and dynamic pose of the falling soldier became entrenched in the collective memory as an iconic image of death. Significantly, Bagiński's photographer doctor Dietrich awaits the definite passing of the fallen soldiers and only then captures their protracted bodies in similarly "dynamic" poses. Adding up many similar images, the dead are reanimated — not in their physical bodies, but on screen.

The positioning of bodies on the ground and photographing them from above in order to reanimate them in stop-motion picture is a method known from recent art practice. It was used by Katarzyna Kozyra in her multi-channel video installation *The Rite of Spring* (1999–2002). Kozyra reanimates the photographs of naked elderly people performing rather demanding dancing figures. At the rate of 1,500 frames per minute, the effect is of a completely smooth, even if sometimes jerky and protracted, dance routine. Kozyra's work caused a scandal worthy of its famous predecessor, Igor Stravinsky's ballet *The Rite of Spring* from 1913. (Walker, 2001, Wróblewska, 2011) She defiantly imposed a different look at ability, aging, beauty norms and gender. Interestingly for this analysis, she reversed Stravinsky's idea of dance as a primordial sacrifice to nature. In the ballet, a girl is chosen as an offering for which she has to dance to death. In Kozyra's version of the rite, people nearing the end of life, or at least not expected to dance wildly, are miraculously empowered to perform difficult and dynamic poses. The photo-filmic apparatus is the agent of that miracle, since the people are only made to perform the poses as tableaux vivants, protected by the sure solidity of the floor. Stravinsky and the choreographer Nijinsky were praised and criticized for resorting to fragmented, stiff and mechanic movement. The dancers were said to move like machines or lifeless puppets. (Rivière, 1913: 722–723) In Kozyra's, and by extension Bagiński's work, the dance actually is a mechanically constructed movement. Kozyra therefore attempted to reformulate that outrageous idea of a sacrificial dance bought at the price of an innocent life. Bagiński, on the contrary, seemingly returns to the despicable idea of sacrificial death.

In theoretical accounts discussed above, a person accidentally falling is often taken as the model humorous situation. Bagiński reverses that model, creating an absurd world where an orchestrated fall, leading to the death of the jumping person, is the beginning and the condition of the creative act of photography. Other artistic examples are not far away. As it happens, several artists working in performative and conceptual paradigms take such orchestrated and controlled fall as their working method, yet their laughter is rather convulsive. Two key works of art on the theme of the fall need to be mentioned: Yves Klein's *Leap into the Void* (1960) and Bas Jan Ader's series of staged falls. The first is known as a single photograph of the artist throwing himself ecstatically from a building into a street, the second encompasses various pieces of video and photography showing the artist falling from a rooftop while seated on a chair, biking into a canal or hanging from a tree and eventually sliding into the water. Klein's *Leap* can be seen as a repetition achieved by a contrivance. Determined to visualize an accidental fall he experienced previously, Klein staged the leap and had it photographed by Harry Shunk and Janos Kender. The final image

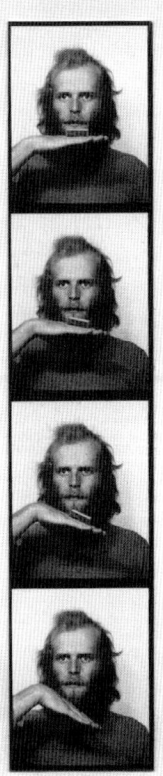

UPADEK   1973.

Figure 1.6

Paweł Kwiek, *Upadek (Fall)*, 1976, series of four photomaton photographs mounted on cardboard, 20 × 30 cm. Courtesy Paweł Kwiek and Arton Foundation.

is a composite photograph. By means of montage, two images were combined in order to conceal the tarp held by a group of friends on the original photograph with Klein falling. The leap into the spiritual void is achieved by carefully staging and crafting the image.

Bas Jan Ader's repeated attempts at capturing his own fall are based on simple performances for the camera. In contrast to Klein's leap, they are "authentic" situations in which the artist's body was put under duress without hidden contraptions. Yet the seeming compulsion with which he repeated these unassuming acts brings them closer to a parodic laughter. (Laermans, 2006) The premature death of both of these artists threw a shadow of seriousness on their oeuvre. Yet their activities disclose the propensity towards irony and distanced self-mockery. Their well-known falls should be expanded, however, into a discussion of some less exposed examples. In the remaining section of this chapter I discuss four cases of the art of falling, coming from the Polish context of the 1970s and the 1980s. They range from what Philip Auslander called performed photography to performance documentation. (Auslander, 2006)

A Photographic Cool

A Fall (*Upadek*) made by Paweł Kwiek in 1975 is a series of four photographs from a photo booth from which the artist, seen in a portrait view typical of an identity photograph, stages a fall in front of the camera. (Fig. 1.6) While the artist's face remains unmovable in the four subsequent pictures, he makes a small box slide off his outstretched hand. The fall occurs in a minutely planned situation. It is one of several series of photo booth art done by Kwiek in this period. In them, photography serves as a means of investigation into visual communication, metalanguage and auto-referentiality. Simple things or gestures by the artist's hands become ideal objects drawn outside of the photographic frame. Kwiek was active between the Łódź film school and the Warsaw artists' milieu centered around Oskar Hansen and the Open Form Studio. Working with the camera to record actions and performances, he was interested in ephemeral and unpredictable processes that could objectively be documented by the photographic and filmic apparatus. His serial photographs can be associated with the so-called contextual art.[11] (Świdziński, 2009)

Kwiek's deadpan expression and the sequential character of the series give this work a serious, scientific allure, even if the experiment seems rather trivial. Following the principles of the Open Form, Kwiek stages and isolates a single operation for which his own presence is only a backdrop.[12] Yet the forcedly neutral presence of the artist gives the

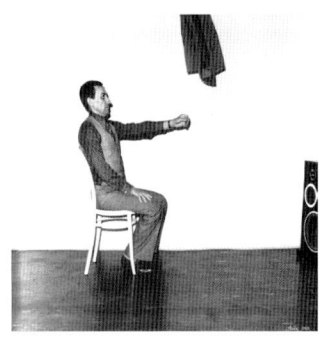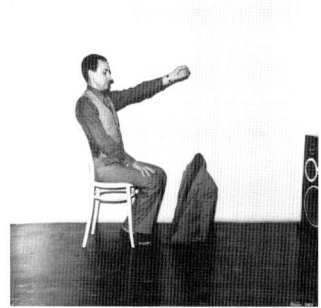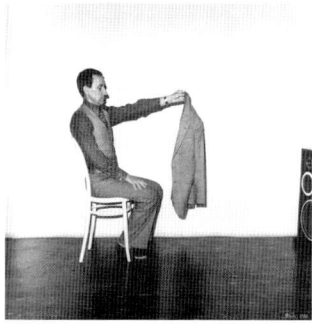

work a humorous twist. It is the artist's body as a usable and inconspicuous material for art which triggers an uneasy laugh. As the viewer focuses on the falling object, what effectively falls out of the visible field is the figure of the artist. Photographing himself in the format and convention of an identity photograph, Kwiek in fact erases himself from the picture.[13]

A similar deadpan attitude can be seen in the series of photographs by Andrzej Lachowicz, entitled *Energy of the Fall* (*Energia upadku*) from 1981. (Fig. 1.7)[14] These sequential shots also show things falling off the hand of the artist. Lachowicz is seated or, in one case, standing, in an otherwise empty interior. Always with the same air of neutral investigation, he holds a coat hanger, a jacket, or a cardigan in his outstretched hand and drops them on the floor in subsequent pictures. In another sequence, the artist performs the fall himself as he stands straight in the first frame and bends to the right or to the left in subsequent frames. Yet in some cases, the photographs are swapped or the object is shown in the upper part of the frame as if the process of falling was reversed. These simple procedures recorded with the camera balance between pure observation of the laws of nature and a playful reversal of those laws. The fall sometimes is and sometimes is not what it seems, while the camera either neutrally registers the action or is complicit in staging a visual trick.

Lachowicz performed the fall more than once and in more than one sense. Initially trained as an engineer in Cracow, he studied art in Wrocław and spent most of his artistic life there. He ran the Permafo gallery and subscribed to the principle of "permanent" art.[15] He had a profound and lasting interest in the idea of the fall, also in an existential dimension. Both Lachowicz and Kwiek went through a conversion to catholicism, which adds to the idea of the fall yet another facet—that of religious symbolism. In the 1980s, he wrote a text under that same title: "Energy of the Fall." In a style not devoid of contradictions and defiant abstractions, he argued for a less negative approach to falling. He defined it as a sort of complicating the world which is relative in terms

Figure 1.7

Andrzej Lachowicz, *Energia upadku (Energy of the Fall)*, 1980, series of three photographs on canvas, collection of Dolnośląskie Towarzystwo Zachęty Sztuk Pięknych, Wrocław (DTZSP), photo by Małgorzata Kujda, © DTZSP.

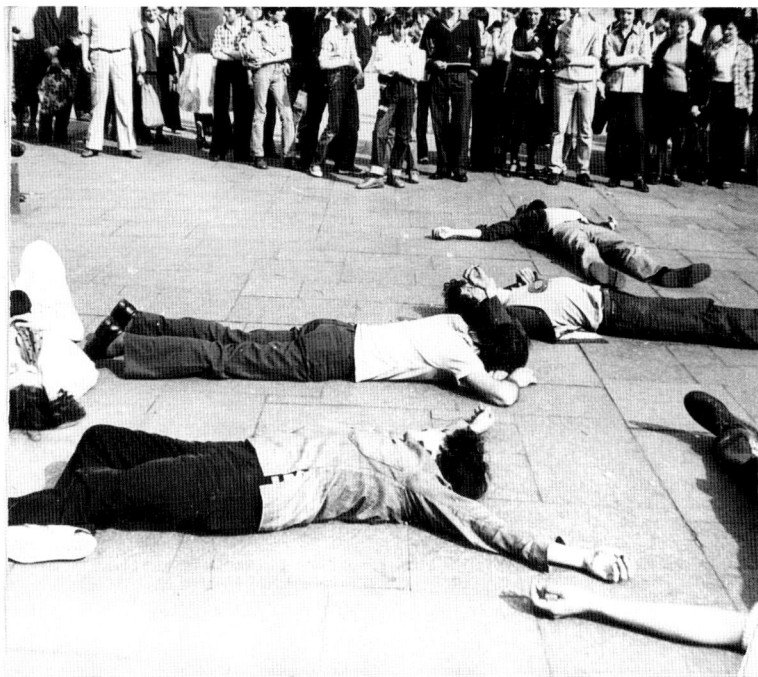

Figure 1.8

Lódź Kaliska, *Upadek
zupełny (Complete
Fall)*. Two photographs
mounted on cardboard,
hand-written and typed
text, 1982, photo by Piotr
Tomczyk. Courtesy of
Lódź Kaliska.

-- Kraków — 13.05.81. Rynek Główny: Łódź Kaliska zrealizowała
akcję „UPADEK ZUPEŁNY"

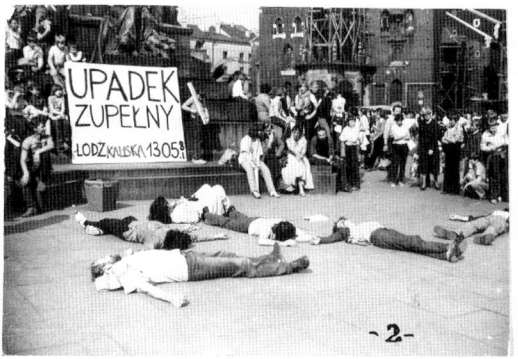

of value and perhaps even necessary in achieving a change. (Piotrowski,
2010) Paradoxically, he posited, the fall itself is not free from falling.
But what would a falling fall lead to? This amusing principle prompted
him to repeatedly experiment with falling in reverse. Apart from the
Energy of the Fall series, he spent a significant part of this life studying a
shape falling in front of him — his own shade. As a life irony, Lachowicz
experienced quite a devastating fall later in his personal life. (Jurecki,
2008) After an ill-fated accident, he was confined to a wheelchair for
the rest of his life.[16]

Quite in contrast to Lachowicz's unfortunate accident and more in tune with Bagiński's fallen art, another artist of the 1980s staged his own fall. Zbyszko Trzeciakowski (1957–2006) started experimenting with falling on a floor covered with lime powder. He registered these performances on two photographic cameras, but these photographs were unfortunately lost. (Truszkowski, 2013: 147) Three years later he performed *The Fall on the Bamboo Sticks* in Poznań (1986). In a private apartment frequented by artists and local punks, he threw himself on the bamboo sticks embedded in the floor. The action was filmed and then photographs were made (by the artist himself) out of the video recordings. The original videos are lost. According to some accounts, Trzeciakowski destroyed them because he thought them too extreme. (Krajewski, 2010: 205) According to others, they were "lost" after an exhibition. (Truszkowski, 2014) The photo captures the artist's out-stretched body in a dangerous tilt towards the bamboo spikes on the floor. This piece belonged to a group of performative works of this artist, which were designed to test the limits of his own endurance. It also ended badly—Trzeciakowski broke several ribs and a jaw. In his own words, he searched for a life-risking situation which would appear in a "non-banal form." (Lisowski, 2014) He argued that in the present-day-reality—the 1980s Poland, after the harsh period of the Marshall Law—he as an individual lacked basic freedoms and in fact could lose his life at any moment in time due to an arrest or an act of aggression by the police. (Truszkowski, 2013: 147) In these circumstances, he wanted to make this choice himself and risk his life in an artistic action. There is an absurd aspect to this practice. On the one hand, the artist seeks an extreme challenge risking his own death; on the other, he remains playful as he searches for an appealing form for such a radical act. It may also be one of the reasons why his works remain little known and his name is almost forgotten in the art history of the period. A witness recalled that shortly after his surprise fall on the bamboo sticks, when the artist lost consciousness due to the shock, a small girl present in the room exclaimed in amusement: "That's so cool." (Truszkowski, 2013: 146) Balancing between dead serious and playful, Trzeciakowski's dark humor proves difficult to place within the art system.

This is also the case with the fourth work on the theme of falling. In May 1981 the Łódź Kaliska art collective and artists associated with Pitch-in Culture (in Polish: *Kultura Zrzuty*)[17] staged and photographed a performance called *Complete Fall* (*Upadek zupełny*). Out of many photographs documenting this performance, several were chosen to represent the event. They show a group of artists lying on the pavement of the Main Market Square in Cracow, in a symbolically charged place next to the monument to the national poet Adam Mickiewicz. (Fig. 1.8) On the pedestal of the monument the artists placed a board with the title of the performance followed by an explanation admitting bluntly that it was an "economic action" (*akcja zarobkowa*), aimed at an immediate material gain. (Kuryłek: 28) The inscription on the cardboard next to the photographs repeated again that the artists' main motivation was their lack of money and added that the event was commissioned by the local club Pod Jaszczurami.

This action was part of a week long program encompassing various interventions and encounters in the city. It was designed in such a way as to create a complete "world of art," intended to become a parallel reality doubling the existing universe. The idea was to live twice, perhaps because, as Walter Benjamin convincingly agued, once is never (*Einmal is Keinmal*). The actions were therefore organized in seven days in analogy to the Biblical story of Genesis and consisted of a permanent play registered on film and photographs. The complete fall of the artists thus acquired the lapsarian dimension typical of Biblical symbolism.

One of the participating artists, Andrzej Kwietniewski, recalls that they lay down, fallen and broken, because they realized this was what an artist in the society of the time was — namely, a bankrupt in social and moral terms (the Polish *upadek* encompasses these various meanings, from Biblical, through physical, to economic ruination).[18] Therefore, while intended as an ironic commentary and a playful reconfiguration of reality into an imaginary world, *Complete Fall* is equally a bitter commentary on that reality and the conditions of living and working as an artist.

The group associated with Pitch-In Culture and the related Łódź Kaliska formation overtly resorted to humor and mockery. Their actions can thus be qualified as advertent humor. Andrzej Lachowicz, whose *Energy of the Fall* played at a reversal of the tragic fall, scornfully rejected the grotesque and mocking attitude of Pitch-In Culture. According to him, all the group achieved was irreverently but clumsily to ridicule the official culture, but the effects of these actions failed and were definitely "not funny." (Banasiak, 2007: 5) In turn, Pitch-In Culture willingly ridiculed the "serious" artistic approach of, among others, Lachowicz. (Stelmach, 2015) An overt and deliberate derision of Kultura Zrzuty seems at odds with the previous examples of falling in art. Without attempting to draw these practices closer to each other, this investigation rather demonstrates how playing at falling results in different forms and figurations of the humorous motive. The four case studies therefore present different variants of the art of falling. Beyond the obvious differences between Kwiek, Lachowicz, Trzeciakowski and Pitch-In Culture, their "falls" offer valuable experimentations into repetition based on the possibilities of the photographic apparatus. Resorting to the doubling and freezing qualities of the machine, they explore the terrain of art infiltrating into life.

In theoretical debates, humor has been connected to an archetypal situation which most of us find funny — a man accidentally falling on the ground. This picture had to be corrected, since humor should involve self-reflexive laughter at oneself (oneself as other), for which photography, equipped to perform the doubling and a repetition of the self, seems particularly suitable. One's own fall should be the proper object of humor, as it entails an encounter, even if fleeting, with one's own death. Humor should therefore be understood as laughter tinged with a darker note. This, however, is a reminder of that paradoxical oscillation between flesh and spirit, living organism and machine, movement and stillness. The short animation by Bagiński derisively replaced the accidental fall with an arranged jump into death, convincing us that dead photographs can be transformed into an on-screen, and lively, performance.

Notes

1. Bagiński's *Fallen Art* (2004) can be viewed online at https://youtu.be/f9OtRxduVNk.

2. One might note echoes of Tadeusz Kantor's vision of dead soldiers shot down again with a camera-gun in *Wielopole, Wielopole.* On the heroic-martyrological complex in the Polish culture, especially in connection with the persistence of romanticism, see the studies of Maria Janion. (Janion, 2000)

3. Other such satires are Charlie Chaplin's *The Great Dictator* to Michael Moore's *Fahrenheit 9/11*. See a discussion of such forms of humor by John Morreall. (Morreall, 2012)

4. See the essay on the fascist aesthetics by Susan Sontag. (Sontag, 1975)

5. I have argued elsewhere that images can "perform" history, but will avoid drawing on that study in order to investigate the hypothesis of photography

performing humor from the perspective of theories of comedy and laughter. (Ruchel-Stockmans, 2015)

6. Not only Baudelaire and Bergson pay attention to the inadvertent falling as a source of laughter. Other authors ruminating on that subject include Anca Parvulescu and Alenka Zupancic discussed below.

7. Literary scholar Anca Parvulescu pertinently argues that there is laughter which has no object (nobody is laughed at), but that has the common aspect (it is a laughing with). (Parvulescu, 2017: 519) There is, according to Parvulescu, something godly in it, as if not laughing at others was almost beyond human capacities. As it will appear below, gripping towards the limits of humanness is very much at the center of this particular theory of humor.

8. The notable exceptions are the studies of Heinz K. Henisch, Bridget Ann Henisch and Louis Kaplan. (Henisch and Henisch, 1998; Kaplan, 2009, 2016)

9. Jack Halberstam made this point in the lecture entitled "On Behalf of Failure" at the 2014 Summer School for Sexualities, Culture and Politics, IPAK Center at Singidunum University, Belgrade. The recorded version of the lecture can be found on http://www.ipakcentar.org/open-lecture-jack-halberstam.

10. As an analysis of the contact sheets shows, Capa was photographing the posing or exercising soldiers while unexpectedly a sniper shot a deadly bullet at the soldier in question. This is one plausible explanation among others, yet its advantage lies in demonstrating how a degree of staging or theatricality can be part and parcel of what otherwise should be considered an "authentic" documentary photograph. A recent survey of the various theories about the *Falling Soldier* can be found in the book-long study by Vincent Lavoie. (Lavoie, 2017)

11. Świdziński formulated his theses on the contextual art against the universalist claims of conceptualism which he perceived from the perspective of a culturally colonized and forgotten Eastern European country. According to him art has to be understood in a set of historical and social circumstances, infrastructures and discourses. As a result, art's significance is never settled but rather evolves through time. (Świdziński; Ronduda 2008)

12. The concept of Open Form was developed by Oskar Hansen in his theory of architecture and planning, but was extended to artistic practice in general.

It moves away from the closed and rigid object-oriented practice towards process, transformation and environment-integrated forms. The attitude associated with the open form is directed not so much on possessing and dominating of the environment but rather at playfully exploring of the chosen situation. (Hansen, 2005a, 2005b)

13. This self-effacement becomes even more apparent when his other photographic works are taken into account. Paweł Kwiek created a series of various experiments based on similar self-portraits in a photo booth. Minor variations in the images, such as an object held in the artist's hand or his index finger pointing outside the frame, are used to stage various experimental situations. While Kwiek investigates the particularities of closed and open systems of visual signification, his own appearance in the picture frame remains constant and thus hardly noticeable.

14. The three photographs reproduced here are in the collection of Dolnośląskie Towarzystwo Zachęty Sztuk Pięknych, Wrocław (DTZSP). There are, however, other versions of this work with a different order of photographs. According to the artist Natalia LL, who was present during the making of the series, the sequence was deliberately reversed by Lachowicz in various versions of the *Energy of the Fall*. This statement by Natalia LL was collected by Wrocław Contemporary Museum's main registrar Dominika Sośnicka. I would like to thank Dominika Sośnicka for her invaluable help in interpreting Lachowicz' work.

15. Permanent art refers to the never-ending registration procedures applied by the group of artists belonging the Permafo group. (Markowska, 2013)

16. This accident happened in the year 2000.

17. Pitch-In Culture is, according to Łukasz Ronduda, a strategy of sharing which emerged out of necessity and was the need to survive without public funding. Its artistic actions were described as nihilistic, Dadaist, anarchist. (Bryzgel, 2013: 170)

18. The action was organized as part of the festival "Manifestacje, performance" launched by Wojciech Sztaba, Artur Tajber and Władysław Kaźmierczak. According to Andrzej Kwietniewski: "We fell, we lay down because we had no money. Being an artist is in fact a collapse [upadek] in a moral and social way" [author's translation]. (Łuczko, 2012)

Bibliography

Philip Auslander, "The Performativity of Performance Documentation," *PAJ: A Journal of Performance and Art* 28, no. 3 (2006): 1–10.

Kuba Banasiak, "Awangarda W Czasach Grozy I Groteski," *Atlas Sztuki* (2007). http://www.atlassztuki.pl/pdf/kaliska2.pdf. (accessed 23.09.2017).

Roland Barthes, *Camera Lucida: Reflections on Photography* Richard Howard trans. (New York: Hill and Wang, 1982).

Charles Baudelaire, *De L'essence Du Rire Et Généralement, Du Comique Dans Les Arts Plastiques* (Paris: Éditions Sillage, 2008 (1855)).

Henri Bergson, *Laughter: An Essay on the Meaning of the Comic* (Mineola: Dover, 2005).

Amy Bryzgel, *Performing the East. Performance Art in Russia, Latvia and Poland since 1980* (New York: I.B.Tauris, 2013).

Oskar Hansen, *Towards Open Form | Ku Formie Otwartej* (Warszawa: Zachęta, 2005a).

———, *Zobaczyć Świat* (Warszawa: Zachęta, 2005b).

Glenn A. Hartz and Ralph Hunt, "Humor: The Beauty and the Beast," *American Philosophical Quarterly* 28, no. 4 (1991): 299–309.

Heinz K Henisch and Bridget Ann Henisch, *Positive Pleasures. Early Photography and Humor* (University Park: Penn State University Press, 1998).

Hobbes, *Leviathan,* Richard Tuck (ed.) (Cambridge: Cambridge University Press, 1991).

Maria Janion, *Do Europy – Tak, Ale Razem Z Naszymi Umarłymi* (Warszawa: Sic!, 2000).

Krzysztof Jurecki, "Upadki Andrzeja Lachowicza," *Obieg* (2008), http://archiwum-obieg.u-jazdowski.pl/recenzje/4166 (accessed 14.09.2017).

Louis Kaplan, *Photography and Humour,* Exposures (London: Reaktion Books, 2016).

———, "Unknowing Susan Sontag's *Regarding.* Recutting with Georges Bataille," *Postmodern Culture* 19, no. 2 (2009).

Leszek Kołakowski, "O Śmiechu," in *Mini Wykłady O Maxi Sprawach* (2009), 82–85.

Piotr Krajewski, "The Hidden Decade: An Outline of the History of Polish Video Art 1985–1995," in *Ukryta Dekada. Polska Sztuka Wideo 1985–1995 | the Hidden Decade. Polish Video Art 1985–1995,* ed. Piotr Krajewski and Violetta Kutlubasis-Krajewska (Wrocław: Centrum Sztuki WRO, 2010), 173–215.

Dominik Kuryłek, "Really, I'm Not a Nihilist. Chosen Aspects of Adam Rzepecki's Work from the Years 1979–1989," in *Preferuję Bardziej Zrzutę Niż Kulturę | I'd Rather Prefer Pitch-in to Culture,* ed. Dawid Radziszewski (Nowy Sącz: Galeria Sztuki Współczesnej BWA Sokół), 23–38.

Rudi Laermans, "Bas Jan Ader," *De Witte Raaf* (2006), https://www.dewitteraaf.be/artikel/detail/nl/3149 (accessed 10.09.2017).

Vincent Lavoie, *L'affaire Capa, Le Procès d'une Icône* (Paris: Textuel, 2017).

Piotr Lisowski, "Oświadczenie. O Sztuce Zbyszko Trzeciakowskiego," *Magazyn Sztuki* (2014), http://magazynsztuki.eu/teksty/oswiadczenie-o-sztuce-zbyszko-trzeciakowskiego/ (accessed 10.10.2017).

Zofia Łuczko, "'Upadek Zupełny' 1981," *www.kulturazrzuty.pl* (2012). http://www.kulturazrzuty.pl/performance-upadek.php. (accessed 21.10.2017).

Jennifer Malkowski, *Dying in Full Detail: Mortality and Digital Documentary* (Durham: Duke University Press, 2017).

Anna Markowska, "Permafo 1970–1981: Zbigniew Dłubak, Antoni Dzieduszycki, Natalia LL, Andrzej Lachowicz," in *Permafo 1970–1981,* ed. Anna Markowska (Wrocław: Contemporary Museum & Motto Books, 2013), 13–101.

Christian Metz, "Photography and Fetish," *October,* 34, (Fall, 1985): 81–90.

John Morreall, "Philosophy of Humour," *Stanford Encyclopedia of Philosophy* (2012), https://plato.stanford.edu/entries/humor/ (accessed October 12, 2017).

Anca Parvulescu, "Even Laughter? From Laughter in the Magic Theater to the Laughter Assembly Line," *Critical Inquiry,* 43, no. 2 (2017): 506–527.

Kazimierz Piotrowski, "Sztuka Upadku. Lachowicz I Jego Cień," *Sztuka.pl*, 4 (2010).

Jacques Rivière, "Le Sacre Du Printemps," *La Nouvelle Revue Française*, 5, no. 59 (1913): 706–730.

Katarzyna Ruchel-Stockmans, *Images Performing History. Photography and Representations of the Past in European Art after 1989*, Lieven Gevaert Series (Leuven: Leuven University Press, 2015).

Debarati Sanyal, *The Violence of Modernity. Baudelaire, Irony, and the Politics of Form* (Baltimore: The Johns Hopkins University Press, 2006).

Susan Sontag, "Fascinating Fascism," *The New York Review of Books*, February 6, 1975, http://www.nybooks.com/articles/1975/02/06/fascinating-fascism/ (accessed October 12, 2017).

Monika Stelmach, "Łatwiej Było Działać W Grupie. Rozmowa Z Zofią Łuczko," *Dwutygodnik*, 168, no. 9 (2015), http://www.dwutygodnik.com/artykul/6135-latwiej-bylo-dzialac-w-grupie.html.

Jan Świdziński, *Sztuka I Jej Kontekst* (Radom: Ośrodek Działań Artystycznych Piotrków Trybunalski and Mazowieckie Centrum Sztuki Współczesnej "Elektrownia," 2009).

Jerzy Truszkowski, "Najbardziej Niepokorny Polski Artysta Zbyszko Trzeciakowski," *Artluk* (2014), http://magazyn.o.pl/2015/jerzy-truszkowski-najbardziej-niepokorny-polski-artysta-zbyszko-trzeciakowski-artluk/#/ (accessed September 14, 2017).

———, *Post Partum Post Mortem. Artyści Awangardowi W Społeczeństwie Socjalistycznym W Polsce 1968–1988* (Bielsko-Biała: Galeria Bielska BWA, 2013).

Gie van den Berghe, *Kijken Zonder Zien. Omgaan Met Historische Foto's* (Kalmthout: Pelckmans, 2011).

Hamza Walker, "Hail Yarilo!," Renaissance Society (2001). http://www.renaissancesociety.org/publishing/66/hail-yarilo/. (accessed October 12, 2017).

Dan Webb, "Discipline and Pose: Imagining the Rights-Based Liberal Subject as Photograph: a Critique," in *Declensions of the Self: A Bestiary of Modernity*, ed. Jean-Jacques Defert, Trevor Tchir and Dan Webb (Cambridge: Cambridge Scholars Publishing, 2008), 57–75.

Richard Whelan, "Proving that Robert Capa's 'Falling Soldier' is Genuine: A Detective Story," American Masters, (28.95.2006) http://www.pbs.org/wnet/americanmasters/robert-capa-in-love-and-war/47/ (accessed April 1, 2018).

Magdalena Wróblewska, "Rite of Spring – Katarzyna Kozyra," culture.pl (2011). http://culture.pl/en/work/the-rite-of-spring-katarzyna-kozyra. (accessed October 11, 2017).

Alenka Zupančič, *The Odd One In. On Comedy* (Cambridge, Mass.: MIT, 2008).

Adding a Giggle: Lee Friedlander's Practice of the "Shadow Self-Portrait"

Ann Kristin Krahn

"I first saw Friedlander's earlier work in 1974 and thought it 'cold,'" confesses former London Curator Mark Haworth-Booth in his essay for *Camera Austria* in 2006, "[i]t took me a few years to realise his photographs are actually 'cool'—i.e., not soul-lessly cerebral but amusingly detached (replacing right-on humanist values with something more authentic, personal, sceptical and witty)." (Haworth-Booth, 2006: 10) Based on that note, Lee Friedlander might not be the very first name to pop up in regard to the theme of "Humor in Photography," despite the fact that there is this typical "Nonchalance" (Haworth-Booth, 2006: 11) to his work, that brings an underlying (self-)irony and wit in almost every picture. Most trenchantly, it is realized in his playful yet reflexive take on the topic of self-portraiture—especially in his shadow self-portraits—which will be the leading theme in this essay.

Lee Friedlander in the Picture: A Deliberate Catalog of Photographic Errors

> Mark my words, you sheep, because it always holds true, the photographer is never in the image. (Kästner, 1989: 23).[1]

About to become one of the most important US-American photographers of the 20th century, Lee Friedlander began his career in the tense political atmosphere of New York in the 1950s and 1960s, working as a freelance for the booming magazine world. It opened a lot of doors to him by meeting art directors, editors, and other professional photographers such as Robert Frank, Walter Silver, Frank Cowan, and Garry Winogrand, or documentary filmmaker Helen Lewitt, who was a confidential advisor to the Guggenheim Foundation, whose Fellowship Friedlander won in 1960, 1962, and 1977. (Galassi, 2005: 17–18) Situated in this educational and inspirational environment, while

Photography Performing Humor

having the opportunity to work on his own art at the same time, he soon developed a style that distinguished itself from the standardized demands of the magazine assignments. Highly influenced by Robert Frank, Walker Evans and Eugène Atget—especially by their photo-books—he pursued a new interest in the minor and vernacular: "This was the lesson that Evans took from Atget and passed on to Frank: that the most ordinary thing—precisely because it is ordinary—can be made to speak through the vernacular language of photography." (Galassi, 2005: 33)

Such new interest in picturing the ordinary in an apparently unar-tistic way went hand in hand with an increasing use of the book as a medium to display and distribute photography. The photobook assem-bles photography in sequences: it is not the single iconic image that is relevant, but the various interactions and cross-references of a group of pictures. The pictures on a double page correlate with each other, and with the turning of pages the beholder experiences the narrative of a photographic layout, its rhythm, its order, the contrast or the repetition of motifs. Like this, photographers "might make purposely open-end-ed, unbalanced pictures that can't stand alone and need to be played off one another in groups or runs in books," as Colin Westerbeck und Joel Meyerowitz argue when it comes to the photographic practice of Robert Frank. (Westerbeck/Meyerowitz, 2001: 34)

Friedlander himself outlined the topic of his personal work in 1963 with the "American social landscape"—a term that stuck and became the catchword to condense a whole generation of photographers, joined in their interest in everyday life but differentiated in their esthetic and approach. Together with Garry Winogrand, Duane Michals, Bruce Davidson and others Friedlander was featured, inter alia, in the 1966 exhibition *Contemporary Photographers: Towards a Social Landscape*, curated by Nathan Lyons at the George Eastman House, Rochester, (Lyons. 1966: n.p.) as well as in John Szarkowski's 1967 major exhibi-tion *New Documents* at the MoMA in New York. (Galassi, 2005: 37) Many of the photographers included here had found their subject in public places with an interest in people, urban life and architecture, but whereas Winogrand for instance covered the heated political moments of the demonstrations for and against the Vietnam War, Friedlander al-ways focused on more formal aspects, on "a moment when the camera lens can frame the visual play of form against form." (Orvell, 2003: 126) Within such photographic practice—where elegance and banality meet and the "photographer's view is constantly on display" (Orvell, 2003: 127)—he got started with an extensive range of self-portraiture in which the examination of his own shadow played an important role:

Looking over his contact sheets and work prints, Friedlander noticed that his shadow or reflection sometimes intruded. This was not surprising: any snapshooter who puts his back to the sun to get good light on his subject will often find his shadow in the picture [...] Friedlander, though, in a manner that was fast becoming a hallmark of his work, went after this idea like a dog for a bone, encouraging his surrogate self to behave like a character with a mindlessness of his own. (Galassi, 2005: 41–42)

In the first decades of his work, Lee Friedlander usually used a Leica with a 28mm or 35mm wide-angle lens; later he took on a Hasselblad Superwide, a middle format camera, which has also a wide angle. (Galassi, 2005: 59) The use of these short lenses highly determined the impression of being "almost amidst" the scenery in his pictures. (Galassi, 2005: 75) In doing so, the intrusion of his own shadow started as a random, but repeated observation: "They began as straight portraits but soon I was finding myself at times in the landscape of my photography." (Friedlander, 2005: n.p.) Looking through Friedlander's many photobooks it becomes clear that his shadow appears in nearly every context of a larger photographic series. Similar to an observer or commentator, the shadow sneaks into the landscapes, the documentary or family pictures, or into the streets. Like this, the intruding shadow soon became more than the occasional photographic incident, but a partner-in-crime, a winking collaborator and a visual trademark, that allowed Friedlander to put himself in every "landscape" of his pictures and to engage in various plays with his environment: "At first, my presence in my photos was fascinating and disturbing. But as time passed and I was more a part of the other ideas in my photos, I was able to add a giggle to those feelings." (Friedlander, 2005: n.p.)

This motif of the photographer's intruding shadow is specifically known from the long history of photographic "mistakes" in vernacular photography.[2] It made its first appearances in the late 19th century—with the birth of the so-called snapshot—when photographic devices like the Kodak "Brownie" had become much more handy and available for a common, amateur application. (Orvell, 2003: 144–147) In his publication *Fautographie* Clément Chéroux discusses a very early article from an issue of Photo-Revue in 1901 that designates the "auto-shadowgraphy" (l'auto-ombromanie) as one of the most common errors among the "small miseries of photography" (les petites misères de la photographie). (Chéroux, 2003: 68–69) As said above, these small miseries derived primarily from the necessary advice for photographers to put the sun at their backs. Judging by the frequency and, to some extent, obviousness of the "error" in many amateur pictures, it is nevertheless surprising how the photographers could have overlooked their own shadow. (Fig. 1.9–1.10) But the focus of the human view tends to concentrate on the center and the object of interest and easily fails to notice such an ephemeral thing as a shadow in the act of triggering a photographic devise. It is this ability of the photographic medium that Walter Benjamin described as the "optical unconscious," whereby a photographer can never perceive or control each detail of his or her chosen field of view. (Benjamin, 2002: 302–303)

At the same time, the shadow of the photographer is a matter of technical progress. Richard Benson, a close friend of Friedlander and a photographer as well, is very familiar with the technical side of the phenomenon and describes how the history of photography is one of a steadily increasing angle of view as focal lengths became ever shorter: "A curious thing happens when one photographs with a short lens: the attentive photographer is often faced with the annoying choice of finding either the sun or his shadow in the picture." (Benson, 2011: n.p.) This quotation points out one more time the importance of technical developments for the history of photography and its specific manifestations, and is supported by other photographers such as Paul Strand: "I always think the material aspect of things is the real basis from which the whole development of photography or anything else flows." (Strand, 1974: 46) He further states: "As photography developed the shutter developed, the speed of the lens developed, and the speed of photographic emulsions increased. These were potent influences on what the photographer could do." (Strand, 1974: 46)

With this, I would like to underline the "agency" of the photographic devices and materials itself, the accidents and coincidences, the whole "potentiality of the material," as Peter Geimer puts it. (Geimer, 2010: 52) The relation of art and technique is thereby thought of as mutually affecting. (Wolf, 1995: 12) To conclude this brief historical and technical round-up, ever since the production of photographic images increased, there has been a flood of "bad photographs." The significance and influence of their visual vocabulary for artists and photographers of the late 19th and 20th centuries cannot be overemphasized:

> The accidents of millions of amateurs devoid of a picture vocabulary—which produced an outpouring of multiple exposures, distortions, unusual perspectives, foreshortening of planes, imbalance—has contributed greatly to the visual vocabulary of all graphic media since before the turn of the century. (Lyons, 1966: n.p.)

Lee Friedlander went for it "like a dog for a bone," as former MoMA Curator Peter Galassi phrased it, showing off his authorship and the technical origin of photography early photographers tried to disguise.

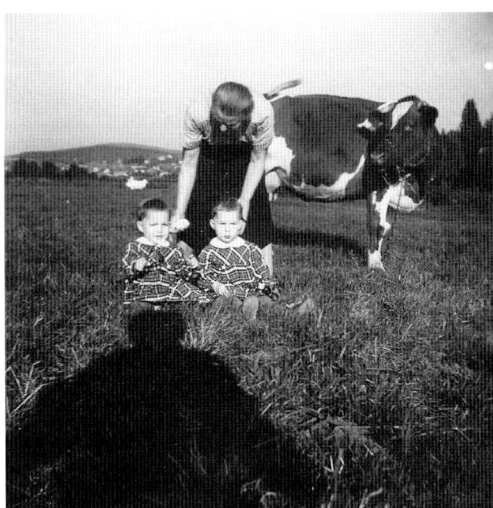

Figure 1.9

Anonymous, *Baby-Twins with Women and Cow*, n.y., silver gelatin print (5,9 × 5,9 cm), Private Collection of the Author.

(Chéroux, 2003: 73) Except for one earlier portfolio, containing etchings by Jim Dime combined with Friedlander's photographs, forty-three of his particular self-portraits formed his first self-published photobook *Self Portrait* in 1970. Here, the motif of his own shadow appears repeatedly and among other forms of self-portraiture, which display unconventional, trivial or unflatteringly rude pictures of the young Friedlander. The cover image is already quite a kickoff and shows the dark silhouette of Friedlander's head in the reflecting frame of a window, whereby his face is erased by a high gloss polished trophy, which is the single prominent object on display behind the glass. (Fig. 1.11)In this self-portrait, we learn less about his physical features (although there is also a tiny, second reflection of his whole figure in the glossy cup) than about his sophisticated skills as a photographer as well as his humor: he hides his face, playing with the expectations of the beholder, and has himself already been awarded a prize, setting the tone for the following content of the book. Throughout, he denies and hoaxes the poses and conventions of classic portraiture. On that account Peter Galassi declares: "Friedlander's work of the '60s is a deliberate catalogue of photographic errors." (Galassi, 2005: 41)

In 2011, he eventually published a 379-page catalog named *In the Picture*, which assembles self-portraits from over five decades of his work. It is a broad overall view of his ironic, nonchalant interest in this topic and his various ways of pushing the boundaries of the portrait genre in photography. The 2011 photobook certainly contains not only shadow self-portraits; very similar to his involvement with his own shadow is his use of mirrors or reflecting surfaces like windows, which increasingly interweave and fragmentize different layers in the

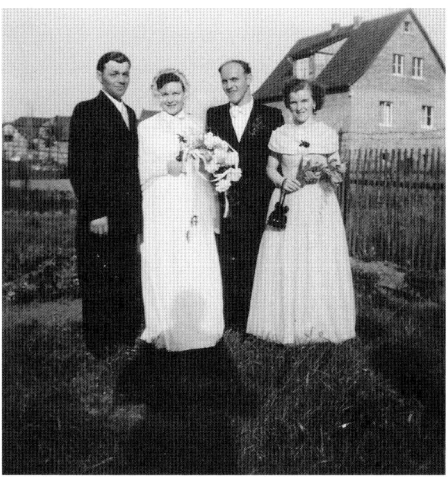

photographic image. Here as well occur surprising contrasts and connections. My interest in this essay is, however, focused on the shadow self-portraits, and I would like to show in the next passages why the motif of the shadow — even more than that of the mirror — is particularly suitable for a humorous photographic practice, for it allows a wide range of unusual interactions between the image content and the photographer's alter ego.

Performing the Shadow-Game

The physical principles of a cast shadow — the clear demarcation of the presence and absence of light — has very distinct premises. While a reflection only becomes visible in the closed area of a window or mirror, the body shadow is a steady companion. Negatively defined as a void, a *hole* in the light, it becomes more or less visible with the intensity of a light source. (Baxandall, 1998: 18) It is the result of photons blocked by a solid body, like a negative track. Like this, a human's shadow is almost a pure indexical reference to a physically present body — its time is the time of the referent only. (Dubois, 1998: 119) With the movement of light and objects it is always changing, transmutable, and able to imitate other shapes, for example if we think of the shadow theater. The notion of the theater might lead us back to Friedlander and the different roles or persona his shadow is adopting: one recurring *type* is the overlaying and interaction of his shadow with a detail in the picture. Like this, the shadow imitates and doubles the shape of a stony monument, wears the sunglasses that a young woman left on her towel, or adopts the head of a decorative Santa Claus in a restaurant window. All these are

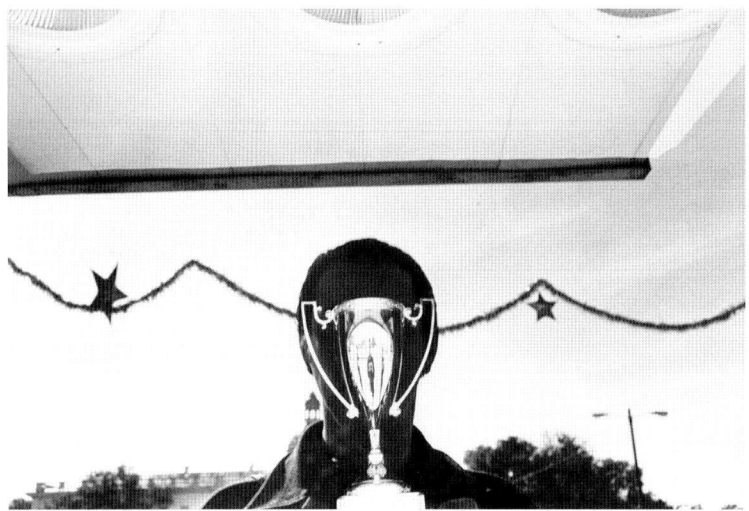

Figure 1.11

Lee Friedlander,
*Tallahassee, Florida,
1969.* © Lee Friedlander,
courtesy Fraenkel Gallery,
San Francisco.

very straightforward jokes, which work with unexpected and therefore witty combinations. The jolly sticker face of Santa in the upper middle of the picture *Mobile, Alabama, 1966* centers our gaze and shows the duality of the shadow's paradox: we know he belongs to the photographer *behind* the picture, yet he is the one returning our look, acting as a subject with a mind of his own.[3] It is a game of disguise, performing between visibility and invisibility. "[O]ne could think of these pictures not exactly as portraits but as sketches of tentative identities being tried out to see if they fit," writes John Szarkowski in the Afterword of *Self Portrait,* and goes on: "[t]hese roles, although obviously based on fact, were not to be taken too seriously as *truth*." (Szarkowski, 2005: n.p.)

In this regard, the shadow is an ideal object for humorous appearances: it can slip into different scenes and roles and temporarily incorporate other objects. Widely used in art, philosophy and literature, it is a metaphorically loaded symbol *per se*, filled with hints and allusions.[4] Its partial transparency allows a layering and forms an ambivalent status between its recognizable human form and its immateriality. It can imitate another shape, becoming its doppelgänger, or blend into another shadow to create a playful moment of confusion. Yet, the shadow of the photographer does not usually belong to our expectations of photographic images. The leading humor theory of incongruity broadly analyses how the perception of such contrasts creates amusement:

> Incongruity is a comparative notion. It presupposes that something is discordant with something else. [...] Comic amusement emerges against a backdrop of presumed congruities or norms.

Moreover, because we assume so many congruities or norms in order to wend our way through the world, there are an indeterminately large number of things that are potentially perceivable as incongruous. (Carrol, 2014: 18)

This applies all the same to our perception of photography and its normalized styles and modes of representation. The more recent example of *Santa Fe, 2008,* for instance, toys with the contrast of human and nature.[5] Friedlander's shadow bends and shifts, until it becomes part of the shadow of a tree on the sidewalk. Whereas his body and head are mostly concealed by the shadow of the trunk—with three spread branches of the treetop acting as head—he still braces his left arm and hand to the side, showing a strange, hybrid status between human and tree. The comedy of this example comes from a certain absurdity, the "surreal" quality of the tree/figure, and makes a reference to the motif of Daphne from Ovid's *Metamorphoses.* He or she who knows the origin can smile with knowledge.

Such lucky findings do not derive from a photographic practice that plans or stages the pictures long beforehand, but keeps an eye open for every possible setting that comes along. With regard to his first photobook *Self Portrait,* Friedlander states, the pictures were taken over "[...] a period of six years and were not done as a specific preoccupation, but rather, they happened as a peripheral extension of my work." (Friedlander, 2005: n.p.) This also applies to *Denver, 1972,* where the low sun throws long shadows on the groomed grass of a park complex.[6] Showing a daring stunt, Friedlander's shadow stands right under the hooves of a shadow-horse, rearing up with its rider on top. Being bold enough, Friedlander holds still and takes a picture. We can recognize the scenery from another photobook of his, *The American Monument,* published in 1976,[7] when we see the pendant of what is obviously another bronze monument of an equestrian statue, standing in the park. With the even grass as his screen, Friedlander arranges and composes the shadow-figures at his will. Being two-dimensional, they become "picture-like" even before they have been fixed in the black-and-white of photography. In their flat world, every shadow is alike: they are all part of Friedlander's role-play, performance and posing.

In some way, in the moment of taking a picture of his own shadow, Friedlander watches himself as *other.* Roland Barthes writes: "For the Photograph is the advent of myself as other: a cunning dissociation of consciousness from identity." (Barthes, 1981: 12) In an even more chiastic interlacing—for he is both photographer and beholder, subject and object—Friedlander navigates in the "field of forces," Barthes described in portrait photography:

Four image-repertoires intersect here, oppose and distort each other. In front of the lens, I am at the same time: the one I think I am, the one I want others to think I am, the one the photographer thinks I am, and the one he makes use of to exhibit his art. (Barthes, 1981: 13)

The Photographer's Shadow: Intrusive, Subversive?

Every so often, Friedlander "exhibits his art" and aims in particular at his own role as a male photographer and the power as well as the desire to gaze at women. A more obscene joke is shown in *East Hampton, New York, 1966*, where the camera's eye and view point of the photographer are pointed directly at a woman's private parts, while she is completely unaware, sleeping and sunbathing.[8] Through the shadow, Friedlander shows very unabashedly what he is looking at, and invites the uncomfortable beholder to do the same. We can observe how the male gaze objectifies a woman's body and how we duplicate this view through the photograph. It is the classic arrangement of sexual imbalance with the juxtaposition of male/active and female/passive, which Laura Mulvey explained in the context of mainstream film. (Mulvey, 1999: 837) Just like this, the phallic shadow becomes threatening. The tangency of the unfelt touch gets highly unpleasant and the shadow of the photographer exposes him as a voyeur. One might think of Susan Sontag, when she says: "The photographer is an armed version of the solitary walker reconnoitering, stalking, cruising the urban inferno, the voyeuristic stroller who discovers the city as a landscape of voluptuous extremes." (Sontag, 2008: 59) The idea of the photographer as a clandestine hunter of images, the understanding of the camera as a (sexualized) weapon, is condensed in the motif of the lurking shadow of the photographer.

While there is this strong momentum of sexism and the mechanisms of superiority cohering with these kinds of jokes — the joy of gloating over somebody's misfortune or weakness — it raises the question if the shadow literally allows another layer of interpretation. (Carroll, 2014: 7) As we try to contemplate or gaze on the picture, we get irritated by the black shade, which is an indexical indicator of the presence of the photographer and his camera. We cannot indulge in looking at the woman. Unlike the conventional narrative cinema (or photography) with its denial of the "intrusive camera presence" in favor of a joyful illusion, the shadow provokes a "distancing awareness" of the spectator. (Mulvey, 1999: 843) Although it offers an identification with the photographer's former voyeuristic point of view, it blocks an easy consumption of the image in favor of an ongoing irritation, for we become aware of the picture's artificiality. Like this, Friedlander not only duplicates, but also discloses common relations between a male photographer or artist and a female model. He dissolves the first impression and offers a second, more self-reflective reading: A joke at his own expense.

This irritation might even become productive by means of the deconstruction of gender, race and class. In *Madison, Wisconsin, 1966*, Friedlander pictures the display of yet another shop window, interleaving the fragmentized layers of the interior, his own reflection on the mirroring glass, and his shadow. (Fig. 1.12) Prominently looming from the middle of the bottom, the silhouette of his head falls on a picture frame, whose oval gab is filled with a traditional portrait photograph of a young black woman. The shape of his head completely covers her face, which returns the eye contact and implies a direct exchange of views. While this contact is somehow forced, just like in the previous example, the direct and sincere gaze of the woman centers the focus of the beholder and defies it. Victor Burgin writes in regard to this particular picture:

> In everyday social life it is the face which carries the burden of identity; in these terms, to exchange one's face for that of another would be to take the others place in society. Friedlander's photograph suggests the idea of such an exchange of identities — if I am white, it invites me to imagine what it would be like if I were black. (Burgin, 2013: 207)

The "burden of identity" — *The Burden of Representation,* as John Tagg's influential book phrases it — refers to the regulative social agencies of portraiture and its use as document and evidence: "The portrait is therefore a sign whose purpose is both the description of an individual and the inscription of a social identity." (Tagg, 1988: 37) The self-portrait as shadow eludes such inscriptions of social or individual characteristics. It has no distinct gender, is mobile, transparent, invisible at times, it is a withdrawal and denial of a fixed (self-)representation, still — through its indexical connection — it directly represents a human presence. It points towards the author of the photograph, while at the same time it is a *blank*, an invitation for the beholder to fill it with his or her own presence and experience. With this in mind, Friedlander evades a fixed or serious meaning of the *self* and clearly undermines and exceeds common forms of artistic self-representation. It might be read as a skeptical comment on the question: What can we know from a person's photograph, other than a surface? As the American journalist Vince Alleti wrote: "Memory, transience, identity, and the impossibility of capturing anything more than a fiction or a mask in photographic portraiture — Friedlander put all these issues slyly into play with

Self-Portrait […]." (Alleti, 2001: 198) The "shadow-self" might even be fulfilling Barthes' wishful thinking:

> "Myself" never coincides with my image; for it is the image which is heavy, motionless, stubborn (which is why society sustains it), and "myself" which is light, divided, dispersed; like a bottle-imp, "my-self" doesn't hold still, giggling in my jar: if only Photography could give me a neutral, anatomic body, a body which signifies nothing! (Barthes, 1981: 12)

To put it pointedly, Friedlander's shadow can be the giggling bottle-imp, jumping from picture to picture, a (nearly) neutral body which is light, divided, dispersed. The shadow functions as a visual hinge that joins the beholder with the former viewpoint of the photographer and might be read as an intrusive *and* subversive visual strategy. With Friedlander there are certainly no explicit moral or political state-ments, no "right-on humanist values," (Haworth-Booth, 2006: 10) but a constant witty unsettlement of photography's esthetical, social and cultural codes.

Laughing Behind the Scenes: The Shadow as Media-Reflexive Joke

> The shadows of photography, its defaults, thus become the privileged place for an exploration of the medium.[9] (Chéroux, 2003: 89)

With the given examples I would stress one more time that the pho-tographer's shadow invites an identification, but at the same time ex-poses a break or crack. If we think of some well-known assumptions about photography, this irritation derives from the *cut* through space and time, (Dubois, 1998: 157) respectively the "that-has-been" of Roland Barthes:

> The name of Photography's noeme will therefore be: "That-has-been," or again: […] what I see has been here, in this place which extends between infinity and the subject (*operator or spectator*); it has been here, and yet immediately separated; it has been ab-solutely, irrefutably present, and yet already deferred. (Barthes, 1981: 77)

A photograph is known to be in stagnation, elapsed, whereas a shad-ow implies an actual indexical connection. The combination sharp-ens the temporal paradox: we see a cast shadow of a human body, a

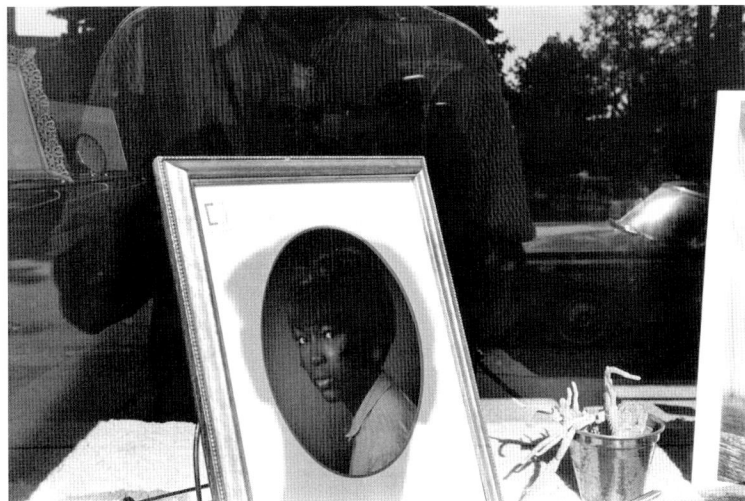

Figure 1.12

Lee Friedlander, *Madison, Wisconsin, 1966.* © Lee Friedlander, courtesy Fraenkel Gallery, San Francisco.

body that is missing in place and time. Just as Mulvey before him, Peter Galassi mentions the "normal" settings we are used to experiencing: "Like movies, photographs are supposed to pretend that the camera isn't there. We take this pretense for granted, putting ourselves in the cameraman's place as if he had never existed." (Galassi, 2005: 41) In contrast, the photographer's shadow makes the beholder aware of the presence of the person *behind* the camera, *in* the photographic act, and invites him or her, to emphasize with this place, to think about the premises of photography. With this in mind, in the motif of the photographer's shadow lies a dynamic quality that bounces back and forth—overplaying the photograph's frame towards the beholder and pointing towards the lost connection of space and time. As Philippe Dubois elaborates it in his publication on *The Photographic Act*, the depicted shadow of a photographer oversteps the boundaries of the photographic frame, since it reaches into the picture from an "outward-off" behind the scene.[10] (Dubois, 1998: 179–180; 182) The photograph can be seen in its ambivalent status: as a virtual window as well as a two-dimensional surface, that is a material object. Over and over, the shadow becomes a reminder for the beholder to be skeptical—an ironic clue of the presence of the photographer and the artificiality of photography.

A shadow is also directly intertwined with the photographical process itself, for it is a chemical reaction based on a sensivity to light. Therefore, to fix one's own shadow is a genuine photographic achievement. In no other art form has it been possible to *shock* it and ban it on a surface.[11] (Dubois, 1998: 126) In this reading what Friedlander is picturing first and foremost is the act of taking a photo itself. As Chéroux states, "more than a simple self-portrait, we are dealing here with the self-portrait in action, as if the operator wanted to photograph himself while photographing."[12] (Chéroux, 2011: 12) Thereby, the technical and practical dispositions of a photograph are displayed and add a meta-humoristic as well as self-reflective comment on the position of the photographer. With a wink, Friedlander manifests his status as a photographer with a media-reflexive "inscription of light."

So I would like to conclude that Friedlander performs quite an elaborate game of what is possible with photography, especially with self-portraiture. Although the motif of the photographer's shadow derives from snapshot photography at first appearance and plays with the allusion of a photographic mistake, the pictures soon reveal very thoughtful and complex compositions, which surpass conventional portraiture. He satirizes common forms of self-portraiture and adds his shadow surrogate as a sly, mocking commentator in the realm of the photograph. Friedlander's humor manifests itself within his daily photographic practice, not as an end in itself, but with a certain "Nonchalance" that reacts on the given circumstances of a setting and enjoys the visual interactions that can be found with an attentive approach. Thereby, the photographer's shadow with its ephemeral qualities is suited to all kinds of exaggerations, unexpected combinations and witty comments and adds — literally — a second layer for reflections about the visuality of a photograph. The shadow self-portraits are no serious epiphany; they are slightly detached, ironic observations on the photographer's view, on the medial premises of photography and its social and cultural codes. In the specific disposition in front of such a photograph, we become aware of the situatedness of the photographer and are encouraged to revive the photographic act putting ourselves in Lee Friedlander's shoes: with a giggle.

Notes

1. Original quote: "*Merke dir, du Schaf, weil es immer gilt, der Fotograf ist nie auf dem Bild.*" Author's translation. This epigram by Erich Kästner is under the caption "Rude Self-Talk."

2. A great survey on this motif offers the private collection of gallerist Jeffrey Fraenkel published in *The Book of Shadows*, ed. Jeffrey Fraenkel (San Francisco: Fraenkel Gallery, 2007).

3. See Lee Friedlander, *Mobile, Alabama*, 1966, in *Lee Friedlander. In the Picture. Self-Portraits 1958–2011*, exh. cat., (New Haven/London: Yale University Press, 2011), 46.

4. We may think of Plato's allegory of the cave (Platon: *Der Staat*, ed. Karl Vretzka (Stuttgart: Reclam Verlag, 1982): V. 514a–514c, 327-328), or the Birth of Painting through the tracing of the lover's shadow by Plinius (Plinius C. Secundus d. Ä., *Naturkunde,* ed. Roderich König/Gerhard Winkler (Düsseldorf: De Gruyter Verlag, 2007): 115). In *The Shadowless Man; Or, the Wonderful History of Peter Schlemihl* of Adelbert von Chamisso, the notion of the shadow shifts towards the uncanny, for he becomes an independent opponent. (Adelbert von Chamisso, *Peter Schlehmihls wundersame Geschichte* (Berlin: Hofenberg, 1814/2005).

5. See Lee Friedlander, *Santa Fe*, 2008, in *Lee Friedlander. In the Picture. Self-Portraits 1958–2011*, exh. cat., (New Haven/London: Yale University Press, 2011), 328.

6. See Lee Friedlander, *Denver*, 1972, in *Lee Friedlander. In the Picture. Self-Portraits 1958–2011*, exh. cat., (New Haven/London: Yale University Press, 2011), 146.

7. See also Lee Friedlander, *The American Monument* (New York: Eakins Press, 1976).

8. See Lee Friedlander, *East Hampton, New York*, 1966, in *Lee Friedlander. In the Picture. Self-Portraits 1958–2011*, exh. cat., (New Haven/London: Yale University Press, 2011), 32.

9. Original quote: "*Les ombres de la photographie, ses défauts, deviennent ainsi le lieu privilégié d'une exploration du médium.*" Translation by the editors.

10. Dubois describes the photographic frame as static: the horizontal cut of the frame is final. Nevertheless, through mirrors or shadows, objects from the vertical axis can reach into the photographic image. This axis means the line between photographer, camera and the chosen field of view and implies a bodily connection. (Dubois 1998: 175f)

11. Most conclusive, William Henry Fox Talbot referred to the photographic process itself as "The Art of Fixing a Shadow." (Chéroux, 2011: 7)

12. Original quote: "*[…] plus que d'un simple autoportrait, c'est là un autoportrait en acte, comme s'il s'agissait, pour l'opérateur, de se photographier photographiant.*" Translation by the editors.

Bibliography

Vince Alleti, "Lee Friedlander. Self Portrait," in *The Book of the 101 Books. Seminal Photographic Books of the Twentieth Century*, ed. Andrew Roth (New York: Distributed Art Pub, 2001), 198–199.

Roland Barthes, *Camera Lucida: Reflections on Photography* (New York: Farrar, Straus & Giroux, 1980/1981).

Walter Benjamin, "Kleine Geschichte der Photographie" (1931), in *Walter Benjamin. Medienästhetische Schriften* (Frankfurt am Main: Suhrkamp Verlag, 2002), 300–316.

Richard Benson, "Afterword," in *Lee Friedlander. In the Picture. Self-Portraits 1958–2011*, exh. cat. (New Haven/London: Yale University Press, 2011), n.p.

Michael Baxandall, *Löcher im Licht. Der Schatten und die Aufklärung* (München: Fink Verlag, 1998).

Victor Burgin, *Thinking Photography* (New York: Palgrave Macmillan, 1982/2013).

Noël Carrol, *Humour. A Very Short Introduction* (Oxford: Oxford University Press, 2014).

Clément Chéroux, *Fautographie. Petite histoire de l'erreur photographique* (Crisnée: Éditions Yellow Now, 2003).

Clément Chéroux, *Ombres portées* (Paris: Éditions Centre Pompidou, 2011).

Philippe Dubois, *Der fotografische Akt. Versuch über ein theoretisches Dispositiv* (Amsterdam/Dresden: Verlag der Kunst, 1990/1998).

Lee Friedlander. In the Picture. Self-Portraits 1958–2011, exh. cat. (New Haven/London: Yale University Press, 2011).

Lee Friedlander, "Preface," in *Self Portrait*, ed. John Szarkowski (New York: Museum of Modern Art, 1970/2005), n.p.

Peter Galassi, "You Have to Change to Stay the Same," in: *Friedlander*, ed. Peter Galassi, exh. cat. (New York: Museum of Modern Art, 2005), 14–80.

Peter Geimer, *Bilder aus Versehen. Eine Geschichte fotografischer Erscheinungen* (Hamburg: Philo Fine Art, 2010).

Mark Haworth-Booth, "Lee Friedlander," in *Camera Austria International*, 94 (2006), 9–24.

Erich Kästner: *Kurz und bündig: Epigramme* (München: dtv Verlagsgesellschaft, 1989).

Nathan Lyons, *Contemporary Photographers: Towards a Social Landscape*, exh. cat. (New York: Horizon Press, 1966).

Laura Mulvey, "Visual Pleasure and Narrative Cinema," in *Film Theory and Criticism: Introductory Readings*, eds Leo Braudy and Marshall Cohen (New York: Oxford University Press, 1999), 833–844.

Miles Orvell, *American Photography* (Oxford: Oxford University Press, 2003).

Susan Sontag, "Melancholy Objects," in *On Photography* (London: Penguin Books, 1977/2008), 51–84.

Paul Strand, in *Aperture: The Snapshot,* Vol. 19, Nr. 1, ed. Jonathan Green, (1974): 48–49.

John Szarkowski (ed.), *Lee Friedlander: Self Portrait* (New York: Museum of Modern Art, 1970/2005).

John Tagg, *The Burden of Representation: Essays on Photographies and Histories* (New York: Palgrave Macmillan, 1988).

Colin Westerbeck and Joel Meyerowitz, *Bystander. A History of Street Photography* (London: Bulfinch, 2001).

Herta Wolf, "Der fotografische Apparatus—wie funktioniert die Fotografie," in *Zugänge zu einer Oberfläche. Vorträge zur Fotografie an der HBK Braunschweig,* (Braunschweig: Hochschule für Bildende Künste Braunschweig, 1995), 12–31.

Performing the Performance Documentation

Kevin Artheron

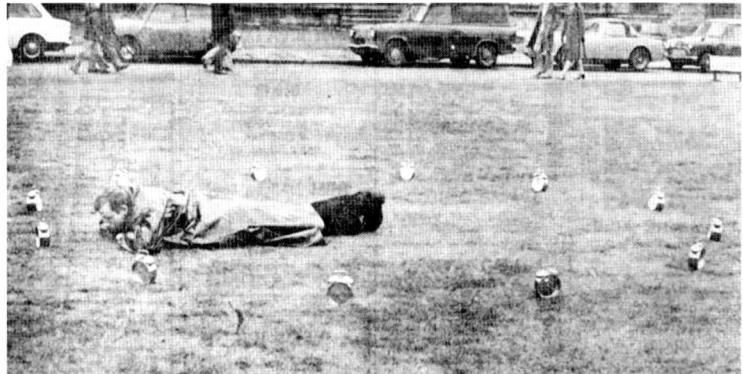

Figure 1.13

Kevin Atherton,
Timepiece, performance,
1974, picture published in
The Northern Echo, 1974.

Brussels, LUCA School of Arts, 14 April 2016. I began my presentation in the standard art school "visiting artist talk" way. Standing in front of an image of *Timepiece*, an outdoor performance of mine from 1974, projected on the screen behind me, I started to talk about the black and white photograph as the only record of the performance. (Fig. 1.13) Before proceeding to use this single image as a visual leaping off point for my verbal riff, I pointed out that a press photographer from the *Northern Echo* newspaper had been responsible for taking the image. I mentioned this deliberately in order to absolve me of the charge of contradicting my resistance to documentation in the early seventies. At the time of the performance, like a number of artists in the early seventies, I had felt that to have a photographer present in the space of the performance mediated the performance itself. All the same, in 2016, despite having issues with the current obsession with preserving the performance art archive, I was glad to have some form of proof that I had actually done the performance back in 1974.

Slipping into a role that I am accustomed to, having talked about *Timepiece* many times over the intervening forty-two years, I described the work as twelve alarm clocks arranged in a circle on the grass rough-ly the radius of the height of my body. The clocks themselves I de-scribed as archetypal "Tom and Jerry" alarm clocks, before going on to describe the site as a square of grassed open space in the centre of Durham, a university town complete with a cathedral in the North East of England.

I explained that the twelve alarm clocks had been arranged in a circle in the middle of the green and at just before 14.00 hours I had walked into the centre of the circle and lay down facing one of the clocks, which at the moment I touched the ground rang. In addition I pointed out the site-specific link to the Cathedral clock, which chimed twice, in per-fect sync with the first alarm clock ringing at two o'clock. Slowly I pro-gressed to the second clock, always knowing what the time was from the three or four clocks within my field of vision. Five minutes later hav-ing edged along the grass, I reached the second clock which dutifully also rang on time.

In the lecture in Brussels, I described the forty-two-year-old perfor-mance as being totally predictable. From the very first minute it was possible to anticipate what was to come for the following hour and that as an example of performance art this predictability hadn't been a problem as I was using myself; not in a theatrical sense, but in a sculp-tural one, as a living element within an installation. Similarly the role required no acting skill; all I had to do was to slowly move my body in time, in a clockwise direction. I was after all the minute finger of a clock. To demonstrate this at one point in the lecture I lay on the floor at LUCA, all the time continuing to talk to the audience.

In describing the audience for the 1974 work, I said that they were mostly passers-by or typically Saturday afternoon shoppers who, hav-ing parked their cars on the edge of the green, had noticed the per-formance before they went shopping. It was fine by me that nobody watched for the full hour because I had been using time in a different way from the way that it is used within the theater where it has to carry a narrative. Rather than use time to tell a story this was a work about time itself. Real time.

At this point in the lecture I departed from the text—although it had always been my intention to do so—into a more conversational style of delivery where I began to describe the job that I was employed to do at the time that I had had the idea for *Timepiece*. I first of all talked about having left art school in 1972 and how at that time I had a very romantic view of what being an artist might involve. My models for this bohemian outlook had been more literary than visual, being drawn from writers such as George Orwell, whose 1933 autobiographic nov-el *Down and Out in Paris and London* had influenced my view of how I thought an artist should make a living, along with the legendary story that William Faulkner, the American Nobel Prize-winning author, had written his first novel whilst working as a night watchman.

So with this as my back-story I described how, when I was a young artist in my early twenties, I not only expected to have to do menial jobs to make a living, I almost demanded to do them. The menial job that I was working at when I conceived of *Timepiece* was that of a "Timekeeper Night Watchman" in a factory, and this had been the only menial job, amongst lots of menial jobs that I had ever done, that connected directly with a work of art that I had made. Having established my historical credentials as a struggling young artist, I proceeded to describe my job as a Timekeeper Night Watchman to the Brussels audience, which had involved me in "clocking on" to work in the Time Office of a large tailoring factory in Darlington in the North of England. The Time Office was a room within the factory which, being glazed on three sides, looked out, as in Foucault's panopticon, over several hundred sewing machines. This was my view during my shift, which ran from six-thirty in the evening until seven o'clock the following morning.

As I continued to talk in this "off-the-cuff" manner, I described how as a twenty-three-year-old I felt that I was being paid for just turning up to a job where I didn't have to do anything. I didn't even have to sweep up, I just had to be there and although I was paid a low wage and worked very long hours, I liked that I got paid for just "being." In the Time Office there was a big clock with a long pendulum, which was connected to the clocking-on boxes that ran all the way down one side of the factory wall and on which the factory workers would daily punch in their cardboard time-cards from which their weekly wages would be calculated precisely to the minute. The large clock in the Time Office controlled the individual clocking-on machines, which on the minute went click as the dial on the mechanism rotated a notch. The only downside to having a job where you didn't have to do anything except be there was, I explained, that if the factory was burgled you might get shot.

I proceeded to describe my chief reason for liking the job of Timekeeper Night Watchman as that it gave me time to read and that I had read a lot of existential and absurdist literature whilst working in the job including *On Being and Nothingness* by Jean-Paul Sartre. This I had connected with being alone in an empty pre-war factory every night. In the middle of the night in the dimly lit factory I described how I could hear the click of the clocking-on machines: there was a click every minute and then every hour there was a clunk, and at midnight there were three sounds: there was a click, a clunk and a sort of shunting noise as the date changed. I talked about how, in the emptiness and silence of the factory, I learnt to look forward to the end of the month so that I would hear an extra sound as the machines ratcheted up for a new digit that marked the change in date. I confessed to the Brussels audience that in 1973 I had volunteered to work on New Year's Eve in order to experience the annual sound of the year digit changing on the machines, describing it to the audience as having been "orgasmic!"

Clearly at the LUCA School of Arts, in a conference about humor, I was now playing it for laughs. I was, however, also making some serious points about the early days of Performance Art, which was still an emerging practice in the UK in the nineteen seventies. As an example of the situation that prevailed I cited that when I applied for the funding to buy the twelve alarm clocks from Northern Arts, the regional Arts Council, my proposal was passed from the Visual Arts Panel to the Theatre Panel as it involved the use of time. This I highlighted as indicative of how narrowly Visual Art was considered in the early seventies but also extremely ironic as the piece itself had sought to establish the difference between performance art and theater.

My application to the Arts Council had been successful and I had received a cheque for £50 to buy the twelve clocks. Still in a casual mode of address with the audience in Brussels, I talked about having gone into "Woolworth's" department store in Durham and engaged in the elaborate process of buying twelve alarm clocks from a shop assistant, making sure that all of the alarms worked. This had involved winding up the clocks and setting off the alarms in the store and the female assistant signing and date-stamping the guarantees for each of the twelve clocks. Paying the assistant in cash, I had anticipated that she would ask me "the inevitable question." I had rehearsed my response to this question as the process of purchasing the clocks had advanced and anticipated that my answer would go along the lines of an articulation of the difference between time in the theater and time in real-time performance art. I would say to the shop assistant that even in the case of the Theater of the Absurd, with writers such as Beckett or Ionesco, there was still a big difference between theater and performance art. I would throw in something about a sculptural use of time as opposed to a linear application of time. The "inevitable question" finally arrived; just as the shop assistant was placing the last clock into the bag she said: "Why do you need twelve alarm clocks?"

Capitulating completely I replied: "To get me up in the morning."

The audience in Brussels erupted with laughter.

I concluded this section of my presentation at LUCA by telling the audience that the shop assistant, thinking my accent was Irish, telephoned the police and reported that a young Irish man had just bought twelve alarm clocks and had seemed particularly concerned that all the alarm mechanisms worked. This had coincided with the fact that the two IRA bombers, the infamous Price Sisters, were about to be moved from Holloway Prison to Durham Prison. The climax to this "shaggy-dog story" was that I was held by the police as a suspected IRA bomber.

At this juncture in the lecture in Brussels I paused to suggest that, as I was talking about performance art from the nineteen seventies, it might be fitting if we were joined by an audience who were also from the nineteen seventies. Constructed behind the audience was a wall onto which I now began to project a series of slide images from a previously unseen second projector positioned behind the first. (Fig. 1.14)

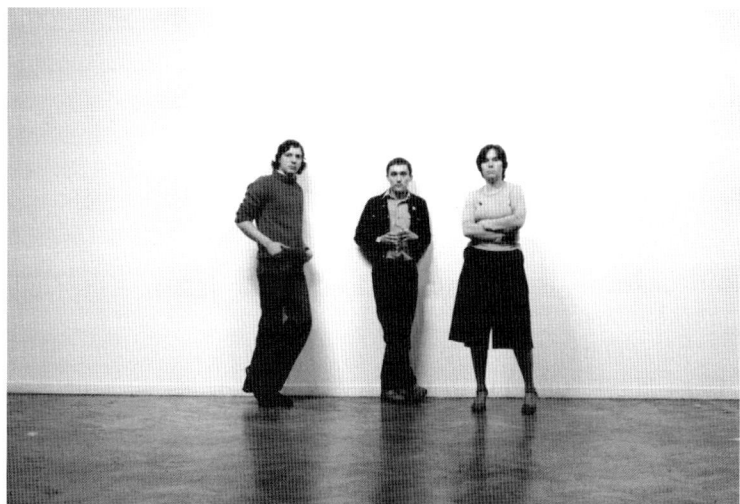

Figure 1.14

Kevin Atherton, *An Audience Arranged 7,* color slide from performance at the Whitechapel Art Gallery, 1978.

I outlined the idea behind the new slides as being a recent work from 2015 where I had re-enacted an audience for a 1978 performance of mine at the Whitechapel Art Gallery. I explained that I had made this recent work as a playful, yet critical, piece that ran counter to what I saw as the current fashion for re-enacting performances from the past. By re-enacting the audience rather than the performance I suggested that we could learn as much about the original performance. After all, we are frequently told that performances are "held" in the memories of the individual audience members who experience them. This then was an attempt to restage an audience doing exactly this: could we make out the 1978 performance in their eyes?

At this point I felt that there was a humorous feel to what I was saying, deliberately heightened, so I thought, by my inclusion of extraneous, if also corroborating, information such as the fact that the Irish Arts Council had supported me in this project by generously awarding me a grant in 2014. To further plant the seed of doubt as to the veracity of what I was saying, in the same ironic vein I also mentioned, for the benefit of any camera buffs in the audience, that I had used Kodachrome color slide film and a Pentax SLR camera in order to achieve the correct seventies feel to the images that we were about to look at. All of this, I of course said with a straight face.

By focusing my attention on the new images projected on the wall in front of me, but behind the audience, I caused the audience to turn their heads, and in some cases their seats, in order that they could see the new slides. The result of this was that the room layout was now disrupted with the audience not sure whether they should be looking forward at me, or behind at the life-size images of the "new audience members," as they individually appeared on the screen behind their heads. (Fig. 1.15) The new work entitled: *Documentation of the Audience at a Performance by Kevin Atherton at the Whitechapel Art Gallery 1978* now appeared on the back wall. The first photograph showed a head-on view of a white gallery wall and floor, including a narrow white skirting board, which horizontally divided the image three-quarters of the way down, the lower quarter of the image being made up of a wooden floor.

This I said was a reconstruction of the upper gallery at the Whitechapel Art Gallery in London as it was in 1978. I had constructed the "set" that we were looking at in my studio in Ireland. This process had proved more complex than at first thought as on revisiting the

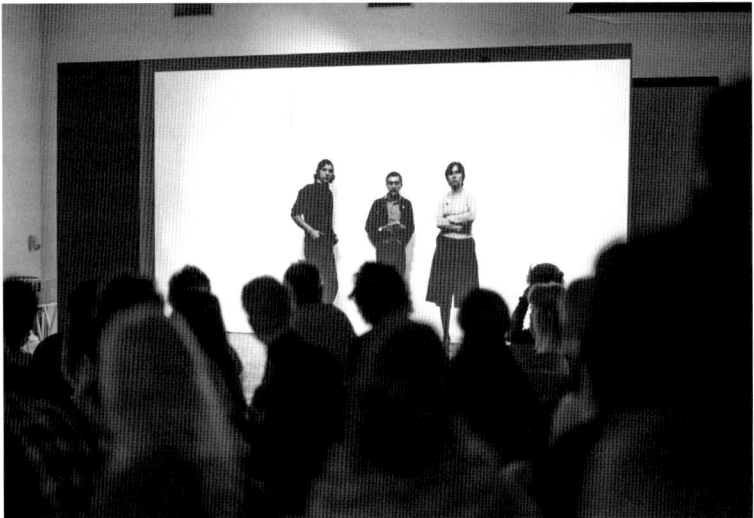

Figure 1.15

Kevin Atherton, screening of *An Audience Arranged 7* during the artist's lecture/performance at Conference "Photography Performing Humor," LUCA School of Arts, Brussels, April 14, 2016.

Whitechapel in 2014, I realized that they had changed the parquet flooring in the upper gallery in the 1990s, where I had performed in 1978. I was therefore grateful for the Carl Andre catalogue, published on the occasion of his exhibition at The Whitechapel in 1978, which proved invaluable in my project. By referring to the installation shots of his *Equivalents* series (the bricks), featured in The Whitechapel catalogue,

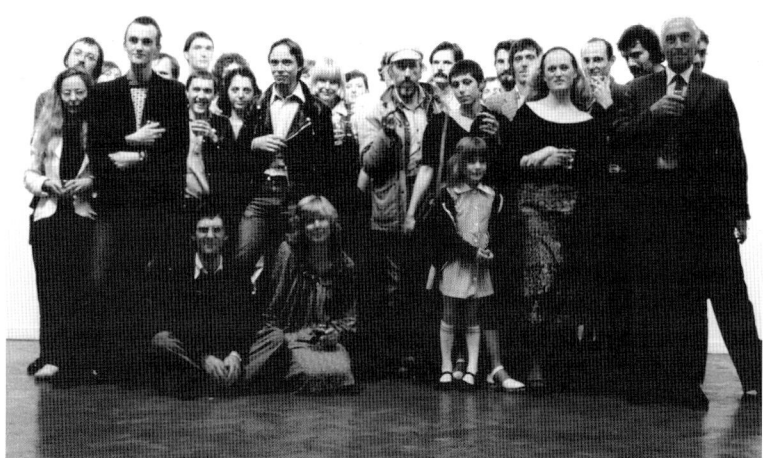

Figure 1.16

Kevin Atherton, *An Audience Arranged 59,* color slide from performance at the Whitechapel Art Gallery, 1978.

I was able to replicate the original worn wooden floor in my life–sized replica set in my studio.

Reading from my notes I began to describe, one by one, the individual audience members from the 1978 performance. Crucial in this process was the fact that my verbalized description of the individuals preceded their appearance as slide images. In this manner each person was introduced as they joined the rest of the audience in the gallery. This device of verbally describing the individuals before revealing them as an image on the screen served to emphasize that I had cast them as "performance art audience types" recreated from my memory of the seventies. I explained that in reality the people I had used were actors supplemented by a few art students that I taught at the National College of Art and Design in Dublin.

As I read out my descriptions of the people as I projected them, the black and white slide of *Timepiece* remained on the screen behind me. *Timepiece*, and my verbal extemporisation about it, had been successful I thought, in both grabbing the attention of the audience in Brussels and revealing to them that humor was a part of my modus operandi. Now in the larger presentation *Timepiece* had taken on a "meta" role as an image of a performance from the nineteen seventies that the projected seventies audience were looking at: they were contemporaneous. (Fig. 1.16)

To enable an understanding by the reader of the extent to which I went to describe each person on screen, below is the written script that I read, and ad-libbed from, as I clicked each person into view on the facing screen:

1. Bring on "The Young Art Administrator" — that's you — the young woman brave enough to wear that seventies classic: the French culottes.

2. Now I'd like "The Bohemian Painter" to come on and join "The Art Administrator." For sure he's a painter but you can tell by the way he stands that he's open to other art forms — not always the case in the nineteen seventies.

3. To bring a critical awareness to things, I need "The Performance Artist." To be authentic you must be smoking a cigarette.

4. Okay, now give me "The Second Performance Artist" — one who looks as if he could be a writer as well — smartly dressed. If the performance artists outnumber the other members of the audience so be it.

5. Now I want "The Freddie Mercury Guy" — could you stand at the front and although you're playing an artist don't be afraid to look confrontational.

6. Now "The Hippy Woman," the girl with the headband and the William Morris dress. Could you come into the frame please and take things down a bit? The people at the back you can relax by leaning them against the wall.

7. The woman playing "The Contemporary Dance Person," could you position yourself on the left? Try to look as if you're a dancer in the stance that you take please.

8. Enter the guy who looks like a Duane Hanson life-size sculpture. You, your job will be to play "The Heckler." The rest of the audience you should slowly ostracize him. If you could indicate your disapproval through your body language that would be good please.

9. "The Child": there always had to be at least one at a performance. This one is not too bad. So if the little girl could come on but remain silent that would be good — like the agency told you to be.

10. Now I'd like if I could, "The Older Male Arti," just to calm things down and moderate 'The Heckler's' behaviour.

11. "The Critic" next, the person who reviews performance for Studio International, could you; in the time-honored tradition, sneak in at the back and try to make yourself unnoticed. Don't forget to do the affectation of the sticky-up collar, another passing fad from the nineteen seventies.

12. I want "The Feminist in the Denim Bib" to stride in confidently and stand in front of the critic deliberately block his view.

13. Speeding up a bit now, could "The Biker in Denim," you with the beard, stand right in the centre and really stare at the camera.

14. "The American Post-Graduate Student" in the pink top, please could you wrap the turquoise jumper over your shoulders, it's the give-away that you're American.

15. Just to break things up a bit here, I would like two people to appear at once now. The guy playing "The Second Biker Artist" only this time in leather and "The Richard Hamilton Look Alike" from the model agency — I want you to be dressed in nineteen sixties clothing as we discussed earlier — the Beatle hat — that's your signature.

16. Now I want "The Very Tall Arts Administrator" in a Laura Ashley dress to enter and for "The Heckler" character to pull a funny face.

17. Could "The Glamorous Looking Female Artist" in the black cloak with long hair come in on the right–look romantic–look Irish if you can?

18. Now I want "the Ambitious Conceptualist in a Scandinavian Jumper."

19. "The Fair-Haired Woman Wearing the Yasser Arafat Scarf," another seventies classic, draped over your shoulders–in you come.

20. Now I want the guy playing "The Gallery Manager" character in the tie and the green shirt to fold his arms and look a bit self-conscious on the left.

21. If "The Young Female Photographic/Installation Artist" with the shoulder bag and red lips could place her hand on her hip and take up her position to the left with the child.

22. Now enter "The Lone Hero Painter" character with the Marlborough Man moustache, if you could stand apart and look menacing.

23. If everyone could move around a bit and make room in the centre for the person playing "The Woman with Red Lips II."

24. Enter "The Nerdy Young Exhibitions Officer" — do your best to look disheveled.

25. I want "The Hippy Dad" in the checked shirt to stand behind his daughter but to carry on drinking.

26. What we need now is "The Third Performance Artist" in a cream linen jacket and white shoes–could we have you at the front please, hurry along!

27. Right–speeding up for a moment. Could I have the woman with the very large glasses in the middle, the very tall person playing "The Male Art History Graduate," and the older woman in the

white dress playing "The Mother of the Arts Administrator" that we saw on the first slide.

28. Now "The Bald Man," act a bit nervous if you could and stand on the left.

29. I want "The Be-spectacled Gallery Education and Outreach Officer" to show his moustachioed head.

30. "The Very Tall Community Muralist" in black should enter now and stand behind "The Child." Also if the two older actors playing "The First Arts Administrator's Parents." Could you all stand together in order to appear like you're a family group?

31. Move around a bit and make room for "The Cheerful Technician Guy in the Jumper That his Mother Bought Him."

32. Okay, now if I could have "The Guy With the Big Hair" come in at the front and "The Woman With the Cream Trousers" nip in at the back. Could the woman playing "The Mother of the Child" show the child some affection and place your hand on her shoulder. "The Child" – you should look down.

33. I want "The Female Structuralist Filmmaker"; you know who you are, to position yourself on the right.

34. Can I have "The Young Art Critic," with the barrel chest to take up a quizzical stance at the front.

35. "The Young Part-Time Art Lecturer" with the curly hair smoking the cigarette and wearing the Ossie Clark blouse could you try to look serious and sexy at the same time by smiling and leaning your head slightly to your right.

36. Now finally, I need "The Cool Conceptual Photographer" in the white shirt to stand right in the center of the group.

At this point the lecture/performance came to an end and I thanked the audience at LUCA who in turn applauded. As the last presentation of the day, and of the conference, I was conscious that I would be followed by a "Closing Remarks" session, but nevertheless I asked the audience if there were any questions. When there were no questions I began to talk about what I felt had just occurred in my presentation, saying that clearly I was attempting something complex, almost, I realized now, like delivering two lectures at once: a lecture within a lecture. Expanding on this point, I delineated between the two separate performances I'd talked about, saying that within the structure of what I had just attempted, the first lecture was also for the benefit of the audience that joined us in the form of slide images at the back of the room. In this way the first lecture had functioned as the content for the second and primary performance. I felt that the first type of lecture, where I used humorous anecdotes as a means of illustrating what can happen when performing in public spaces, presented a problem. Amusing though this method of talking about work might be, there was a dilemma in presenting performance art in this way. By re-framing *Timepiece* through story-telling within a lecture theater context I had contradicted its original intention of marking out the territory for performance art as a non-linear practice.

Having outlined the mise en abyme relationship between the two stylistically contrasting performative lectures that I had just presented, I then, almost casually, pointed out that the major difference between them was that the first had actually happened and the second was a fabrication. The audience's response to this announcement was a resounding silence.

It transpired that they had believed what I had said to them about constructing a replica of the Whitechapel Gallery in my studio and that the Irish Arts Council had funded me to do so; that I had used students and hired actors from a theatrical agency to play the characters in the work. I'd spent a fortune on the wardrobe for all these people to appear as convincing characters from the nineteen seventies. All these thoughts suddenly rushed through my mind at once. It had been my intention to de-stabilize the audience in Brussels but the audience's response had just had the reverse effect and had completely thrown me.

I first began to use fiction in my performances and video pieces almost thirty years ago and know from experience that the humor of the work is based in large part on the audience realizing the fiction for themselves. This would be ruined by me revealing the structure of the artistic conceit at the outset of the lecture. I cannot say: "What I am about to tell you is a bunch of lies," I can only perform in a manner that eventually makes this apparent. It is the virtual space that opens up in the mind of the audience during this process that I am interested in. My presentation at the Brussels conference had set out to challenge the performance art archive and what I see as its problematic desire to tie everything down through photographic documentation. As a performance artist active in the seventies, I view this desire to document everything as a contravention of the original spirit of the performance art movement but felt, certainly immediately after my presentation at LUCA, that I had failed to demonstrate this point through my presentation. This question of success or failure spilled out into the space of the foyer after the closure of the conference and followed me back to Ireland where it has continued to occupy my thoughts.

The humor and wit of the Canadian sociologist Erving Goffman runs as a constant seam throughout his writing, to such an extent that I suspect that he is being provocative when he says: "He who reports jokes, in a lecture on humor, has a right, and perhaps the obligation, to tell bad ones, for the punch line is properly to be found in the analysis, not in the story…" (Goffman, 1981/1995)

By taking the stance that it is not the primary role of the lecturer to be funny when talking about humor but that the emphasis should be on providing insights into the nature of humor, is Goffman really saying that even as a tool humor is barred from the lecture theatre? Surely the joke that provides the example in Goffman's lecture on humor might as well be a good joke as a bad one.

To successfully pursue the answer to this question the lens needs to be more finely focused on the category of humor I applied in Brussels. In my use of the lecture as a performative vehicle at LUCA, I am aware that I used myself in the role of the artist talking about his work in a "self–conscious manner" and in this way deliberately embarked on a Menippean satire where I sought to establish myself as my own figure of ridicule. This I did as a form of a parody, the first rule of which, in order that it works at all, is that the audience recognizes the figure being parodied. In my presentation the figure I played was intended to be the familiar one of "The Egotistical Contemporary Male Artist" who is accustomed to getting what he wants. He thinks nothing of building a section of a gallery in his studio in order to re-enact an audience from a forgotten performance of his from forty years ago. The audience in Belgium recognized this figure, but for my purpose did so rather too readily. LUCA itself needs a credit for the role it played in this process, acting as it did as the frame for my performance. The institution gave much more than an architectural space to perform in; its esteem gave legitimacy to my presentation in a way that rendered it totally believable. What I had thought of as preposterous had been presented as credible.

As individual audience members said to me afterwards: "This is exactly what artists do these days Kevin. Why wouldn't an audience in Belgium believe an artist of your generation coming from another country confidently telling them about his work?" From this response I feel that my original concept had backfired in the absence of the audience's knowledge of my previous work, I had been too convincing in performing the parody, or alternatively the audience had, in an age of the celebrity artist, been too accustomed or too willing in accepting it.

Again Goffman provides a useful view of what might have occurred at LUCA when he says:

> And he who lectures about lectures does not have a special excuse for lecturing badly; his description of delivery faults will be judged according to how well the description is organized and delivered; his failure to engross his listeners cannot be reframed retrospectively as an illustration of the interactional significance of such failure. Should he actually succeed in breaching lecturing's constraints, he becomes a performing speaker, not

a speaking performing. (He who attempts such breaching, and succeeds, should have come to the occasion dressed in tights, carrying a lute. He who attempts such evasion and fails – as is likely – is just a plain schmuck, and it would be better had he not come to the occasion at all.) (Goffman, 1981/1995)

Bibliography

Erving Goffman, *Forms of Talk* (Pennsylvania: University of Pennsylvania Press, 1981/1995).

Part II

Making Fun of Photography through Tricks and Montage

Ghosts Just for Laughs: Spirit Photography and Debunking Humor

Louis Kaplan

"Humour is the debunking of humanity, and nothing is funny except in relation to human beings."

George Orwell, "Funny, But Not Vulgar"

The Ghost Dialectics of Spirit Photography: Brewster contra Mumler

If photography has been theorized as having an intimate relationship with death and mortality from Roland Barthes to Susan Sontag and if the affective correlate of this has been the serious work of mourning, then it can also be said that the medium has had recourse to a morbid sense of humor as a natural response or antidote to its death-drive over the course of its history. In other words, photography's dark comedy serves as the flip side to this somber state of affairs in marking the return of the (humorously) repressed. Beginning with the failed Hippolyte Bayard's prankish performance *Self-Portrait as a Drowned Man* (1840), photographers have "played dead" and turned to this photographic sense of black humor as a mode of comic relief. A range of genres and fascinating case studies in the history of photography typifies this morbidly comic sensibility whether these images stage macabre stereographic skeletons on parade, the poses of Surrealist *humour noir*, headless photographic cut-ups, or Conceptual artistic pratfalls.[1] The debunking humor that seeks to undermine spirit photography as a serious Spiritualist practice and religious belief affords another excellent case study that mocks this somber equation of photography with (the return of) the dead. While spirit photography is closely related to the work of mourning for those believers who invest in these images as supernatural keepsakes of their dearly departed, the debunking of spirit photography and the creation of "ghosts just for laughs" in popular

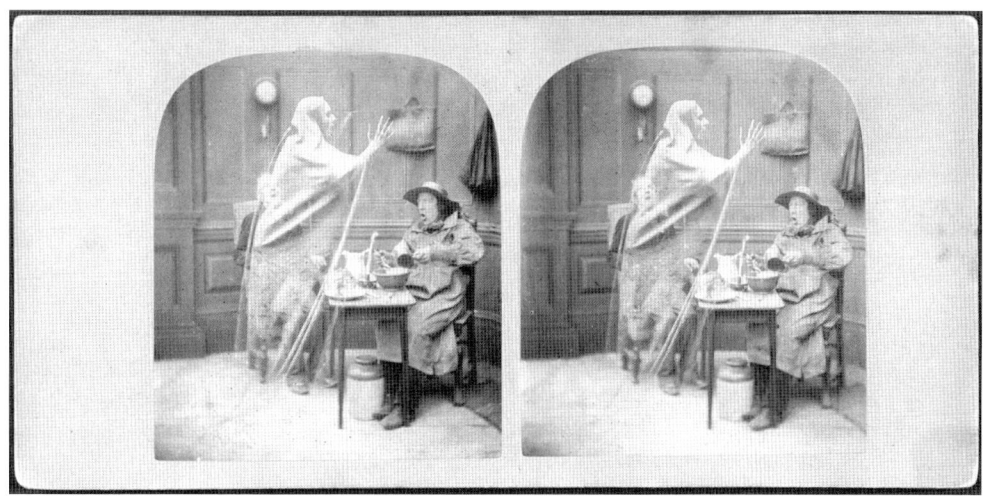

visual entertainments laugh in the face of death and offer the return of the comically repressed.

In "Ghost Dialectics: Spirit Photography in Entertainment and Belief" that serves as his contribution to the pivotal exhibition catalogue *The Perfect Medium: Photography and the Occult* (2005), curator and editor Clément Chéroux uses a haunting figure to think about the Janus-faced status of spirit photography as it shuttles back and forth between the pious seriousness of a religious belief and the lighthearted amusement of a popular visual entertainment. He writes, "The ghost of death shadows the specter of derision. They haunt us together." (53)

Such ghost dialectics and their superimposition of two frames of interpretation (the one mystifying and the other debunking) can be traced back to the earliest manifestations of spirit photography itself and its contest of meaning. In the beginning was the specter of derision and it took the form of "The Ghost in the Stereoscope." (Fig. 2.1) This refers to the British visual entertainment and commercial practice instituted by George Swan Nottage of the London Stereoscopic Company circa 1856 with the mass dissemination of a series of ghoulishly popular and humorous 3-D cards. These stereographic images were a direct application of the method for the photographic production of "ghosts" suggested by the esteemed British scientist Sir David Brewster as outlined in the chapter of his treatise entitled "Application of the Stereoscope to Purposes of Amusement." Framing the appearance of the spirit as a photographic amusement, the materialist scientist retraces the mechanics of the magic trick that delivers the illusion of something supernatural: "For the purpose of amusement, the photographer might carry us even into the regions of the supernatural. His art, as I have elsewhere shewn, enables him to give a spiritual

Figure 2.1

London Stereoscopic Company, *The Ghost in the Stereoscope* (kindly suggested by Sir David Brewster), ca. 1856. Albumen silver prints from glass negatives with applied color. The Metropolitan Museum of Art, New York.

appearance to one or more of his figures, and to
exhibit them as 'thin air' amid the solid realities
of the stereoscopic picture." (Brewster, 1856: 205)
According to Brewster, the ghost stages an amusing performance and he even focuses on this matter of stagecraft in his description of how this new
special effect can be achieved. In this case, it is a
matter of comic timing on the part of the female
lead who takes up the role of the "aerial personage" and who exits the stage at the right time.
Brewster relates, "When the party have nearly sat
the proper length of time, the female figure, suit-
ably attired, walks quickly into the place assigned
her, and after standing a few seconds in the proper attitude, retires quickly... If this operation has
been well performed, all the objects immediately
behind the female figure, having been, previous
to her introduction, impressed upon the negative
surface, will be seen through her, and she will
have the appearance of an aerial personage, unlike the other figures in the picture." (205–6)

Meanwhile, we encounter the case for belief
in the resurrection of the ghosts of the dead with
the "spiritual photography" of the Boston photographic medium William H. Mumler beginning in 1862. (Fig. 2.2)
Mumler's successful practice was built on the assumption that he
could deliver the ghosts of the dead in the form of cartes-de-visite to
those who were mourning the loss of their loved ones and who would
be willing to pay handsomely for such an otherworldly service. This
was clearly the case for the wealthy Wall Street banker Charles F.
Livermore who turned to Mumler to manifest the spirit of his recently
deceased wife, Estelle. (Fig. 2.3) Framed in terms of Spiritualist doctrine and the belief that communication with the dead was possible,
Mumler's spirit photographs moved the ghosts from the stereoscope
to the supernatural, and this would pave the way for their debunking.
Yet even here we find a telling anecdote in Mumler's memoir that he too
interpreted his first ghostly exposures as nothing but a joke. This passage was written in 1875 or six years after his notorious trial and public
shaming in New York that will be discussed in further detail. Mumler
recalls there that before his conversion to Spiritualism he thought of
the first spirit image in terms of an accidental double exposure. "One
day a gentleman visited me who I knew was a Spiritualist; and not at
that time being inclined much to the spiritual belief myself, and being
of a jovial disposition, always ready for a joke, I concluded to have a

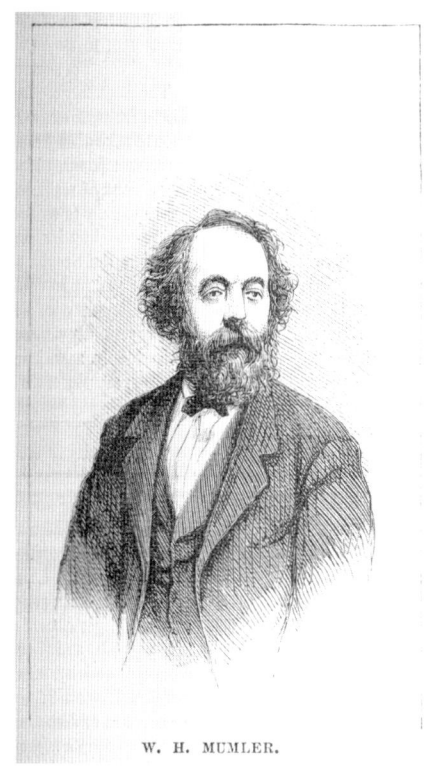

W. H. MUMLER.

Figure 2.2

"W.H. Mumler", *Harper's
Weekly*, May 8, 1869,
cover, wood engraving
after photograph.

little fun, as I thought, at his expense. I therefore showed him the picture, and with as mysterious an air as possible, but without telling an untruth, which Mr. P.T. Barnum calls 'drapery,' I stated to him 'that this picture was taken by myself when there was no visible person present but myself.'" (Mumler, 1875: 5) Mumler claims that it was only after the insistence of Dr. H. F. Gardner and other known Spiritualists that there was something more serious to entertain in these ghostly developments that he took up a Spiritualist interpretation of his botched self-portrait. However, Mumler omits an important point in his memoir that differs from his statement about what happened in the initial reports about the new phenomenon of spirit photography as published in A.J. Davis' journal *The Herald of Progress* and in *The Spiritualist Magazine*. In this earlier account, Mumler does not find himself alone in his photographic studio but rather in the shadowy presence of his dead cousin who is taken to be the first spirit extra. Mumler confirms: "This photograph was taken of myself, by myself, on Sunday, when there was not a living soul in the room beside me — 'so to speak.' The form on my right I recognize as my cousin who passed away about twelve years since." (C.M.P., 1862: 562) It is this explanatory addition that takes Mumler's photograph out of the realm of photographic amusement and that aligns it with Spiritualist ideas about the afterlife and communication with departed spirits. Following Chéroux's terms, Mumler's ghosts of death were shadowing Nottage's specters of derision.

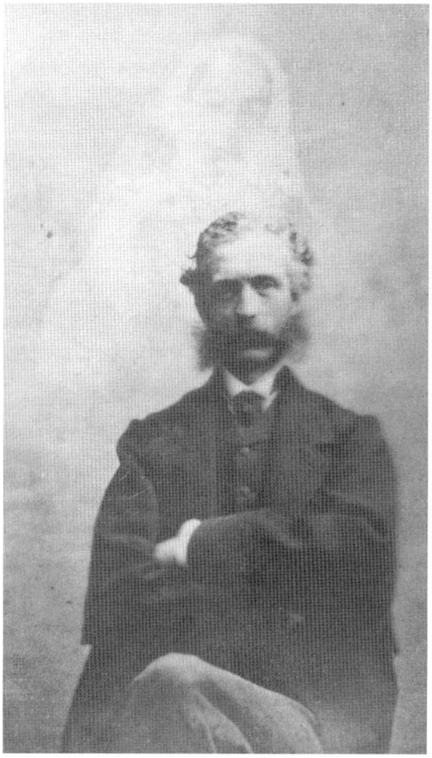

Figure 2.3

William H. Mumler, *Charles Livermore with the Spirit of his Wife*, 1869. Albumen silver print. The J. Paul Getty Museum, Los Angeles.

Thus, there always have been two ways to reflect upon the ghosts conjured by and as spirit photography. The "ghost of death" signifies and signals the belief system of Spiritualism as a religious doctrine that frames spirit photography as a medium (technological and occult) that enables visual communication with the dead. In contradistinction, the "specter of derision" is the flip side of the equation that stands ready to entertain spirit photography as a hoax and a con job and to register its disbelief in the form of a mocking and tendentious laughter. Chéroux elaborates further upon the ghost dialectic in the following manner: "On the one hand, [spirit photography] reinforced the spiritualist hypothesis by demonstrating the possibility of communicating, if only visually, with the dead. On the other, it gently mocked this belief." (2005: 46) It is the goal of this essay to expand upon and to reframe

Chéroux's "specter of derision" (and its deriding of the specters) as a type of debunking humor that turned spirit photography into the target and the object of its ridicule. In contrast to Chéroux, it is my contention that this brand of debunking humor was much harsher and more pointed in its execution than mere gentle mocking. Instead, it was more in the order of the iconoclastic and in line with "the liberating privilege of comic sacrilege" (465) that the American literary critic Leslie Fiedler (1971) described as central to the debunking humor of Jewish-American writers-comedians such as Philip Roth and Woody Allen half a century ago. We should not forget that Spiritualism was a religious system of belief and faith that had many adherents in the mid-19th century and with which a sizable segment of the American population was affiliated. In light of this point, the lampooning critique against spirit photography staged by the skeptical and secular stars of our show constituted a type of comic sacrilege against Spiritualism. The debunking of spirit photography (and spirit photographers) deployed such skeptical humor as a mode of demystification. There is a comedy of deflation at work and play here that pokes holes in the lofty and supernatural assertions made in the name of spirit photography. This comedy broke out when the magical, mystical, and supernatural claims that adhere to spirit photography were debunked and when they were demonstrated to be the result of pure mechanism alone—as a tinkering in the toolbox generated by merely natural and technical means. This constitutes a breaking of the idols in a blasphemously satirical vein that resonates with the superiority theory of laughter attributed to Plato and Thomas Hobbes. For debunking humor always constitutes a condescending or insulting form of "laughing at" rather than a gregarious and convivial "laughing with." From P.T. Barnum to Harry Houdini, this corrosive and debunking humor laughed at those who believed in spirit photography and deployed such derogatory and insulting terms as delusion, superstition, and ignorance in the process. (Kaplan, 2017) All in all, this constituted a mean-spirited laughter directed against the spirit photographic faithful.

Mechanical Illusionists as Debunking Humorists

The legal historian and theorist Jennifer L. Mnookin provides an astute analysis about the status of the evidence submitted at the Mumler trial in "The Image of Truth: Photographic Evidence and the Power of Analogy." Mnookin asserts that there were two ways by which to evaluate Mumler's spirit photographs and that these correspond to the positions held by Spiritualist believers and scientific skeptics. On the one hand, the serious believers saw such images as examples of a "supernatural realism" that provided evidence of physical traces of a heavenly referent in the indexical medium of photography. On the other hand, the skeptics saw these same images as examples of "mechanical illusionism" asserting that these conjured spirits on glass plate negatives only provided evidence of photographic manipulation and therefore that such "spirit photographs" documented nothing but lies and falsehoods. The dialectical relationship staged here between the spiritual revelations of supernatural realism and the magic tricks of mechanical illusionism parallels the long-standing debate as to whether photography should be viewed as an objective and scientific medium that generates truthful images or whether photography should be viewed as a constructed medium that generates manipulated images. Mnookin's terms also help us to better understand the critique of spirit photography through the staging of debunking humor. In other words, debunking humor demystifies any claims made about spirit photography as a discourse of "supernatural realism" and exposes it as a discourse of "mechanical illusionism." In this way, the dialectic between the "ghost of death" and the "specter of derision" translates into a contest between the magical and the mechanical. We move from a magical investment in spirit photography as a supernatural belief with its somber revelation of the "ghosts of death" to the mechanical debunking and demystification of the "ghosts in the machine" as mere illusions and made in the mocking spirit of derision and ridicule. In this manner, the dramaturgy of spirit photography shifts from a religious belief to a visual entertainment, from pious faith to a comic prank or hoax. As Samuel Beckett reminds us in his novel *Watt*, debunking humor and its rhetoric of exposure constitutes the "hollow laugh" that "laughs at that which is not true, it is the intellectual laugh." (39) Beckett's categorization fits neatly into this narrative wherein the skeptical intellect and the rational faculties take aim at the leap of Spiritualist faith or what it takes to believe in the "ghosts of death" captured on film as truthful and credible spirits rather than as manipulative and fraudulent pranks that warrant only derisive laughter.

If we undertake a historiographical survey of spirit photography, there is a recurrent pattern whereby one encounters a series of arch-debunkers seeking to demystify the medium through the use of ridicule and mean-spirited laughter. Each of them made use of a different exclamatory utterance to serve as his catchphrase in the service of a mocking and debunking humor. Their goal was either to bring the magical and the mystical down to the level of the mechanical or to find the trace of the mechanical in the so-called magical. This latter point aligns with Simon Critchley's assertion that humor constitutes "the return of the physical into the metaphysical." (Critchley, 2002: 50) They lashed out with these barbed and mocking epithets—Humbug! Fraud! Flim-flam!

Bullshit! This history of spirit photographic debunking begins with America's greatest showman of the 19th century P.T. Barnum and his comic and taunting attacks on William H. Mumler when he testified as the star witness for the prosecution at Mumler's trial for fraud and larceny in the spring of 1869. Here, the accusation of humbug became the mocking chant against the swindles of Mumler's spirit photography. After all, Barnum claimed that he knew a humbug when he saw one given that he was a master of the art of deceptive visual entertainments. After World War I and into the 1920s, we witness both Harry Houdini's and Harry Price's mockery of the Crewe Circle in Great Britain as well as the debunking of other spirit photographers elsewhere. (Fig. 2.4) In his damaging and damning exposé *A Magician among the Spirits* (1924), the wisecracking Houdini devoted a full chapter to debunking spirit photography and he proclaimed it to "reek of fraud" and delusion like all Spiritualist phenomena. (xix) Later, the Canadian-born conjurer James "the Amazing" Randi (1982) made the wondrous "thoughtography" of the Chicago elevator operator Ted Serios in the late 1960s the target of his skeptical ridicule, asserting that such paranormal activities were nothing but flim-flam and a result of Serios' sleights of hand. Most recently, the popular entertainers Penn and Teller took up the mantle of debunking humor in a potent and attractive combination of magic and comedy. Their successful television program on the Showtime network *Penn and Teller: Bullshit!* aired for eighty-nine episodes in the period between 2003 and 2010. The aggressive and tendentious humor of the show revolved around their skeptical debunking of paranormal beliefs and any claims of supernatural powers. With the vulgar cry of "bullshit" and its overtones of scatological humor and their "you've got to be f***ing kidding me approach," Penn and Teller brought the supernatural back to earth with a great deal of levity. They mastered the art of ridicule as a mode of entertainment in a mocking exposure of contemporary quacks and charlatans.

In each of these four moments in its fascinating history, we observe that the greatest opponents of spirit photography, Spiritualism, and supernatural phenomena in general were stage magicians and/or visual

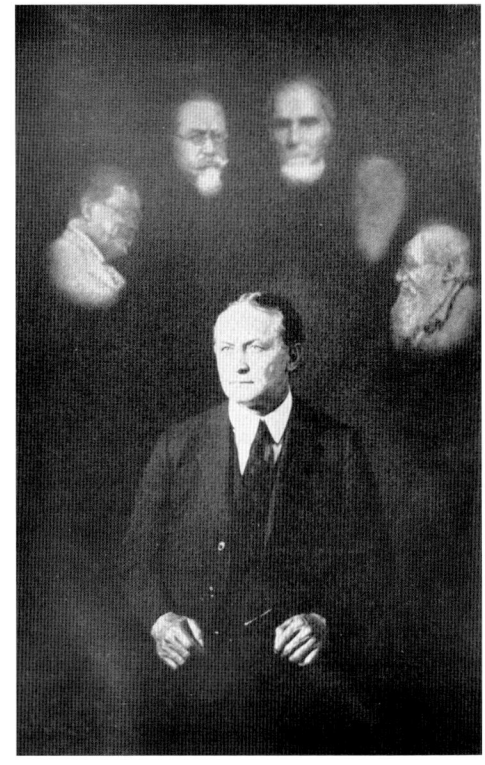

Figure 2.4

Photograph of Houdini made by Alexander Martin at Denver, Colorado, on May 10, 1923, showing so-called "Spirit Extras." Reproduced in Houdini, *A Magician Among the Spirits*, 1924.

illusionists themselves—for Barnum also belongs to this latter category even though he was not a magician by trade—who insisted upon the materialist basis of their craft and the tricks of their trade. As a master magician, each of these debunkers made a living from visual entertainments and excelled in the arts of mechanical illusionism. This recalls further that when we invoke the word "magician" and "magic" we are actually referring to two different phenomena with a dual structure of belief that is quite similar to the Janus-faced nature of spirit photography. We may be referring either to those who believe in magic as actual manifestations of the supernatural and the occult or to those who practice magic to create the illusion of the supernatural while never denying the natural and mechanical basis of their tricks. While the first definition of magic continues to dwell in a world that taps into religious or mythic powers, the second category of magician performs illusions in a secular world ruled by mechanics alone.

In this regard, it is fascinating to recall a text by the British magician and psychic researcher Harry Price that reviews his debunking of William Hope and the Crewe Circle of Photographers among other phenomena. "The Mechanics of Spiritualism" (1939) begins with a succinct and categorical statement that sums up the debunking operations that I am tracing here. It is a mocking maneuver that unmasks the magical as the mechanical. Price begins with the following bold assertion, "The history of spiritualism is a history of fraud." (190) As his title suggests, Price cannot efface the trace of the mechanical in spirit photography and Spiritualism in general. Like his friend and colleague Houdini, Price warns his readers that if they were so foolish as to believe in these Spiritualist and spirit photographic frauds and hoaxes, then the joke would be on them.

Playing the role of the debunker, the magician and showman therefore are likened to a specific type of entertainer possessing many of the same characteristics as the comedian. The deflationary slippage from the magical to the mechanical—or the incongruity and ironic reversal of a burst of stage magic suddenly appearing in the space of the mechanical—was enough to produce a debunking brand of humor utilized in the accusatory campaigns waged by the likes of P.T. Barnum and Harry Houdini as adept mechanical illusionists against the spirit photographers of their day. In the next section, I want to review the attack on the spirit photographs of William Mumler staged by his adversary from Barnum's ironically entitled chapter on "Spiritual Photography" in *The Humbugs of the World* (1866) to his debunking testimony and mock-spirit photographic work (with Abraham Bogardus) at Mumler's infamous trial.

Barnum and Bogardus Conjure Lincoln's Ghost at Mumler's Trial (1869)

> Q. Were you conscious of a spiritual presence?
> A. I did not feel any thing of that sort. (Great laughter).
>
> Testimony of P.T. Barnum at The Mumler Trial

It is important to recall that Barnum's comic debunking of Mumler did not begin with the trial. Barnum begins his testimony providing further context to his interest in mocking spirit photography and he elicits debunking humor in the process. "I wrote to Mumler that I was publishing a book exposing humbugs of the world (great laughter) and I wished to expose the humbugs of the spiritual photographs." ("The Mumler Trial," 1869: 55) Barnum's Chapter XIV in *Humbugs of the World* (1866) is full of mockery in that he not only frames Mumler and his practice as a humbug but he also makes fun of those who invested in these "spectral illusions." (119) Whether Spiritualist or not, Barnum derides Mumler's customers as deluded and delusional and he insists that his comic efforts at demystification were made "for the purpose of opening the eyes of the people to the delusions daily practiced upon the ignorant and superstitious." (119) The text focuses specifically on the case of the politician William "Colorado" Jewett who organized the failed Peace Conference of Niagara Falls in 1864. Jewett wanted Mumler to conjure the spirits of elder statesmen to illustrate that they supported his efforts to end the Civil War. Barnum exposes the ruse of so-called "spiritual photography" using the debunking language of mechanical illusionism: "The spectral illusions of Adams, Webster, Jackson, Clay, and Douglas were readily obtained from excellent por-traits of the deceased statesmen, from which the scientific operator had prepared his illusions for Colorado Jewett." (119) One also notices that Barnum refers to Mumler as a "scientific operator" to further cast off any suspicions upon his use of occult powers. At the trial, Barnum also testified that his relationship to Mumler included his request for exam-ples of these spirit photographs for exhibition purposes. He recalls that he bought the series of Jewett photos for two or three dollars each and he hung them as one of the many visual attractions in his American Museum. They were put on display as "bogus spirit photographs" (in the words of the prosecutor Elbridge T. Gerry) until the building burned down in a spectacular fire in 1865. (Kaplan, 2008: 168)

But Barnum did not stop with these derisive accusations. The show-man decided that a much more effective and sensational means of mak-ing his case would be to simulate "the ghost of death." Thus he teamed up with the highly respected New York photographer Abraham Bogardus the day before his court appearance in order to create a mock-spirit photograph of President Abraham Lincoln, and this was submitted as an exhibit for the prosecution at the trial. (Fig. 2.5) The overall aim was to have the public get a chuckle as to how easy it was to manufacture fake images of ghosts. Bogardus was a highly skilled photo-technician who had worked in the profession for nearly twenty-three years at the time of his testimony and who had served as the President of the National Photography Association for five years. His haunted exemplar demonstrated that he had no problem reproducing the supernatural effect by purely mechanical means. The use of the still mourned and iconic figure of Lincoln added to the comic sacrilege of this particular phony spirit photograph. (One recalls that President Lincoln had been assassinated just four years prior to the making of Bogardus' spirit photograph in the key of parody.) Barnum relates his visit to Bogardus' studio as part of his testimony and his account already elicits great laughter from the audience when Barnum utters his favorite epithet with a large dose of irony. ("The Mumler Trial," 1869: 55) "I went on to ask him if he could take a spirit photograph, as I would like to have my likeness taken with the spirit in the background; but I told him that I did not want to have any humbugging in the matter (Great laughter)." One notes the layers of irony in the exchange presented here. The audience (or at least the skeptics in the audience) break into great laughter as the master of the spectacular humbug asks facetiously for a genuine spiritual photograph (i.e., some photographic magic) from Bogardus knowing full well that he will not deliver upon any supernatural promise "in the matter" (and on account of matter). Then to make things even more ambiguous, Barnum testifies, "He said he could do it." One notes the open-endedness of the antecedent for "it" here. It could mean that Bogardus was able to perform the task of producing a genuine spirit photograph without any humbugging (hence the implication of another tongue in cheek statement or downright deceit). However, it also could mean that he could produce a spirit photograph using the mechanical means at hand and thereby that he would be able to reproduce and duplicate Mumler's manipulative humbug. If the latter meaning, then Bogardus' resultant spirit photograph must be viewed as the parodic performance of debunking humor.

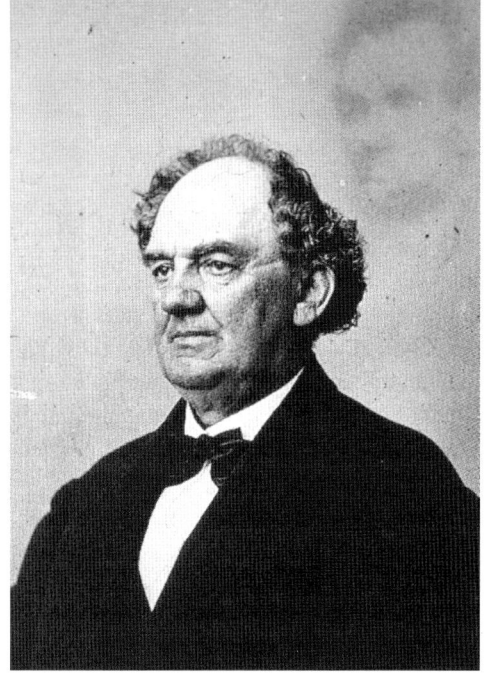

Figure 2.5

Abraham Bogardus, *P.T. Barnum with the Spirit of Abraham Lincoln*, 1869.

Barnum then proceeds to play the part of the scientific investigator himself as he examines Bogardus thoroughly in the attempt to locate the source of the mechanical illusion but he was not able to locate anything improper. One should note that the first part of the next portion of testimony did not serve as a source for merriment. "I told him that I wished to examine the thing. He gave me liberty to do so, and so I investigated about the plate glass, went into the dark-rooms and saw the process of pouring over the first liquid; after it was placed in the nitrate of silver bath, then it was put in the camera; there was a little break upon the glass, so that I could distinguish it all the time; went through the operation; had my shadow taken, and that of the departed Abraham Lincoln came also upon the glass. (Great laughter)." ("'Spirit' Photographs," 1869: 1) This burst of "great laughter" derives from the incongruity between the preceding dry technical accounting and the unexpected and magical result in the sudden appearance of Lincoln's ghost which functions as the punch line to Barnum's account. The ensuing scornful and skeptical laughter gets directed at the bogus spirit photographer as Bogardus "stands in" as the double for the duplicitous Mumler.

The prosecutor Elbridge Gerry then asked Barnum to identify the photograph in court and he produced the visible evidence. This led to another witty and curious retort on Barnum's part containing the amusing earmarks of debunking humor.

> Gerry: Is that it [showing the picture]?
> Barnum: Yes, that's the critter. (Renewed merriment.)
>
> ("The Mumler Trial," 1869: 55)

Here again one is left to wonder about the ambiguity of reference in the use of antecedents. Does the use of the slang term "critter" refer to the mock-spirit photograph or to the ghost of Lincoln in the photograph? Why would Barnum refer to the mock-spirit photograph of himself with the ghost of Honest Abe Lincoln as a "critter"—this informal term for a living creature that also can mean a domestic animal or a person? Are we to believe that Bogardus caught Lincoln's ghost as one would catch an elusive critter? In casting the photograph or great Lincoln's ghost as a living creature and thereby attributing to it a type of animation, the ironic Barnum is in effect marking the gap between what the photograph actually is (an inanimate material object) and what the Spiritualists wish it to be (a reanimation of the spirit, a resurrection of the dead President).

At the conclusion of Barnum's testimony, Gerry sets up a final joke by offering the suggestion that he and Bogardus should have conjured a second photographic ghost in keeping with one of the master showman's most famous hoaxes. This refers to the young Barnum's exhibition in 1835 of an elderly African-American woman named Joice Heth under false pretenses. (Fig. 2.6) In that visual spectacle, Barnum made the outrageous claim that Joice was none other than the one hundred sixty-one years old nurse of George Washington. In the cross-examination, Mumler's lawyer John Townsend hoped to discredit the witness by reminding Barnum and the court of his many entertaining hoaxes over the years including this duplicitous racial spectacle. Townsend's line of questioning implies that if Barnum has the audacity to accuse Mumler of humbugging his spirit photographic spectacles, then he should take a look at himself in the mirror. Thus, when Gerry asks Barnum if he considered the possibility of manufacturing the ghost of Joice Heth by mechanical means, the prosecutor seeks to return attention to the humbuggery at hand and recall that Mumler was the conman on trial and not Barnum. Interestingly, there are two published accounts of this last exchange but both

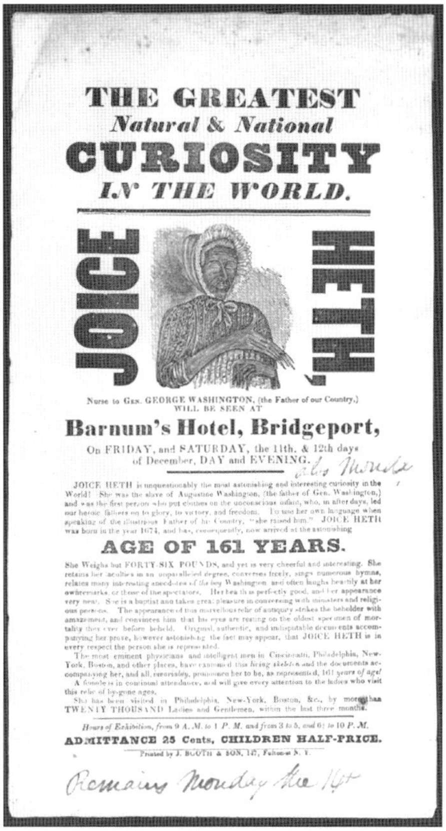

Figure 2.6

Printed Handbill, *Joice Heth: The Greatest National and Natural Curiosity in the World*, ca. 1835.

of them report that Barnum's testimony ends in "great laughter." The difference in transcription revolves around whether Bogardus or Heth was the subject of the sentence and the butt of the joke. In the first version, Barnum sarcastically suggests that the ghost of the aged nurse would not have had enough vitality to be resurrected.

> Gerry: When you were with Bogardus, did you want George Washington's nurse to appear?
> Barnum: He said that she had no vitality left. (Great laughter, during which Mr. Barnum left the stand and left the court-room, the examination having been conducted)

("'Spirit' Photographs," 1869: 1)

In the second version, it is rather Bogardus who was exhausted from producing the likeness of Lincoln and who had had enough for one day. The punch line rings of debunking humor in expressing the certainty ("I have no doubt") that the supernatural hoax can be replicated by

Bogardus' technical wizardry. One notes the final aside that comments on the overall humor of Barnum's testimony and signals the tendentious laughter stirred up by his debunking of spirit photography.

> To Mr. Gerry—I went to Mr. Bogardus' gallery, and asked if he could produce the likeness of the nurse of George Washington; he said he had not enough of vitality left, but he could do it at some other time; I have no doubt he could. (Laughter.) The humorous manner in which this witness gave his testimony elicited considerable laughter from the audience.
>
> ("Spiritualism in Court," 1869: 2)

In contrast to Barnum's highly ironic style of testimony that professed outrageous truths at times only to entertain doubts, Michael Leja sees Mumler's downfall as his being stuck in an old paradigm that demanded an authentic belief in religious miracles. In clinging to the ghosts of the dead rather than occupying a shiftier and more self-ironic subject position on the question of the spirits, Mumler was not able to put quotation marks (or even scare quotes) around his chosen profession. After that early Barnumesque encounter with Gardner (as related earlier), Mumler committed himself to Spiritualist doctrine. In consequence, he found himself trapped in an inflexible subject position that foreclosed the "specter of derision" or the mixing of magic and comedy as one finds in the contemporary antics of Penn and Teller. In contrast to Barnum, Leja writes, "[Mumler] would not acknowledge his mischief and allow his patrons to share his secret. His allegiance to the old supernatural forms of magic prevented him from following the course charted by Barnum, which might have proved at least as lucrative." (2007: 55) In other words, Mumler was condemned to wear the wizard's hat to the trial and was not able to take it off. Interestingly, the *World* (1869) printed a story at the time of the trial associating Mumler with such magical wizardry and asserting that this was exactly the reason why Barnum—who played dumb when defending his own humbugs and thereby incited much laughter—could not tolerate this phony spirit photographer striking the pose of supernatural realism. It reads: "Mumler as a magician revolts [Barnum's] else universal credulity. … Who will pretend a trust in the preposterous pretensions of the spiritual photographer?" (4) Barnum's strategy then was to exploit this mistrust in deflating and debunking Mumler as a humbug.

Finale: Mumler's Resurrection of the Presidential Ghost with Mary Todd Lincoln (1872)

Believe it or not, Mumler was not finished yet. Three years after the trial, the somber "ghost of death" would rise again and the "specter of derision" would be veiled once more in a heavy cloak of grief and mourning. For this is exactly the way to interpret Mumler's most famous spirit photograph of Mary Todd Lincoln that was accompanied by the return of the ghost of her late husband and their dearly departed son Thomas (Tad) when viewed from the Spiritualist perspective. (Fig. 2.7) In his memoirs, Mumler (1875) recalls the grave appearance of "a lady dressed in black, wearing a crape veil" visiting his Boston studio, thereby bringing the question of bereavement to the forefront of his narration. (30) The "in cog" visitor introduced herself as one Mrs. Lindall and she did not remove her veil until the very moment of the exposure as if to demonstrate

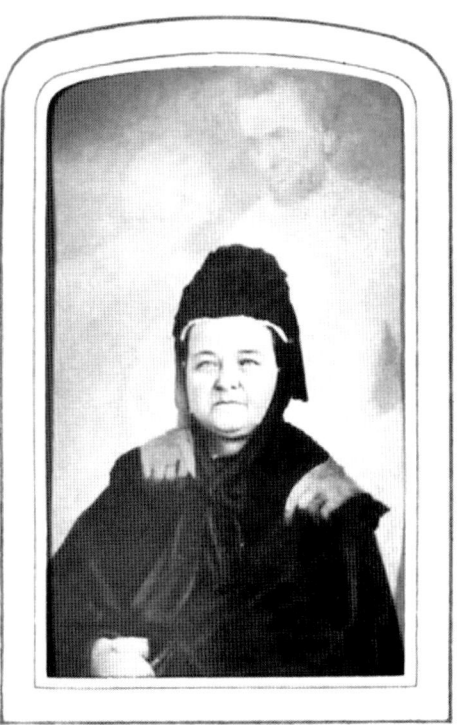

that Mumler could not have practiced any trickery. Striking the pose of the innocent, Mumler recounts in his memoirs: "I had not the slightest idea that I had had such a distinguished sitter." (30) Mumler also reports that in the spooked photograph President Lincoln "is seen standing behind her, with his hands resting on her shoulders, and looking down, with a pleasant smile." (30)

In terms of the ghost dialectics traced here, the Lincoln spirit image of 1872 stages the inverse of the Barnum/Bogardus mock-spirit photograph, for it represents the disgraced spirit photographer's last-ditch effort to re-inscribe the magical and supernatural in the place of the mechanical. In other words, the resurrection of the ghost of Lincoln can be viewed as Mumler's magical revenge. For Mumler, the late President's ghost was not to be taken as a laughing matter but as the way to cover over the peals of skeptical laughter with solemnity, with mourning and melancholy. Nevertheless, one is tempted to ask if Mumler was just copying Barnum (or even parodying him) in staging this particular photograph. For the Lincoln ghost produced by Mumler's camera in 1872 puts the spirit photograph staged by Barnum/Bogardus at the 1869 trial in a new light from the debunker's point of view. It was as if Mumler had a look at Barnum's photograph at the trial and thought to himself, "Wow, what a sensational idea for a spirit photograph! I will

Figure 2.7

William H. Mumler, *Mary Todd Lincoln with the Spirits of Her Husband President Abraham Lincoln and Son Thomas (Tad)*, 1872. Reproduced by kind permission of the College of Psychic Studies, London.

have to try that someday." The fortuitous visit of the ardent Spiritualist (and, by many accounts, mostly mad) Mary Todd Lincoln to Mumler's Boston studio during her round of consultations with spirit mediums after the recent death of her son gave the besieged spirit photographer a golden opportunity to quash the "specter of derision" yet again. But the disbelieving debunkers did not share Lincoln's "pleasant smile" for they had always thought of Mumler as a conjuring con artist and they insisted that this mystification was only replaying Barnum's earlier prank on the ghost of Honest Abe. In appropriating and parodying great Lincoln's ghost, Mumler's pious defense of spirit photography and his serious Spiritualist rhetoric masked a devious grin. In this way, the specter of derision was always already in play.

Thus, the strange case of William Mumler and his spirit photographs demonstrates that humor is not only "the debunking of humanity" in George Orwell's sense. For P.T. Barnum and company, it was also the debunking of the ghosts. (Fig. 2.8)

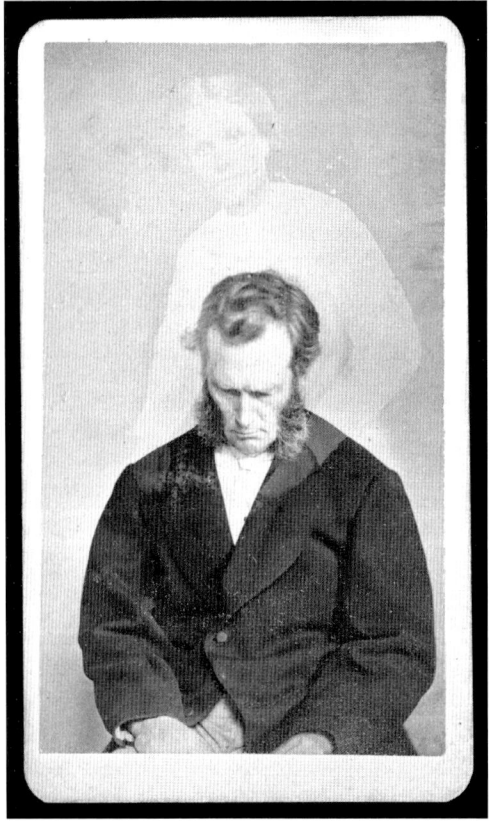

Figure 2.8

William H. Mumler, *Bronson Murray in a Trance with the Spirit of Ella Bonner*, 1872. Albumen silver print. The J. Paul Getty Museum, Los Angeles.

Notes

1. I review these examples and others in the final chapter of my recent book *Photography and Humour.* (Kaplan, 2016) These case studies were also part of my keynote lecture ("A Morbid Sense of Humor: Reflections on Photography's Dark Comedy") at the symposium upon which the present volume is based. I thank Mieke Bleyen and Liesbeth Decan for inviting me to participate and for their valuable editorial comments, suggestions, and corrections.

Bibliography

P.T. Barnum, *Humbugs of the World: An Account of Humbugs, Delusions, Impositions, Quackeries, Deceits and Deceivers Generally in All Ages* (New York: Carleton Publishers, 1866).

Mackenzie Bartlett, "Mirth as Medium: Spectacles of Laughter in the Victorian Séance Room," in *The Ashgate Research Companion to Nineteenth-Century Spiritualism and the Occult,* eds Tatiana Kontou and Sarah Willburn (New York: Routledge, 2012), 267–284.

Samuel Beckett, *Watt* (London: Faber and Faber 2009).

Sir David Brewster, *The Stereoscope: Its History, Theory, and Construction, With Its Application to the Fine and Useful Arts and to Education* (London: J. Murray, 1856).

C.M.P., "Spirit Photographs: A New and Interesting Development," reproduced in *The Spiritual-Magazine* 3, no. 12 (December 1862): 562.

Clément Chéroux, *The Perfect Medium: Photography and the Occult* (New Haven and London: Yale University Press, 2005).

Simon Critchley, *On Humour* (New York: Routledge, 2002).

Leslie Fiedler, "Cross the Border – Close the Gap," in *The Collected Essays of Leslie Fielder* (New York: Stein and Day, 1971).

Elbridge T. Gerry, *The Mumler "Spirit" Photography Case* (New York: Baker, Voorhis & Co., 1869).

Harry Houdini, *A Magician Among the Spirits* (New York and London: Harper & Brothers, 1924).

Louis Kaplan, *The Strange Case of William Mumler, Spirit Photographer* (Minneapolis, MN: University of Minnesota Press, 2008).

———, *Photography and Humour* (London: Reaktion Books, 2016).

———, "A Magician among the Spirit Photographs: Reflections on Houdini's Doubt," in *Photography and Doubt*, eds Sabine T. Kriebel and Andres Mario Zervigon (New York: Routledge, 2017), 59–78.

Michael Leja, *Looking Askance: Skepticism and American Art from Eakins to Duchamp* (Berkeley, CA: University of California Press, 2007).

Jennifer Mnookin, "The Image of Truth: Photographic Evidence and the Power of Analogy," *Yale Journal of Law and the Humanities*, 10, no. 1 (1998): 1–74.

William Mumler, *The Personal Experiences of William H. Mumler in Spirit-Photography* (Boston: Colby & Rich, 1875).

Harry Price, *Fifty Years of Psychical Research* (London: Longmans, Green & Co., 1939).

James Randi. *Flim-Flam! Psychics, ESP, Unicorns, and Other Delusions* (Buffalo, NY: Prometheus Books, 1982).

"'Spirit' Photographs," *World*, New York (April 29, 1869): 1–4.

"Spiritualism in Court," *New York Daily Tribune* (April 29, 1869): 2.

"The Mumler Trial," *The Circular*, Oneida, New York (May 3, 1869): 54–55.

Comedy Performs Photography: Imaginations of Photography in Silent Film Comedies

Hilde D'haeyere

In June 1895 Louis Lumière was filming *Le Débarquement du congrès de photographie à Lyon*, showing a group of photographers with their equipment disembarking from a boat, when one of the gents stopped to snap a photograph of the movie camera filming the event. This moment is booked as the first time photography was captured on film. (Campany, 2008: 7) It started a long tradition in which the new technology of cinema looks at its ancestor photography, with photography gazing back.

This text delves specifically into the *comedic* possibilities of picturing photography on film. Rather than dealing with humor in photography, it examines photography as the very subject of humor in moving images. How, when, and why photography became the subject of merriment and ridicule is traced in a selection of silent film comedies of the first decades of the 20th century that feature, among others, slapstick comedians Charlie Chaplin, Charley Chase, Mabel Normand, Harold Lloyd, Buster Keaton and Harry Langdon. Their gags depict stumbling photographers at work, failing photographic equipment, clumsy posers, mistaken portraits, darkroom flirtations and female photographers, to cite but a few examples. Organized into seven subcategories illustrated with a pair of film frames, each section deals with one aspect of the representation of photography as comedy subject. In fact, the distorted mirror of slapstick comedy reflects how photography is perceived in the era of the silent cinema, and which technological changes and social implications are in need of comedic exploration and digestion. Why particularly silent slapstick comedy is a suitable film genre for such a study of photography is the subject of this essay.

1. Ambimodern Photography

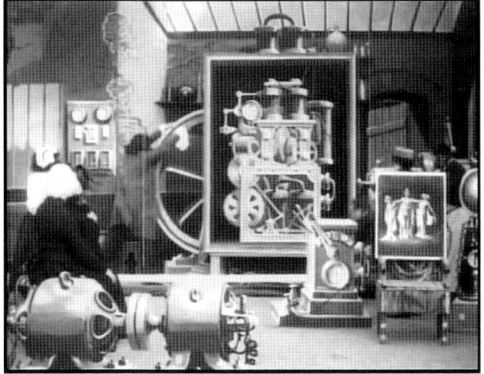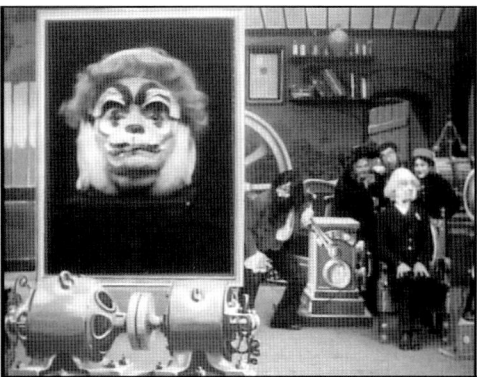

One of the earliest examples that picture the trials and tribulations of a photographer at work is George Méliès' *Long Distance Wireless Photography*. In this 1908 comedy an elderly couple visits a photography studio and, after a demonstration of the procedure by the photographer, poses for a portrait.

Remarkably the photographic equipment in the studio is not fashioned after historical or current models; it is in fact the only comedy in this line-up that proposes a totally novel conception of photography, detached from existing practices. Nor is Méliès' visualization of photography shaped after the paraphernalia of magic or alchemy. As is widely known, before his career as film director Méliès had been a stage magician and the effects-laden films he made between 1896 and 1913 remain steeped in the aesthetics of 19th-century magical theater, while being realized with photographic trick techniques. Yet, in *Long Distance Wireless Photography* the craft of photography is not pictured as a transformative act with potions, explosions and smoke screens to mask changes on the stage. Instead, Méliès' photographic machine is an open construction composed from mechanical parts like nuts, bolts and flywheels, operated by the pulling of a lever. It is a bulky industry-sized piece of machinery, like a steelwork plant or steam locomotive, the enlarged version of a clockwork or telegraph recorder. While the inside of a typical photographic view camera is merely an empty space through which light travels on its way from the lens to light-sensitive material in the back, this camera is filled to the brim with mechanical parts. With this room-sized machine Méliès conjures up a concept of photography as a medium that transmits, by means of a wireless electrical impulse, the likeness of a subject and throws it onto a screen. For instance, when presented with a painting of three goddesses in draperies, the machine pictures three scantily dressed women. (Fig. 2.9a) They turn gracefully

Figure 2.9

Photographie électrique à distance [Long Distance Wireless Photography], dir. George Méliès, 1908 (digital frames).

with waving arms to show their three-dimensionality in motion. The photo-in-the film is realized by a double exposure in a blackened part of the frame, a technique used in 19th-century spirit photography.

Surprisingly, this early depicting of photography on film presents photography as a telepathic medium with the faculty to reproduce movement. Every subject, be it a two- or three-dimensional, still or living original, is transformed into moving pictures on a screen. At first glance, Méliès' machine more closely demonstrates aspects of cinema than of photography. Exactly like the Lumière brothers promoted their invention of the *Cinématograph* as "photographie animé," this comedy demonstrates cinema's relation to the older medium of photography, designed like gear from 19th-century mechanical modernity. Still, more advanced than the then-current state of cinematography, Méliès' comedic version not only transmits moving images wirelessly, it can also see beyond the visible, teleporting grotesque caricatures as well as actual features. When a nice old lady is presented, her smiling face appears enlarged on the screen. But when the distinguished older gentleman is sat in front of the electrical photo camera, the face projected on the screen is that of a monkey. (Fig. 2.9b) Indeed, Méliès' re-imagination of older mechanics makes a proverbial monkey out of a gentleman, as it turns a photo session into a film screening or television show.

The mixed temporality in this retro-futuristic representation of photography remains a trait in later American slapstick comedies, coloring what Ben Singer in 2009 called the "ambimodernity" of the comedy genre characterized by old-fashioned fantasies, infantile plots, and pre-modern sensibilities. Precisely from the clash between the photo camera's 19th-century industrial features, the then-novel technology of film projection and the futurist imagination of wireless revelations, humor emerges that undermines the hyperrealist expectations connected to machine-media.

2. Newscomedies

Slapstick humor crosses the Atlantic Ocean from Europe to America in the company of Charles Chaplin. After a career on music-hall stages with the British Karno troupe, Chaplin's appearance in *Making a Living* marks his debut in the American film industry. The comedy was filmed in January 1914, during his first week employed by the Keystone Film Company in Los Angeles. Chaplin plays a hobo stealing the camera from a reporter who has just witnessed a spectacular car accident and photographed it. (Fig. 2.10a) The vagrant cashes in on the scoop by selling the pictures to the local newspaper that publishes an extra edition on the event.

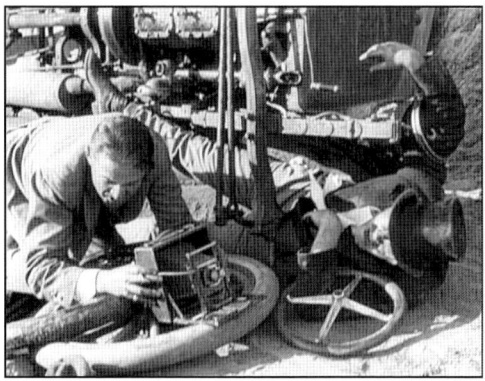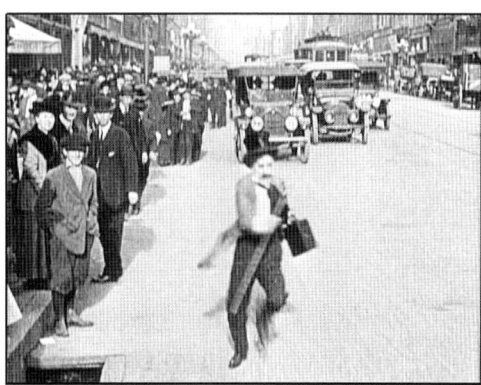

The stolen object is a baseboard camera fitted with a collapsible bellows, which makes a compact package for transportation. The shutter is handled by a squeeze in the rubber bulb on the cable release. Baseboard cameras were widely used as field cameras by photographers who required a lightweight, portable camera that could be operated handheld. Professional users included newspaper reporters, war journalists, scientific explorers, and detectives. What these professions have in common is a form of photography that is performed in the outdoors, outside of the photo studio. Portable cameras, faster emulsions, and mechanized photo reproduction techniques like rotogravure thus create a new type of photographer: the photo journalist. (Albert and Feyel, 1998: 363) Such a reporter-photographer Chaplin's character aspires to become.

In his new profession, taking photographs of catastrophes and beating the competition in having the pictures published is, of course, standard procedure. Yet it is interesting to note that also the shooting of this comedy film is perceived as a newsworthy event in its own right: large numbers of onlookers are crowding the frame to witness Chaplin's slapstick actions performed in the streets of downtown Los Angeles. (Fig. 2.10b) In 1914, shooting a film in the streets is novel enough to be worth reporting on...in the newspaper. (D'haeyere, 2012: 163–165) *Making a Living* then documents a self-serving slapstick cycle of "using news to make news": comedies that reference news facts—so-called "newscomedies"—profit from actual events, on-site crowds, authentic locations and press coverage, without adding to production costs or logistics. The spectacle of a comedy crew at work, in turn, stirs up a crowd, which provides a fresh angle for journalists to report on. Furthermore, newscomedies appeal to the collective memory of the audience that is already familiar with photographic or cinematic images of the events from newspapers and newsreels, with whom they are possibly even paired in the same film program. We can, then,

Figure 2.10

Making a Living, dir. Henry Lehrman, 1914, with Charles Chaplin (digital frames).

imagine the intermedial life of a news item: traveling from witnessed event to news photograph, illustration in the paper, moving pictures in a newsreel and a comedy re-enactment in a slapstick film–all in a day's media experience.

In 1914, slapstick's newscomedies are among the timely film formats that explore how to cope with the horrible news facts pictured by photo journalists who are making a living by photographing the events that sell newspapers. Comedic takes on such reporters-photographers in action work to dilute the bad news-shows in cinemas around the world, on the eve of World War I.

3. Photographic Pests

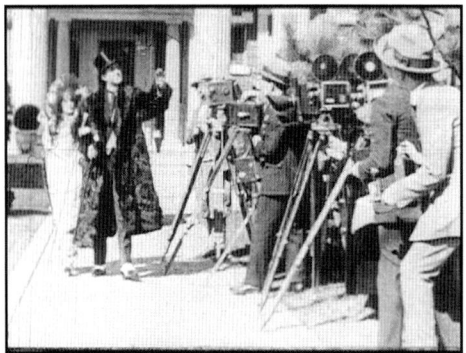 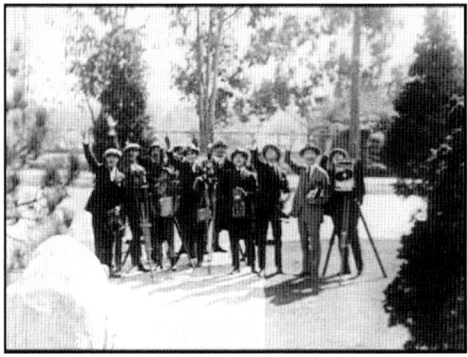

A decade later than Chaplin in *Making a Living* (1914), comedian Charley Chase confronts press photographers in *The Rat's Knuckles* (1925). As the inventor Jimmy Jump, he devised a humane mousetrap that, he imagines, will make him rich and famous. In a daydream, his imagined state of celebrity is visualized by a flock of paparazzi that follows him around, pointing cameras on every aspect of his existence. (Fig. 2.11a) "These photographic persons are such pests," an intertitle declares. Befittingly, his invention of a trap for pests makes him a pestered person, bugged by photography.

That the profession is going through major changes is visible in the line-up of reporters and cameras on his doorstep: a mixed set of cameras for film and photography, on tripods and hand-held, of different sizes and functionalities is present. (Fig. 2.11b) Among some Bell & Howell 35mm film cameras on tripods stands a 8×10" view camera covered with a dark cloth. Hand-held are a baseboard field camera and two Press Graflex 5×7" cameras, recognizable by the tall viewing hood on top.

Figure 2.11

The Rat's Knuckles, dir. Leo McCarey, 1925, with Charley Chase (digital frames).

The Press Graflex is the first camera specifically designed to meet the needs of the emerging press photographer who wants a reliable, sturdy camera with a sheet film magazine, loaded with twelve photographic plates to avoid reloading after each take, with a format large enough to allow insertion in a newspaper without enlargement, while still preserving the option of portability. Added to this is the need for speed: fast lenses, high-sensitive emulsions, and short exposure times. In the early 1920s the different designs of the Graflex settle into a single-lens reflex camera with a swinging mirror and a through-the-lens viewing mechanism, which allows for framing and focusing via the ground glass, hence the pop-up viewing hood. The operation at waist level enables a fast response and a discreetly snapped shot.

The sight of such a well-outfitted journalist expands on Umbo's famous 1929 image of the journalist Egon Erwin Kisch as a mechanical man with prosthetic extensions that enhance his human performance with the benefits of the recording apparatus: a ratting reporter with a tripod for multiple legs, pens for fingers, and lenses for faceted eyes. The photographer as a merger of man, machine, and vermin swarms the streets on the lookout for movie stars and sports celebrities to photograph, in order to feed the constant demand for pictures for illustrated journals and fan magazines in the infectious cult of stars and celebrities that unfolded after World War I.

The American street photographer had yet to discover the best photo camera for such omnipresent and all-seeing journalism: the Leica, while designed in Germany in 1924, was introduced only in the US in 1932. In addition to being compact, this rangefinder camera is practically inaudible without the sound of a swinging mirror. Exactly at the time photography becomes silent cinema starts to talk, which, paradoxically, necessitates the muffling of the whirring sound of film cameras, too. That the Leica is specifically built to accommodate the use of standard cinema 35mm film stock (transported horizontally and not vertically as in film cameras), is yet another example of how photography's imprinting on film makes it benefit from the mobility, speed, and silence of motion picture photography. Thus, cinema gives photography its decisive moment. Yet photography offers film comedies a new character of modernity: the ratting reporter, the detective, the police photographer, who silently lift an individual out of the crowd and identify a person within an anonymous mass, crafting photographic evidence of misconduct or celebrity. (Gunning, 1995: 15–45)

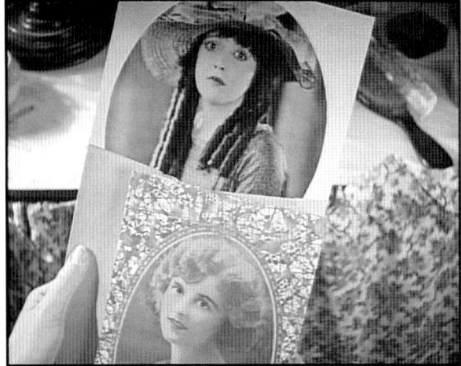 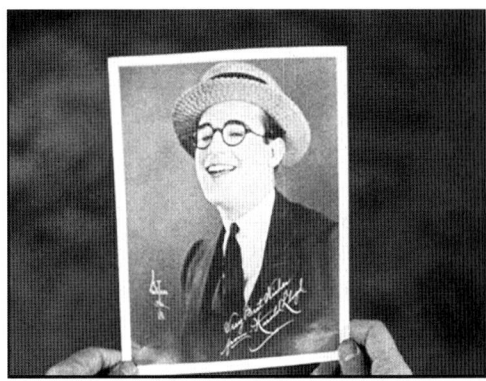

Figure 2.12

The Extra Girl, dir. F. Richard Jones, 1923, and *My Stars*, dir. Roscoe Arbuckle, 1926 (digital frames).

Photography in the early 20th century develops in the context of other image-based industries and distribution systems for publishing, advertising, inventorying, and controlling, which results in the manifestation of photographs in every segment of life. These developments trickle down into slapstick films in which photography's impact on aspects of identity and privacy is explored. Given the emergence of photographic portraits as means of identification, slapstick comically inverts the narrative and explores the mayhem that arises when portraits are switched or people assume a new identity by using someone else's photo. The value of a photographic portrait as a truthful stand-in for a person in official documents is frequently undermined in slapstick gags on mistaken identity and errors with look-alikes. For instance, in *The Extra Girl* (1923), the portrait Mabel Normand's character sends in for a beauty contest is switched for the cookie-box print of a lovely lady by her love rival. (Fig. 2.12a) By exchanging the photographic image for a printed page, the rough-and-tumble hayseed girl transforms into a fine-featured poster lady, which triggers a comic tale of misunderstandings that ultimately proves the physical bravery of the tomboy more useful than the uniform beauty of the cookie model.

Also in the 1920s, a very diverse range of institutions starts amassing photographic portraits in files and image banks, among which are police forces, casting agencies, insurance companies, prisons, schools, and matrimonial bureaus. But the largest producer of portraits with, arguably, the widest distribution is the film industry itself: the publicity portrait is the key component in a star system that sells the glamorous likeness of actors to bolster the loyalty of fans. *My Stars* (1926) pokes fun at such fandom by portraying Johnny Arthur as a boyfriend who tries to please his girl by impersonating the movie stars she admires. Unfortunately, the girl keeps changing her favorites each time the postman brings a new delivery of movie star pictures. The short is punctuated by shots that show a publicity photograph of, among others, slapstick comedian Harold Lloyd, in the hands of the admiring girlfriend. (Fig. 2.12b) She animates the still picture by holding and stroking it while pausing long enough to give audiences the time to recognize the represented star. Unlike film images, photographic prints are objects with a reverse side, so comedy moves, flips, upends, and exchanges the prints to explore the plus side of photographs on film. In turn, also the boyfriend animates the promotional pictures by dressing up like each star and imitating their behavior to impress the girl. At the romantic closure, the narrative stills again when the motions prove too much for the girl who realizes she prefers plain Johnny. They unite in a final embrace. The opposed dynamics of stillness and movement are thus represented by photography and cinematography, but not in the most obvious distribution: while slapstick comedy brings still pictures into motion to mock their static flatness, cinema's frantic goings-on inevitably arrest in the ultimate emblem of a happy ending. In so doing, photography and cinematography inhabit the rhythm of stopping and starting that defines slapstick comedy.

5. Dysfunctional-Family Portraits

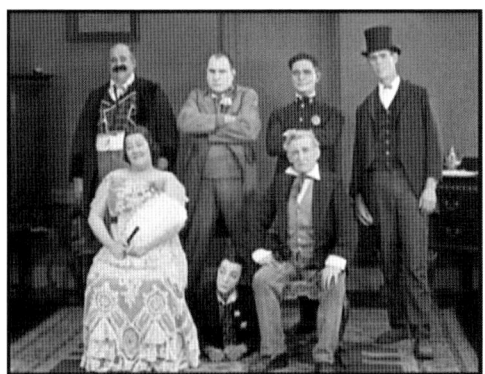 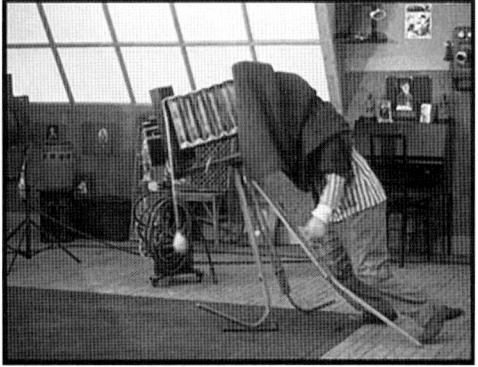

In *My Wife's Relations* (1922), by a perfect misunderstanding Buster Keaton marries the woman he literally falls for on a street corner. The marriage certificate is handed over like a prison sentence and the tense relation with his new bride and her relatives is cemented in the family portrait taken after the wedding. While generally expected to document the highpoint of such a happy social occasion, thereby affirming family ties, this wedding portrait offers a picturesque battlefield that reframes the social hierarchy. (Kaplan, 2017: 91–92) Initially Buster, the

Figure 2.13

My Wife's Relations, dir. Buster Keaton and Edward Cline, 1922, and *Smile Please,* dir. Roy Del Ruth, 1924, with Harry Langdon (digital frames).

groom, is accorded only the tiniest of spaces in the picture — as he is in the family. After being kicked out of the composition repeatedly, he finally finds a spot on the floor in between the legs of his brother-in-law. (Fig. 2.13a) The collective posing in this photo session visually establishes a pecking order from tall and stout to tiny and short. Even the tripod can't handle the tensions and it goes limp, sinking slowly down to the floor, which leaves the family no alternative but to follow the route the tripod dictates. Finally, an exploding flashlight reshuffles the set-up again. Only when Buster kicks out the incompetent photographer does he eventually earn the respect of his in-laws. Posing for a family portrait is thus pictured as the site of a constant negotiation between standing still and moving about, a fight between up and down, the battling of bulk and wit — all visualized in a succession of posing arrangements.

Moreover, the fixed stillness by which the people are asked to pose is comically inverted by the movement of the recording equipment, when the rugged stability of the tripod gives way under the strain of the situation. While a photographer in slapstick cinema is mostly pictured as an insensitive and incompetent artistic type, the photographic machinery proves its intelligence by picking up tensions and emotions, to which it responds like a sensing person. For instance, in the 1924 slapstick movie *Smile Please* the tripod becomes weak at the knees and faints in response to a strong stink. (Fig. 2.13b) In *My Wife's Relations* the embodied behavior of the tripod dictates the composition of the portrait, much like the flashlight prompts a new and chaotic arrangement of people. The photographic apparatus in fact conspires to reframe the social ranking in the family to favor Keaton's position. Henri Bergson already in 1900 noted the force of comedy as a social corrective and famously defined the comic as "something mechanical encrusted on the living." Aided by the corrective force of exploding flashlight and smart tripods, slapstick upends his dictum by also exploring the comedic side of something living encrusted upon the mechanical.

6. Darkroom Dangers

Harry Langdon in *Smile Please* (1924) holds the double position of sheriff and photographer, which share the professional activity of shooting. Harry starts his courtship of Alberta Vaughn by rescuing her from a run-away horse, continues it by photographing her in the beach-set in his photo studio, after which he braces himself to move to the next level. "Let's develop this together," he proposes, invitingly opening the door of his darkroom. The verbal pun also translates into the visuals: the photographic darkroom is clearly the site where chemical reactions are expected to happen between liquids and film, as between men and

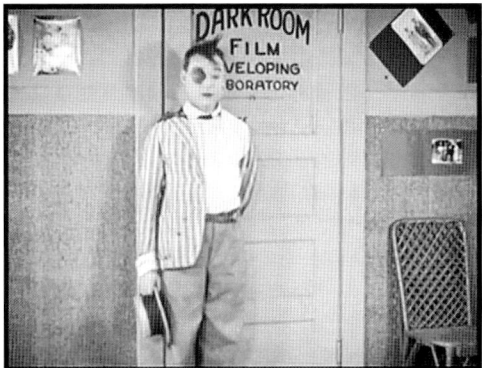 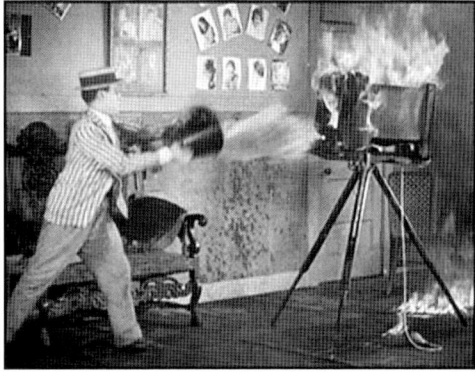

women. Lost in the black-and-white film is the red light of such a room: these colored safelights permit the handling of light-sensitive material without fear of exposure, but also signal a red-light district where sexual activities are semi-secretly performed. In this, the photographic darkroom is closely related to the movie theater. Film development and exhibition share the activity of watching images appear in the dark, linking the first step in the production process of image making media with a photographic base to its last. In fact, movie theaters were among the first spaces where spectators of different class, sex, and age were present in each other's company in the dark. (Elcott, 2016: 67) It goes without saying that such mixed-sex attendance covered by a cloak of darkness resulted in a lot of chemistry among the attendants.

In *Smile Please*, the attraction is one-sided as Harry emerges from the darkroom sporting a black eye. (Fig 2.14a) His fervent feelings ignite a fire of jealously in his rival who sends up the entire photo studio in flames. (Fig 2.14b) Particularly the burning camera is a powerful image that speaks of the dangers connected to the chemical base of photographic media and, on a different level, of the flaming desire that travels through the camera between photographer and sitter.

That the entire second reel of this slapstick short is devoted to events that happen *after* the moment of exposure complicates the idea that taking photographs is a matter of simply pressing a button—as in effect it had been marketed since 1901, the year Eastman Kodak introduced the Brownie. The purchase of this inexpensive cardboard box camera included the photo-finishing service. Using the tagline "You press the button—we do the rest," Kodak targeted a mass market of amateur photographers with the promise to reduce the entire craft to a single push and have the photographer focus solely on the snapping of the shot. In contrast, by amply demonstrating the photographic developing process, the actual dangers connected to the delicate mixing of the formulae, the flammability of photographic chemicals and the fragility

Figure 2.14

Smile Please, dir. Roy Del Ruth, 1924 with Harry Langdon (digital frames).

of the expensive equipment, slapstick comedy acknowledges the expert craftsmanship involved in the professional photographer's trade.

7. Camerawomen

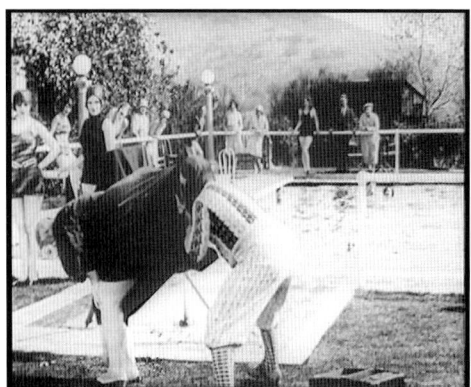 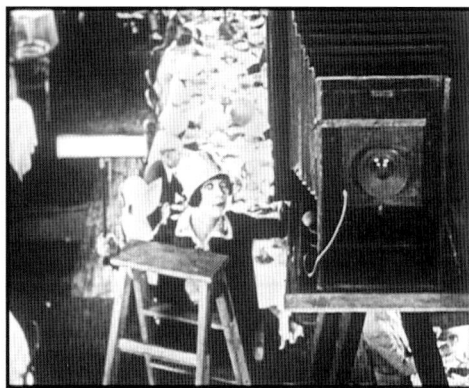

Figure 2.15

The Golf Nut, dir. Harry Edwards, 1927, with Madalynn Field, and *Hold Still*, dir. William Watson, 1926, with Anne Cornwall (digital frames).

    The position of women in slapstick comedy relates the changing agency of women in early 20th-century society. In silent slapstick films mostly young, white, and shapely women appear as decorative elements to dress up the scenes. They are strictly not to be laughed at. Slapstick rules that no humor is directed at beautiful women, their sheer youth and beauty protects them from physical stunt work, violent treatment, or pie-in-the-face gags. (Sennett, 1918: 70) But women with different body types, ladies dressing down into hayseed characters, or actresses who adopt a silly walk, those have free reign: they can be the clown or the butt of pranks. Only when visibly deviant from beauty standards can women be active participants in slapstick jokes.

    Such is the case for star-comedienne Mabel Normand (Fig. 2.12a) and for the tall and rotund actress Madalynn Field. In *The Golf Nut* (1927), the latter strolls past a swimming pool filled with hordes of beautiful babes in bathing suits who are modeling for a photographer. With remarkable timing, exactly when the photographer turns away to pick up the film plates, Madalynn bends over to fix her shoe. Thinking her long skirt is the cloth that covers his view camera, the clumsy lensman takes a long and hard look up her dress. (Fig. 2.15a) Granted, two legs wearing a skirt does bear *some* resemblance to a tripod and camera blind, and the anthropomorphic conflation of person and prop is perfectly in line with Bergson's comedy concept of "something mechanical encrusted upon the living." Even so, the objectification of the female character is humiliating and the power dynamics of the joke offensive for today's audiences. The joke comes entirely at the expense of the plus-size actress, with connotations of peeping and groping.

Only slightly more female agency has Anne Cornwall in *Hold Still* (1926). She is promised a job as press photographer if she manages to make a portrait of a very reclusive senator. After two failed attempts with compact and mobile machines, a Graflex and a tin-type camera, she finally succeeds in snapping a picture of the senator eating his lunch, by using the enormous view camera that is set up atop a high ladder in a restaurant, ready to take a banquet portrait. (Fig. 2.15b) By comically inverting expectations, Anne only succeeds in stealing the sneaky snapshot with the help of the least unobtrusive machinery: a 20×24" plate camera and a massive flashlight. Both operate with the violence of warfare: *shooting* a picture by *firing* the flash. The blinding light relays the aggressive force of the photographic execution onto the targeted subject. Fittingly, flash powder and nitrate film share a chemical kinship with military pyrotechnics and dynamite, which explains the deployment of photographic equipment as weapons. Shot and explosion not only mark the moment a picture is taken, the resulting smokescreen also masks the rearrangement from order to chaos, revealing a totally destroyed room once the smoke lifts. Luckily, the blow-up produced a great close-up.

In spite of her explosive rite of passage into the profession, Anne ultimately turns down the coveted job of press photographer, when her boyfriend asks her to choose between the professional offer and his marriage proposal. With photographer and wife being presented as mutually exclusive jobs, she gives in.

Confusingly, the imagination of a camerawoman as comedy character serves a double agenda: it musters acceptance for female professionals while also pleading their return to the hearth. The idea of a freelance female photographer is certainly ridiculed in slapstick comedy, as is the idea of women in other professions then usually reserved for men, like the female sailor (Alice Day in *Shanghaied Lovers*, 1924, dir. Roy Del Ruth), auto racer (Mabel Normand in *Mabel at the Wheel*, 1914, dir. Mack Sennett and Mabel Normand), firewoman (Gale Henry in *Her First Flame*, 1920, dir. Bruno C. Decker), she-bandit (Mabel Normand in *Should Men Walk Home?*, 1927, dir. Leo McCarey), and many more examples. Yet the very presence of female professionals like camerawomen also accustoms audiences to the expanded professional possibilities for the New Women in the post-World War I era. Likewise, the visibility in slapstick shorts of female comedians of a variety of different builds, sizes and weights broadens the limited options for women that are pictured in commercial contexts like advertising or fashion, and the beauty standards expected of dramatic lead actresses. In both cases, female comedians effectively act as emancipating forces and role models.

Endnotes

To end, some general remarks that shine through all of the above visualizations of photography in silent film comedy.

Time wise, it is enlightening to study slapstick comedy's take on photography because at precisely that time the latter is in the process of undergoing major technological changes and its social functions and cultural implications are shifting. Comedy is in the habit of baring such fields of tensions, aiming straight at the most painful spots. A study of the visualizations of photography then unveils the new developments photography deals with in the first decades of the 20th century, issues that concern the rapid instalment of a visual culture based on photographic images that pervade all aspects of society.

Given slapstick's specific propensity for visual humor based on physical conflicts, comedies mostly fool around with the visual components of every phase of the photographic system, giving room to the extensive examination and abuse of its logistics. In playing with camera(wo)men, cameras, flashlights, tripods, and photo prints, slapstick explores the challenges of mechanization, industrialization, dehumanization, and duplication that pervade 20th-century society — the very conditions that bore the machine-media of both photography and cinematography.

Of course, silent slapstick films do not necessarily paint a truthful picture of the state of photography; we mostly see which changes comedy responds to *on film* and must definitely also tabulate the sensitivities of cinema into its look at photography. Sure enough, the representation of photography in slapstick cinema is also a teasing game between the related media of photography and film. Cinema shares with photography the technological base of a machine-made medium. Thus, by picturing the visual system of photography, cinema also looks at itself — its older, mature, artistic, unmoving, silent self. Particularly those components of photography that cinema feels it also confronts or has surpassed are under fire: the bulkiness of the equipment, the expert handling it requires, and the lack of time, movement or uniqueness embedded in single, still images. Inevitably, such anachronistic looking back at the former recording medium from the position of the new "improved" version is a revenging and ever-frustrated look that also demonstrates cinema's shortcomings to be that quasi-perfect recording medium that manages to capture the whole fleeting experience of reality. (Beckman, 2003: 89, 91) Those components photography most obviously "lacks" for a holistic picture, that is: time and motion, those cinema can provide, hence its manhandling of photographs on the screen, its animation of photographic equipment, and its lingering over the making of photographic memories, that overcome the static, momentary, and morbid nature of photography. The coming of talking film after 1927 moves *silent* film to the position of most closely related, obsolete version of itself. Indeed, talking film comedy adds voices and noises to its quotations of silent film to ridicule the lack of sound of its mute forefather. Something similar happens with the emergence of color film, when black-and-white sequences come to stand for the silly ol' days of yore. Each new and "improved" version consumes its ancestor in ridicule.

The many depictions of photography in silent slapstick comedies of the first decades of the 20th century, then, express the changing perception of photography in the age of its cinematic reproducibility, moving between a salute to a kindred medium, ridicule for imagery that lacks movement and time, fear for a modern technology that employs chemistry and electricity, distrust of the multiplication of images in print runs and press circulation, and reverence for the male and female professionals that handle all the aspects of its own creation process.

Bibliography

Pierre Albert and Gilles Feyel, "Photography and the Media," in *A New History of Photography,* ed. Michel Frizot (Köln: Könemann, 1998), 359–369.

Karen Beckman, *Vanishing Women: Magic, Film, and Feminism* (Durham: Duke University Press, 2003).

Walter Benjamin, "The Work of Art in the Age of Its Technological Reproducibility, Second Version [1936]," in *The Work of Art in the Age of its Technological Reproducibility, and Other Writings on Media,* eds Michael W. Jennings, Brigid Doherty, and Thomas Y. Levin (Harvard Mas.: Harvard University Press, 2008), 19–55.

Henri Bergson, "Laughter: An Essay on The Meaning of the Comic [1900]," in *Comedy: A Critical Anthology,* ed. Robert W. Corrigan (Boston: Houghton Mifflin, 1971), 471–477.

David Campany, "Photography in Film," in *Photography and Cinema* (London: Reaktion Books, 2008), 94–118.

Hilde D'haeyere, *Stopping the Show: Film Photography in Mack Sennett Slapstick Comedies (1917–1933)* (Ghent: University Ghent, 2012).

Noam M. Elcott, *Artificial Darkness: An Obscure History of Modern Art and Media* (Chicago: University of Chicago Press, 2016).

Laurent Guido and Olivier Lugon (eds), *Between Still and Moving Images* (East Barnet, UK: John Libbey Publishing, 2012).

Tom Gunning, "Tracing the Individual Body aka Photography, Detectives, Early Cinema and the Body of Modernity," in *Cinema and the Invention of Modern Life,* eds Vanessa R. Schwartz and Leo Charney (Oakland, CA: University of California Press, 1995), 15–45.

Louis Kaplan, *Photography and Humour* (London: Reaktion Books, 2017).

Mack Sennett, "The Psychology of Film Comedy," *Motion Picture Classic* (November 1918): 20–21, 70.

Ben Singer, "The Ambimodernity of Early Cinema: Problems and Paradoxes in the Film-and-Modernity Discourse," in *Film 1900: Technology, Perception, Culture,* eds Annemone Ligensa and Klaus Kreimeier (East Barnet, UK: John Libbey Publishing, 2009), 37–51.

Paul Young, *The Cinema Dreams Its Rivals: Media Fantasy Films from Radio to the Internet* (University of Minnesota Press, 2006).

Feminism, Laughter, and Photomontage: Comedic Effect and Grete Stern's *Sueños*

Anna Corrigan & Susana S. Martins

During the early years of Peronism, in 1948 Buenos Aires, a surprising photographic collaborative venture was shaped on the pages of the popular juvenile feminine magazine *Idilio.* This carefully designed publication included numerous pieces — ranging from photo-novels to lifestyle tips, to appearance or behavior — that reinforced the representations of stylized and idealized femininity proliferating during those years in Peronist propaganda and commercial visual culture. Every week between 1948 and 1951, *Idilio* also included a distinctive column titled "El psicoanálisis te ayudará," later changed to "le ayudará" ["Psychoanalysis will help you"]. (Bertúa 2012)[1] This advice column mobilized terms and associations from Jungian and Freudian psychoanalysis to function as a sort of "consultorio sentimental" or agony aunt. (Enrique Butelman 1983 quoted in Priamo 2003: 17) The column consisted of a dream interpretation conducted by Professor Richard Rest, allegedly an American psychoanalyst who exhorted readers to participate, promising help with social problems, doubts, anxieties, self-knowledge, etc. In order to submit her dream for interpretation, a reader would fill out a questionnaire (answering a series of 27 questions on subjects ranging from her social behaviour to her biggest fears to her childhood) and send this to *Idilio* with a description of her dream. The analysis of selected dreams would then be published, together with a photomontage that seemingly illustrated the dream under consideration. While the mere description of such psychoanalytic consultations may already strike our contemporary minds as amusing, the humorous aspects of this column exceed the circumstances of its publication.

"El psicoanalisís le ayudará" involved the collaboration of three individuals. Professor Richard Rest was in fact a fictional character designed, and impersonated, by sociologist Gino Germani and editor Enrique Butelman, named after their mutual Italian friend Ricardo

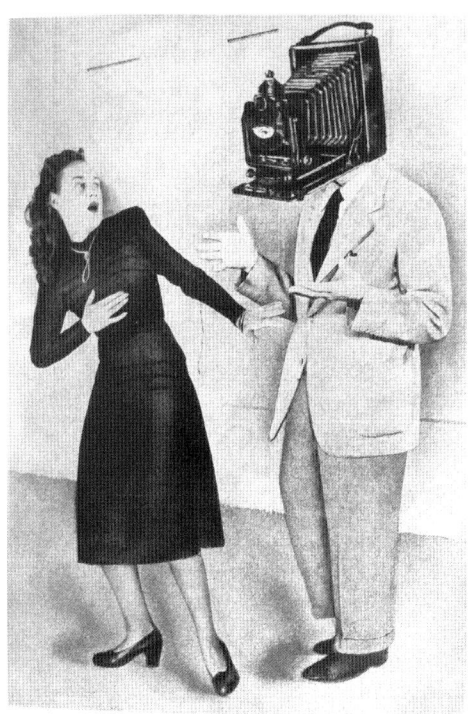

Figure 2.16

"Sueño numero 86: Sueños de fotografía," in *Sueños: fotomontajes de Grete Stern (serie completa),* ed. by Luís Príamo (Buenos Aires: Fundación CEPPA, 2003). Published 1950.

Resta. Germani was born in Italy and fled the rise of Fascism to Argentina in 1934. Though he later founded the sociology department of the University of Buenos Aires and came to be recognized as the founder of modern Argentine sociology, during the time of the column's publication Germani was academically and intellectually marginalized. (Priamo 2003: 17) Enrique Butelman studied under Carl Jung in Switzerland, and later founded *Paidós,* a publishing house specializing in psychoanalytic and psychological content, in Buenos Aires in 1945. After 1957, Butelman became a principal organizer and professor of the psychology department at the University of Buenos Aires. (see Plotkin 1999) The column also included the crucial participation of the German-Argentinian visual artist Grete Stern. Stern was enlisted to provide the images accompanying the published analysis of these dreams, and chose to do so through the medium of photomontage, producing the artistic corpus that later became known as the *Sueños* series. (Fig. 2.16)

Although the *Sueños* were powerful and visually compelling compositions, they were not artistically valued at the time that they were produced, which may help to explain why half of the original images are lost. The only way to access the series in its entirety is through the collected copies of *Idilio.* (Priamo 2003: 18)[2] Despite this, the photomontages of the *Sueños* series have recently enjoyed renewed attention from critics and scholars in Argentina and abroad, and have been exhibited at institutions such as The Museum of Modern Art in New York (2015) and MALBA in Buenos Aires (2013), among others. Since the early 2000s, scholars like Maud Lavin, Luis Priamo, Paula Bertúa, and Hugo Vezzetti have contributed significantly to understanding the series' reception and impact. (Lavin 2002; Priamo 2003; Bertúa 2012; Vezzetti 2003) These studies point to the multitudinous possible readings of Grete Stern's work. We hope to contribute to the existing considerations of Stern's work by identifying a feminist agenda presented in this series through the comedic character of photomontage.

Concretely, this chapter seeks to demonstrate how the *Sueños* series forges a sense of humor, enabled by the medium of photomontage, that challenges conventional terms of femininity in mid-century Argentina. In keeping with surrealist readings of this series, we argue that it does this by rendering the traditional unfamiliar or strange, enabling a perspective that frames certain conventions and ideologies as "funny." While the content of *Idilio*, as well as the written segment of this column, reinforced a status quo that encouraged conservative standards of appearance, behavior, and lifestyle, the *Sueños* invited women to reflect upon (and laugh at) the terms of femininity produced and circulated in popular visual culture at the time.[3] The type of laughter these images invite is significant beyond just the scope of this column, historical moment, and the medium of photomontage. Indeed, it reveals how female-ness is formed and performed at the level of visual culture, thus asserting the possibility for an alternative to conventional presentations or performances of womanhood.

Political and Feminist Potentials of Photomontage

Though the inclusion of photomontage in a lowbrow feminine magazine such as *Idilio* may seem unprecedented, in 1948 the medium itself was far from new. Authors like Mia Fineman importantly place photomontage in a tradition of photographic fabrication that is as old as photography itself. (Fineman 2012) However, classic studies on the topic, such as Dawn Ades' *Photomontage*, tend to highlight how photomontage has been mostly an avant-garde practice, represented by well-known figures like John Heartfield and Georges Grosz. More specifically, Ades states that the artistic and political applications of photomontage became especially significant just after the end of the First World War, around 1916, when the Berlin Dadaists began to introduce photographs and fragments of newsprint or magazine clippings into their work. (Ades 1986: 12) At this point, the technique involved an emphasis on "the comic arrangement of photographs" and "the subversive potential of the medium." (Ades 1986: 14)

Photomontage was not new to Grete Stern either. Though her career began years after the height of the Dadaist movement in Berlin, Stern was clearly aware of the political legacy of photomontage that foregrounded her work. In her lecture entitled "Apuntes sobre fotomontaje," delivered in 1967 at an exhibition opening of her work at the Foto Club Argentina, she refers to the significance of photomontage in Dadaist and surrealist movements in Berlin. She states, "photographers were not the first to play this game [the disassembling and reassembling of images] with photographs.. but fine artists who were involved in the Dadaist and Surrealist movements." (Stern 2003: 31) George Grosz, John Heartfield, Man Ray and André Breton are all mentioned by name in her speech.

Stern was personally acquainted with the Berlin art scene referenced in this speech. As a young woman, she lived in Berlin, where she studied photomontage for two years under Bauhaus photographer Walter Peterhans. It was also there that she, together with Ellen Auerbach, opened the commercial photography studio ringl + pit in 1929. (Mandelbaum 1995) Until 1933, the two produced humorous and inventive advertising images for products directed at women that undermined many codes of commercial production: these were typically cut-up assemblages of objects, mannequins, and silhouettes that simultaneously addressed the masquerade of femininity and critiqued the consumer culture of Weimar Germany. (Fig. 2.17) Despite the limited commercial success of these pictures, they offered an ironic take on femininity and consumerism, and granted the authors a certain amount of recognition in artistic and avant-garde circles. In 1933, for instance, ringl + pit won first prize at the *Deuxième Exposition Internationale de la Photographie et du Cinéma* in Brussels, for the poster advertising *Komol* hair treatment. (Béatrice Didier 2015)

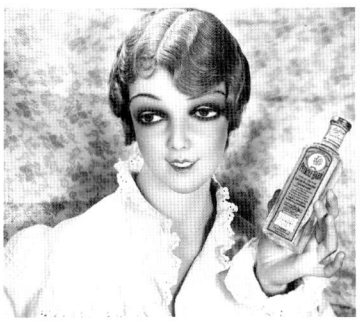

Figure 2.17

ringl+pit, Petrole Hahn (1931-33).

These advertising images, ultimately designed to sell a product, reveal a parody of the female subject consumed by her own emancipation and/or emancipated only through commercial consumption. In her book *Clean New World*, Maud Lavin points out how, in the German advertising culture in which the ringl + pit studio functioned, women were typically represented as empowered either through the consumption of commodity objects or through their representation as commodity objects themselves. "Advertising images were complex representations of the anxieties and desires concerning new identities for women... In these ads, women were addressed as 'empowered' buyers, but often only insofar as their power was limited to purchasing products that would enable them to construct themselves—through make-up, shampoo, powder—as exchangeable objects, commodities." (Lavin 2002: 51) The advertising images of ringl + pit poke fun at this conflation of woman and commodity, calling into question the phenomenon of the female consumer who buys while being sold as a product herself.

In 1933, Stern fled the rise of National Socialism in Germany and the activity of ringl + pit was consequently halted. She first traveled to London, where she married the Argentine photographer Horacio Coppola in 1935. In the following year, the two settled in Buenos Aires, where Stern lived and worked until her death in 1999. Her European background and experience may help to explain why, today, Grete Stern is considered one of Argentina's most important and influential photographers and is often credited, together with her husband, with bringing modernist photography to the country. The *Sueños* series she came to produce for *Idilio*, albeit conceptually and contextually divergent from the images of ringl + pit, drew on several aspects already present in her earlier work. The *Sueños* not only activated a related photographic language, but also similarly explored the conflicting forces emerging from the desire to both perform and disrupt social conventions of femininity. Overall, though, the scope of the work Stern produced over her lifetime testifies to her ability to see beyond the frame of the national, cultural, and social spaces she occupied. As a migrant female artist in the mid-20th century, Stern's work reflected the worlds she inhabited from a critical distance. The photomontages she produced in both Berlin and Buenos Aires deconstructed the tropes associated with femininity propagated by the mainstream visual culture of each city and historical moment through parody and play.

Comedic Effect and Visual Incongruity

This chapter aims to investigate the presence and function of humor staged in the *Sueños* series by analyzing some of the individual photographic montages more closely. Before doing so, however, it should be noted that this series of images—produced by someone with an artistic background for a mainstream magazine—could easily reawaken old debates about the non/artistic properties of photography. Yet, for Grete Stern, who was fully aware of the central role photography played in realms that transcended both fine art and commercial circulation, such discussions were dismissed as useless. As she articulated some years after the series' publication, "to discuss whether or not photography is a fine art seems like a waste of time, because the domain of definitions is infinite, worn-out and constantly changing. No definition can deny the significance of photography to the social, political, and expressive life of man today." (Stern 2003: 30) Accordingly, in the *Sueños*, her use of photography as a powerful visual language clearly worked beyond this division of art and life, and was more concerned with creating a humorous, alternate language for feminist futurity, to borrow a concept from Tina M. Campt's book *Listening to Images.* (Campt 2017)

In the images she produced weekly for the pages of *Idilio,* Grete Stern resumed her pioneering approach to photomontage. (Fig. 2.18) Surrealist in style and enigmatically funny in nature, these compositions continued a long tradition uniting Surrealism with the domain of the oneiric. Moreover, they were an ingenuous solution to the question of how to illustrate the dream interpretations of Professor Rest while also visually portraying a process of free association that was integral to the deciphering of dreams. In a note on her

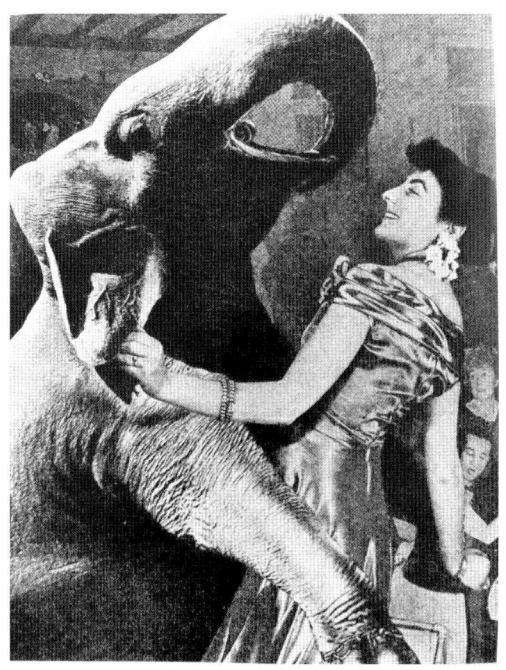

Figure 2.18

"Sueño numero 36: Los sueños de absurdos," in *Sueños: fotomontajes de Grete Stern (serie completa),* ed. by Luís Príamo (Buenos Aires: Fundación CEPPA, 2003). Published 1949.

technique, Stern describes photomontage's ability to represent the uncanny by reproducing a credible relationship between dissimilar objects or constructing unlikely scenarios. "A distorted perspective will always give the effect of the uncertain or the implausible." (Stern 2003: 29) Even though Stern usually drew a preliminary diagram to organize the different photographic elements that would form the final montage, she highlights that her decision was ultimately more visual than intellectual. This might have been the case because Gino Germani frequently set the compositional standards of the images, and stipulated how the dreams were to be illustrated: "Before I began my work, Germani and I spoke about the interpretation. Generally, Germani would request a certain layout: that the image should be horizontal or vertical, or with a foreground that is darker than the background...other times he would tell me that the figure should be doing this or that, or he insisted that I include floral or animal elements in the image." (Stern 2003: 29) Despite the specific instructions she received, Stern's images would consistently play with or undermine the content of the written analysis provided by Germani and Butelman.

In addressing the comedic effect of Stern's *Sueños*, the fact that she received explicit direction from Germani is particularly interesting, as working under such decisive constraints may have stimulated or influenced the humorous strategy of her dream representations. Moreover, considering how closely Stern and Germani collaborated, the frequent contrasts and contradictions between the written and visual components of this column are all the more notable. As Paula Bertúa points out, "while the verbal element reinforced—through the perspective of a medical/psychoanalytic hygienicism—the most traditional stereotypes of femininity, the visual element of the photomontages undermines this model with a critical and ironic gaze." (Bertúa 2008: 19) Through the subversion of Rest's analysis, these photomontages decisively convert the conservative, moralizing and formulaic approach to femininity present in *Idilio* into a photographic joke.

Curiously enough, the conditions of comedic effect are parallel to the practice of photomontage, in that interrupting, fragmenting, or scrambling the viewer's expectations serve to overturn convention and meaning. By juxtaposing elements of incompatible scale, or objects originating from different contexts in the same scene, "a good photomontage has," in the words of George Lukács, "the same sort of effect as a good joke." (Lukács 1980: 43) This, of course, is not the case with every photomontage. Many other examples—from 19th-century combination printing developed by Rejlander or Peach Robinson, to tactics of photographic manipulation and falsification often used in authoritarian regimes—function differently. In these cases, the process of photographic manipulation was meant to be imperceptible, conveying a case of myth masquerading as fact. In the modernist avant-garde mode of photomontage, however, the image is invested in displaying the illusion of this masquerade, emphasizing, sometimes quite centrally, the process of fabrication that is present in the construction of the image. As John Berger points out, in a photomontage "appearances themselves are suddenly showing us how they deceive us." (Berger 2001: 186) In this way, the photomontage possesses the ability to critically reflect upon its own content. Because "the natural continuities within which these things normally exist have been broken, and because they have now been arranged to transmit an unexpected message, we are made conscious of the arbitrariness of their continuous normal message." (Berger 2001: 185) The distance and fragmentation that are so essential to the political function of the photomontage also imbue the medium with great potential for a distinctly humorous effect.

Modernist photomontage practices of fragmentation destabilize accepted norms, producing incoherent, illogical or absurd effects. Comparably, the incongruity theory of humor holds that "what is key to comic amusement is a deviation from some presupposed norm—that is to say, an anomaly or an incongruity relative to some framework governing the ways in which we think the world is or should be." (Carroll 2014: 17) That which deviates from the norm is always potentially comedic, according to the circumstances under which we encounter this deviation. Because humor "is primarily a source of social information about the norms that govern the cultures we inhabit—the cultures that are us," and because through laughter we confront these given norms, jokes can be understood as a type of social intervention and criticism. (Carroll 2014: 76) When we laugh, we laugh as members of a group with a shared vocabulary. In order for a joke to have comedic effect, it must be received by a particular community who are subject to the rules governing the social expectation that is altered, ignored, or disregarded in the joke. "Our converging laughter serves as a signal to each and all of us that we are bound together by shared assumptions." (Carroll 2014: 76) In this way, comedy has the potential to forge community amongst individuals laughing at the shared set of rules or circumstances they are subject to.

What's so Funny? A Closer Look at Three Sueños

The incongruity of Stern's pictures creates the potential for a doubling of meaning: on the one hand, it challenges the norms of conventional femininity presented in the magazine *Idilio*. On the other, it disrupts and diverges from the moralizing discourse forged by Professor Rest. As a result, Stern's composition is a form of suggesting the possibility for personal transformation and social change. The incongruity theory describes comedic effect as a probable result when deviating from a "governing framework." In turn, Henri Bergson's theory of humor, as described by Martin Shuster, argues that comedic effect takes place when certain rigidities that result from our behaving according to convention are pointed out. (Shuster 2013) A joke—in this case a visual one—reveals the conventions and the expectations that dominate a personality or behavior at any given time. Shuster claims that laughter serves to correct the imbalance of convention by illuminating how one is, in any given moment, too fixed or rigid in the roles one performs.[4] In Stern's *Sueños*, one can also observe the performative, unexpected elements of refusal that humorously challenge rigidities of social behaviors and expectations. Given how incongruent Grete Stern's *Sueños* appear to be in both form and content, it is vital to further interrogate what specific norms and expectations these images are actually subverting. What are the codes and conventions disrupted here to frame images as laughable? In what follows, we discuss this question and analyze a few individual photomontages in greater detail.

In 1948, two years after the political rise of Juan Domingo Perón and in the first year of the *Sueños'* publication, Argentina experienced rapid economic growth and an influx of rural populations into city centers, especially Buenos Aires. (Horowitz 2012) Such changes in social mobility and economic distribution inspired profound transformation in the urban centers of Argentina, especially in regard to the position of women in society. (Bertúa 2010) Through the 1940s, and increasingly with Eva Perón's growing popularity from 1946, standards of beauty and appearance shifted towards an image of the professional, happy, active and educated woman; these images of modernity defined new standards of beauty and feminine performance, and also created new roles for women to fill. (see also Newman 1990) Images of women engaged in both domestic and professional activities dominated: "In posters and illustrations, in newspapers and magazines, images proliferated that showed conventional representations of women taking care of their children, their husband, or as high-powered professionals in the modern, industrialized world, taking advantage of their newly-won civil and political rights." (Bertúa 2010: 9)

Idilio was a product of its time. Directed at the newly emergent urban middle class of Argentina, this popular magazine sought to reflect the anxieties of the "mujer moderna," overburdened with her obligations to occupy the role of political actor, professional, wife and mother. The analysis provided in "El psicoanálisis le ayudará" incorporated many of the social codes that enforced these conventional expectations of women. (Vezzetti 2003: 149) In some readings, the column promoted a picture of traditional femininity and domesticity: "In the network of relationships and dependencies that surround the life of these women there is always a husband, a boyfriend, or a father at the center of the conflict. And any advice given about love adheres to a strict sexual morality." (Vezzetti 2003: 154) Stern's images, however, employ the symbols and iconography circulated by cultural and political institutions (such as domestic appliances, the figure of the baby, or the style and fashion worn by many of the dreamers) to first define a picture of acceptable feminine behavior and then visually reimagine the narratives constructed around this picture.[5]

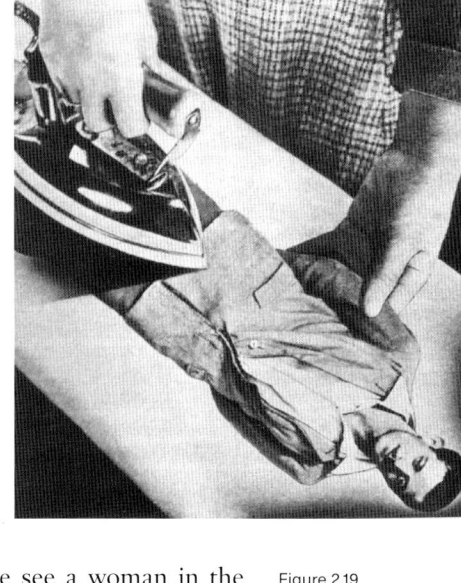

Figure 2.19

"Sueño numero 93: Sueños de conflictos matrimoniales," in *Sueños: fotomontajes de Grete Stern (serie completa)*, ed. by Luís Príamo (Buenos Aires: Fundación CEPPA, 2003). Published 1950.

In one of the photomontages (Fig. 2.19), we see a woman in the act of ironing what appears to be a miniature, flattened man wearing a wrinkled shirt. She cradles his limp figure in one hand and with the other passes an iron over his legs, in front of his genitals. Though the woman's face and head are not included in the image, her clothing style, jewelry and the iron she holds suggest an upper-middle context, much like those in which Stern's protagonists typically appear. Her long checkered skirt is very pragmatic; she wears the modest clothing of a housewife. The hand that grasps the iron wears a bracelet and ring. The male figure is pictured upside-down on the ironing board and his gaze is directed away from the viewer. He is held by his wife's hand but appears to turn away from her slightly, as though lazily struggling to escape her grip. In Stern's illustration, the husband is a thin piece of material pressed against the ironing board and held between his wife's two fingers, as lifeless as a puppet or prop.

Because the magazine did not publish the descriptions of the dreams originally sent in by the readers, one can only guess at their content through Professor Richard Rest's printed response. In this case, he describes the domestic duties carried out by the dreamer as "a symbol of the home life and the tranquility and peace of the family." (Richard Rest quoted in Priamo 2003: 137) As opposed to these peaceful and tranquil associations, however, the act of ironing here supposedly implies the deep turmoil this young wife experiences in her marriage. Rest looks to the definition of "planchar" (to iron), or "to smooth something out, remove the creases or crinkles, to leave something in the necessary conditions for it to be used comfortably." Thus, he concludes that a lack of mutual understanding is at the root of this imagery. "There was asperity between them, and this is exactly what the wife seeks to remove." According to this analysis, the act of ironing symbolizes the wife's desire to smooth out the creases in her relationship. Stern's visual interpretation, however, suggests another reading.

In ironing out her husband, the wife seeks to remove the "wrinkles" in her relationship by carrying out her domestic duties and adhering to her role as wife and homemaker. The strategic placement of the iron over the man's genitals, though, suggests that the housewife is symbolically castrating her husband. The iron in her hand becomes a phallus, positioned as a sort of punch line to the conflict of the unhappy housewife. The symbolic weight lent to the act of ironing is converted into a cartoonish illustration of the tensions involved in the domestic dynamics between husband and wife. The housewife is depicted as a homemaker/castrator, violently ironing out the wrinkles in her marriage to be found upon her husband's flat physique. While Rest's analysis suggests the explanation of the dream is as logical as the seamless relation between domestic chores and the peace and tranquility of the home, in Stern's illustration this equivalence between household appliances and domestic tranquility plays out as darkly comedic. Though only pictured from the waist down, the dreamer appears as the dominating, decisive force in fate of her relationship. The husband, like the tranquil home life ensured by the dreamer's domestic diligence, is represented as an unsubstantial and "thin" fantasy. In Stern's montage, this domestic drama plays out as a humorous criticism of the superficiality of the roles allotted to husband and wife.

In a different image, one of the *Sueños de muñecos* in the series, the figure of a chubby baby in the foreground, arms outstretched and advancing on the female protagonist, dominates the frame of the image. (Fig. 2.20) The dreamer stands at a distance, recoiling and clutching her hands over her face. She is pictured in formal, modest clothing. At first glance, the image could be a still from a noir film: two tall, shadowy walls enclose the anguished dreamer, as an insurmountable threat bears down on the protagonist. In this case, the threat is an oversized baby, with a mass and height equal to hers. Both figures face each other on a narrow sidewalk. In her dream, the subject encountered this doll and felt simultaneously drawn to and repulsed by it.

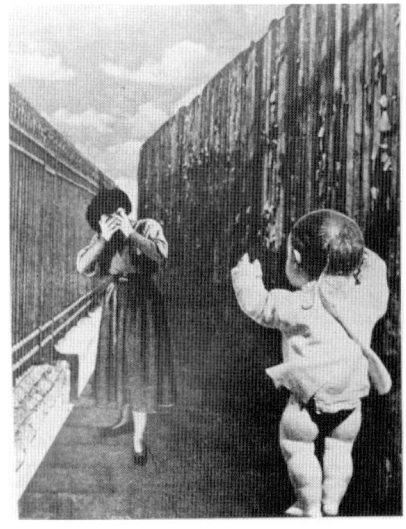

Figure 2.20

"Sueño numero 39: Los sueños de muñecos," in *Sueños: fotomontajes de Grete Stern (serie completa),* ed. by Luís Príamo (Buenos Aires: Fundación CEPPA, 2003). Published 1949.

This scene of terror and anguish is punctuated by a sense of the absurd: the baby, the embodiment of harmlessness need, inspires a terror in the dreamer that seems overstated and incongruous given the situation. However, in the photomontage it is evident that it is the pressure of maternity and motherhood this dreamer recoils from. The image of a person recoiling from a baby, perhaps even a doll, may at first seem silly. Yet, even a baby can be frightening. One possible reading of this scene is related to the pressure to bear and raise children that women faced under the renewed emphasis on the family under Peronism. Stern represents this anxiety and societal pressure surrounding maternity and motherhood through distorted parody.

The "monster" in question (an animated baby doll the dreamer is both attracted to and repulsed by) is terrifying in its need for and pursuit of the dreamer. The humor in this photomontage resides in the dreamer's seemingly inappropriate fear when confronted with the figure of an apparently harmless, yet disproportionate baby doll. Here, it is clear that "incongruity does not involve only a play with spatial dimensions." (Kaplan 2017: 16) The perceived incongruity reveals the expectations held by the viewer surrounding how a woman fitting a certain profile should react to a baby reaching out to her, namely with care and affection. Through exaggeration, we experience a direct contradiction or deflation of this expectation that again holds a tragicomic result. The photomontage is at once sympathetic and empowering: the dreamer, instead of cowering and refusing to face this monster, must confront and identify the true source of her anguish.

Finally, in a third image titled *Los sueños de reminiscencias,* a young girl swoons outside a stark concrete building. (Fig. 2.21) Above her, a man dressed in a suit and tie reaches his arms out of an upstairs window and looks down to her. She stands on a ground of jagged, loose rock. The sky visible above the top of the house looks stormy and dark. The cubic, almost windowless structure overwhelms the frame of the image, and in its center is a net, which seems to fall from the man's outstretched arms and onto the young girl. The dreamer is pictured as literally trapped in romantic entanglement. Interestingly enough, this scene can be read as a subversion of the standard narratives of romance and courtship, riffing on iconic balcony scenes in love stories, such as that of Romeo and Juliet. In the photomontage, gender roles are reversed as the woman stands beneath the window reaching above her toward the object of her affection: the man at the balcony. Stern's image proposes that as long as the dreamer's liberation lies within her inflated expectations of romantic love, she is already ensnared.

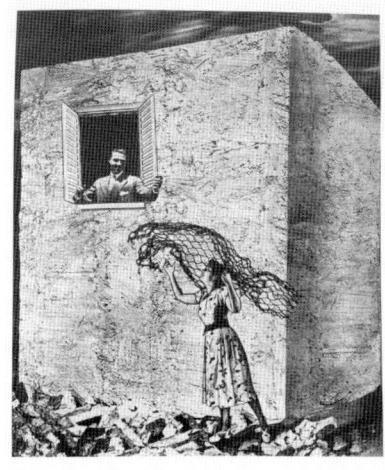

Los sueños de reminiscencias
Idilio n° 22 — 19/4/1949

Figure 2.21

"Sueño numero 22: Sueños de reminiscencias," in *Sueños: fotomontajes de Grete Stern (serie completa),* ed. by Luís Príamo (Buenos Aires: Fundación CEPPA, 2003). Published 1949.

    In Richard Rest's analysis, he easily concludes that the dream refers to long lost love. The concrete structure represents the house from her adolescence with a young man in it whom she has long associated with friendship and affection. As Rest reports, "once again we see here how the unconscious reveals the true significance behind a relationship." (Richard Rest quoted in Priamo 2003: 120) In this passage and elsewhere, Rest positions the subconscious as a kind of authority who reveals the truth behind these dreams. The house contains no doors or windows, other than the one through which the dreamer sees her friend. Equating the house (according to Rest, "a typically feminine symbol") with the dreamer's adolescence or youth, Rest concludes that the dreamer is being told by her unconscious to return to her youth and confront her romantic love for her friend. While Rest's analysis sticks closely to the formula of a storybook romance, Stern's image proposes an alternative interpretation. The centrally placed net that is about to fall directly onto the dreamer is mentioned nowhere in Rest's text. In fact, Rest describes the dreamer "dancing in front of the house of her adolescence" with no reference to the net that is pictured in Stern's illustration as about to ensnare her. The home is nightmarish and unwelcoming. However, the dreamer seems entirely unaware of these hostile surroundings: she and the man in the window wear placid, smiling expressions.

    In this example, the dreamer is pictured as oblivious to the confinement in her future. The photomontage can be read as a foreboding depiction of what awaits the dreamer if she were to take Rest's advice.

The comedic effect of this dream's visual analysis resides in its subtle but clear subversion of the fairytale romance that is predicted by the written analysis. The photomontage warns the dreamer of the unrealistic expectations Rest encourages her to adopt, expressed as a trap she is dancing straight into. The subtle reversal of conventional gender roles and expectations pictured here contributes to the comedic effect of this image. The dreamer's obliviousness increases this comedic effect, emphasizing the incongruity of the lovers' expressions and the situation in which they find themselves.

Photographic Humor as Fugitivity

In their effort to undermine convention, Grete Stern's *Sueños* can be interpreted as an artistic operation wherein humor is used as a political device that articulates alternative possibilities for conceiving of female subjectivity. Moreover, Stern meaningfully addresses the complicated sexual politics of Surrealism — a movement saturated with an eroticizing male gaze that often contradicted the principles of agency and freedom integral to the movement's very ideology. In fact, as Jo Anna Isaak has pointed out, in this male-dominated movement where women are simultaneously celebrated and excluded, "the role for women was that of agent or sexually liberal muse, not fellow revolutionary." (Isaak 1996: 192) In this context, it is all the more significant to see how Stern, like many other women artists working closely with Surrealist circles (from Meret Oppenheim to Claude Cahun), employed comedic effect as an efficient tool of feminist intervention.

The fact that most contributions made by female artists to the Surrealist movement have remained largely absent from the movement's official recorded history may not be surprising. In this chapter, however, our intention is not to unveil the silent history of Stern's peculiar project, but rather to suggest how the *Sueños* may crucially participate in critical revisions of the role of women artists in the Surrealist movement. In feminist reinterpretations, Surrealism becomes a platform from which to question conventional and commercial terms of womanhood. In the book *Mirror Images: Women, Surrealism and Self-Representation*, Whitney Chadwick describes how the Surrealist movement offered women the possibility to "escape what they perceived as the inhibiting confines of middle-class marriage, domesticity, and motherhood." (Chadwick 1998: 5) This movement's resistance to the conditions set by middle-class convention inspired artworks that consider femininity a category defined by social and cultural institutions. As Chadwick notes, the works of female Surrealist artists are concerned with "a self-consciousness about social constructions of femininity as surface and image, a tendency toward the phantasmic and oneiric, a preoccupation with psychic powers assigned to the feminine, and an embrace of doubling, masking, and/or masquerade as defense against fears of non-identity." (Chadwick 1998: 6) The *Sueños* share with this feminist Surrealism a treatment of the feminine as artifice or masquerade, and it constitutes an example of how the oneiric landscape can become political terrain.

In accordance with the Freudian description of humor as not resigned but rebellious, comedic strategies played a decisive role in this artistic intervention, as the case of Grete Stern's *Sueños* well demonstrates. Jo Anna Isaak's book *The Revolutionary Power of Women's Laughter* considers how laughter serves as a platform of social and political analysis in feminist art. Feminist art is understood in this context not to be a homogenizing category, but rather "an agency of intervention—an ongoing activity of pluralizing, destabilizing, baffling any centered discourse." (Isaak 1996: 4) Given this impulse to destabilize and "baffle" social convention, laughter appears as an appropriate method of intervention into the "centered" discourse of male-dominated art movements. As Isaak argues, "in providing libidinal gratification, laughter can also provide an analytic for understanding the relationships between the social and the symbolic while allowing us to imagine these relationships differently." (Isaak 1996: 5)

Though Stern never explicitly elaborated on the function of humor in this series, her photomontages as a whole consistently critiqued the place of women in society through parody, calling attention to the rigidity of convention. The political force of the *Sueños* series thus depends upon this critical and collectivizing power of laughter, which functioned as a kind of counter-propaganda, revisiting George Orwell's idea that every joke is a tiny revolution. As Paula Bertúa highlighted, the dreams depicted in the photomontages "are not individual but collective." (Bertúa 2008: 13) The fact that the series was originally destined not for the art world but for a popular magazine expands the nature and intensifies the impact of Stern's images. Not only because it reached a wider audience, but also because it challenged, from within, the institutional framework of the feminine magazine wherein these pictures were published.

In conclusion, the *Sueños* series is a productive example of a kind of feminist vision that uses laughter as a subversive strategy, or a "mode of dissent against established authority." (Kaplan 2017: 76) Furthermore, Stern's pictures for the psychoanalytic column make clear how laughter itself is a process of analysis. It allows us to imagine new or different relationships between the "social and the symbolic" and the codes that define constructions of behavior, circulation, and performances of womanhood. Given its insubordinate quality, humor may function as a site of empowerment for whoever is laughing. According to this understanding, laughter also becomes a strategy for imagining female agency in a misogynistic culture or society.[6] Similarly, Stern's photomontages crucially disrupted the terms of the female subjection that these practices—of the magazine as a whole and of Richard Rest's interpretations in particular—were designed to create and arrest. Moreover, they also offered its viewers the power to imagine and perform (in the present) a different future, a future that has not happened yet, but must. Thus conveying aspirations of mobility, agency and freedom, Grete Stern's *Sueños* are much more than unusual photographic illustrations of women's dreams; they are profound images of fugitivity.[7]

Notes

1. "La sección comenzó llamandose 'El psicoanálisis te ayudará.' A partir del décimo número ese título fue reemplazado por 'El psicoanálisis le ayudará.' El cambio de pronombre, que denota mayor formalidad en la apelación a los destinatarios probablemente estuvo motivado por la voluntad a convocar no sólo a un público lector juvenil, sino a la franja etaria adulta." (Bertúa 2012: 42). [The section was first called 'Psychoanalysis will help you' [informal]. After the tenth issue that title was replaced by 'Psychoanalysis will help you' [formal]. The change of pronoun, which signifies greater formality in the address to the readers, was probably motivated by a desire to speak to not only a juvenile readership, but also an adult age bracket.] [all translations are ours]

2. "Only a bit more than half of the complete works of the *Sueños* are known. The only way of accessing this collection is through printouts of the copies of *Idilio*... Two thirds of the complete production of the *Sueños* have no second generation negatives that would enable the production of an excellent photographic copy today." (Priamo: 2003: 18)

3. "The photomontages hugely exceeded their original motivation and turned into a rebellious authentication that staged the oneiric fantasies of the readers, but which also undermined the verbal discourse with operations of diversion, questioning, irony, and confrontation." (Bertúa 2012: 25)

4. "One perhaps focuses on one convention to the detriment of others, thereby instantiating rigid action. One becomes too much a fire marshal (as in Jim Carrey's famous character on *In Living Color*) or too little a rational agent (as in various varieties of slapstick). Amusement is the recognition, social in nature, of this occurrence, and laughter its result." (Shuster 2013: 622)

5. "Stern appropriated and reelaborated areas of artistic iconography and rewrote, through visual configuration, stories constructed about the woman." (Bertúa 2010: 14)

6. Isaak, citing Bakhtin's *Rabelais and his World*, notes, "in the course of his writing a history of laughter, Bakhtin reveals not just that women have historically been aligned with the popular comic tradition, but that they have a political stake in this site of insurrection." (Isaak 1996: 19)

7. This work was supported by FCT Portugal – Fundação para a Ciência e a Tecnologia under projects SFRH/BPD/79102/2011, UID/PAM/00417/2013 and PTDC/CPC-HAT/4533/2014.

Bibliography

Dawn Ades, *Photomontage*
(London: Thames & Hudson, 1986.)

Béatrice Didier, Antoinette Fouque, Mireille Calle-Gruber, *Le Dictionnaire universel des créatrices (Grete Stern).* (Paris: Éditions des femmes, 2015).

John Berger, "The Political Uses of Photomontage," in *Selected Essays of John Berger*, ed. Geoff Dyer (New York: Vintage International, 2001).

Paula Bertúa, "Sueños de Idilio: los fotomontajes surrealistas de Grete Stern," *Boletín de estética*, 6 (August 2008): 7–32.

———, "Relatos modernos, centramientos y descentramientos de género: Los Sueños de Grete Stern en Idilio," *Mora (Buenos Aires)*, 16, 1 (2010): 7–33.

———, *La cámara en el umbral de lo sensible: Grete Stern y la revista Idilio, 1948–1951* (Buenos Aires: Editorial Biblos, 2012).

Tina M. Campt, *Listening to Images* (Durham: Duke University Press, 2017).

Noel Carroll, *Humour: A very short introduction* (Oxford: Oxford University Press, 2014).

Whitney Chadwick, *Mirror Images: Women, Surrealism and Self-Representation* (Cambridge MA: MIT Press, 1998).

Mia Fineman, *Faking it: Manipulated photography before Photoshop* (New York: MetPublications, 2012).

Joel Horowitz, "Populism and its Legacies in Argentina," in *Populism in Latin America*, ed Michael L Conniff (Tuscaloosa, AL: University of Alabama Press, 2012), 23–47.

Jo Anna Isaak, *Feminism and contemporary art: the revolutionary power of women's laughter.* (London – New York: Routledge, 1996).

Louis Kaplan, *Photography and Humour* (London: Reaktion Books, 2017).

Maud Lavin, *Clean new world: Culture, politics, and graphic design*: (Cambridge, MA – London: MIT Press, 2002).

Georg Lukács, "Realism in the Balance (1938)," in *Aesthetics and Politics*, ed. Fredric Jameson (London: Verso, 1980).

Juan Mandelbaum, Ringl and Pit . Geovision [online film streaming], 1995

Kathleen Newman, "Modernization of feminity: Argentina (1916–1926)," in *Women, culture and politics in Latin America* (Berkeley: University of California Press, 1990), 79.

Mariano Ben Plotkin, "Tell me your dreams: Psychoanalysis and popular culture in Buenos Aires, 1930–1950," *The Americas*, 55, 4 (1999): 601–629.

Luis Priamo, *Sueños: fotomontajes de Grete Stern: Serie completa* (Buenos Aires: Ediciones Fundación CEPPA, Centro de Estudios de Politicas Públicas Aplicadas, 2003).

Martin Shuster, "Humor as an Optics: Bergson and the Ethics of Humor," *Hypatia* 28, 3 (2013): 618–632.

Grete Stern, "Apuntes sobre fotomontaje (1967)," in *Sueños: fotomontajes de Grete Stern: Serie completa*, ed. Luis Priamo (Buenos Aires: Ediciones Fundación CEPPA, Centro de Estudios de Politicas Públicas Aplicadas, 2003).

Hugo Vezzetti. "El psicoanálisis y los sueños en Idilio," in *Sueños: fotomontajes de Grete Stern (serie completa). Edición de la obra impresa en la revista Idilio (1948–1951)*, ed. Luis Priamo (Buenos Aires: Ediciones Fundación CEPPA, Centro de Estudios de Politicas Públicas Aplicadas 2003), 149–159.

Part III

Photographic Wit in Conceptual Art

Keeping a Straight Face: Photography and the Performance of Conceptual Art

Heather Diack

In June 1971, the artist Douglas Huebler asked his ten-year-old daughter to pose for a series of photographs. His only directorial instruction was for her to keep a so-called "straight face." This ostensibly simple task was made more challenging by the fact that her sister and brother, beyond the frame of the picture, were simultaneously encouraged to try to make her laugh. Huebler photographed her lack of resilience as the young girl inevitably and touchingly failed the test by breaking into laughter, spurred on by her siblings' antics. As with much conceptual art, a plain-faced pseudo-bureaucratic typed-text accompanies the exhibited work: "Twenty three photographs join with this statement to constitute the form of this piece." As a work of art, *Variable Piece #28, Truro, Massachusetts* (1971) is deceptively simple, and nearly banal. Yet it is also a piece that performs disruption—evading the strictures of control, in terms both of its subject (in this case, Huebler's daughter) and the artist's professed intention, as well as the subjective positioning of the viewer and the discourse of photography more broadly. Additionally, through such disruption, the photographs point to an underlying and yet underexplored comic quality in conceptual art.

Certainly, there is something funny about conceptual art. Frequently awkward, often absurd in its blatancy, one detects humor in the ways that the ordinariness of content so often seems to undermine its declarative seriousness. Think for example of Joseph Kosuth's eponymous *One and Three Chairs* (1965), Robert Barry's *Inert Gas Series* (1969), or Eleanor Antin's *100 Boots* (1971–73). More than artworks that engage ideas of representation, materiality, and perception while using photography, each of these embeds humor as a connective tissue prodding the viewer with irresolvable questions regarding the ultimate status and meaning of art. Staring back at the viewer blankly, they suggest a deadpan aloofness by mingling purposeful withdrawal with situational preposterousness.[1]

Like much art emerging from the vein of conceptualism, these are presented as self-evident, *as is*, in other words, as straightforward. And yet, I argue, this professed clarity and plainness of presentation paradoxically provides a crucial source of trenchant ambivalence. Conceptual art turns the combined emphasis on the notions of being straight-forward and keeping a straight face in against itself. Moreover, photography is a central means through which this dubious challenge is enacted. Whereas Jeff Wall accounted for the work of conceptual artists using photography as functioning as a kind of "social cipher," because, as Wall stated unequivocally, "Only an idiot would take pictures of nothing…" (Wall, 1995: 265) I counter that the subversive potential of photoconceptualism is less an encrypted game and more of an invitation to question perceptual experience and social dynamics. In part, I am taking my cues from Huebler here, and his admitted desire to "mitigate or eliminate" visual experience, (Huebler, 1972: n.p.) as a foray to a more expanded approach to thinking about the world and one's relation to it. I would like to push this claim even further — to say that one of the key ways in which conceptual art enacts humor is precisely through photography, not simply as medium or subject, but moreover as a performative mechanism that deliberately plays on the limits of visibility and knowledge.

The medium of photography, even when "strait," is notoriously reticent and oblique. Not coincidentally, an economy of means typifies much conceptual art from the late 1960s onwards. In other words, a tone of expressionlessness and restraint runs throughout. Yet, this seriousness is often simultaneously galvanized by the ludicrous and motivated by a sense of critique. Despite the fact that conceptual art has been largely historicized as one of the most boring of 20th century art movements, I argue that humor as a form of critique was at its core. Moreover, photography instigated and instantiated the very possibility of humor in conceptual art. The following chapter considers key works of early conceptual art, in order to highlight the ways humor shares photography's ability to access phenomena that are otherwise invisible to ordinary vision, demonstrate how the dynamism and duality of the photograph framed the radical incongruence of everyday life in the 1970s, and expose the resultant inability for either photography or conceptual art to maintain a "straight face."

Say Cheese!

Arguably, the affective logic of smiling threads throughout the history of photography. In 1872, Charles Darwin asked Oscar Rejlander to produce photographs depicting people in various emotional states, as

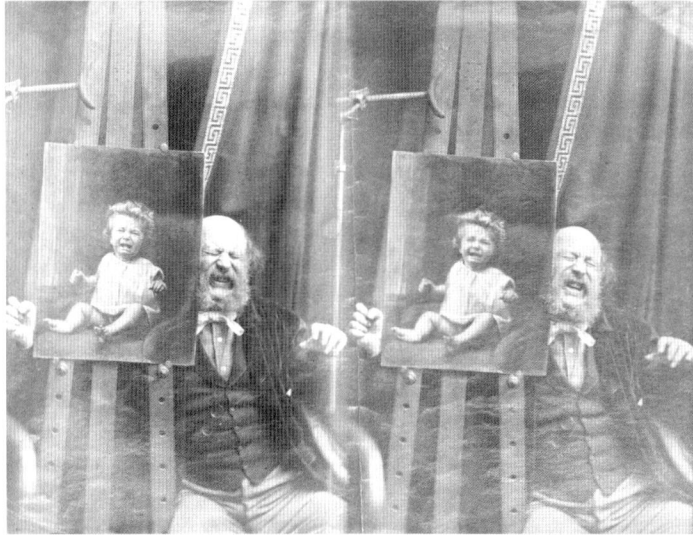

Figure 3.1

Oscar Rejlander, *Laughing/ Crying (Rejlander mimicking Ginx's Baby)* (1871-1872). © Darwin Papers, Cambridge University Library. Reproduced by kind permission of the Syndics of Cambridge University Library (MS-DAR-00053-00001-000-00407.TIF) (DAR 53:1, P. C95r).

means of providing visual evidence to support his theories regarding the physiology of facial expressions for his publication *Expression of the Emotions in Man and Animals.* (Davis, 2013: 42) From this series, the most infamous image became a widely circulated carte-de-visite, dubbed "Ginx's Baby" after a character in a popular contemporary novel by Edward Jenkins. (Fig. 3.1) The photograph was intended to visually show the uninhibited reaction of a child in a fit of rage. Within the grainy black and white image a lone babe with ruffled hair sits with mouth agape, eyes winced, and fists clenched. Though praised at the time as an imitable example of the natural reaction of an upset infant, Rejlander immediately saw the ambivalent potential of the photograph, and the slippery ways in which it inevitably resisted the status of proof. In order to expose the disconnect between the image and its claim to veracity, Rejlander made a second set of images, featuring himself mugging for the camera in a fit of laughter with "Ginx's Baby" displayed on an easel, alongside his face. It is difficult to distinguish between Rejlander's laughing self and the baby's cry, as their expressions are absurdly similar. How can we distinguish anguish from hilarity? Even in the 19th century, Rejlander's joke performed the conceptual contingency of the photograph, by contrast to substantiating a claim to either veracity or knowledge.

From the outset, practices of vernacular photography and portraiture have been shaped by the imperative to smile/or not to smile, and this dynamic has provided fodder for innumerable mix-ups and mirth. The bizarre imperative "say cheese," a deliberately silly saying, has a long history as an invocation to smile, and moreover an instruction regarding how to "act" in front of the camera. More than simply an expression, it is a means to provoke an expression, and moreover to mark the moment of photographic capture with the improv of humor. Cueing the reaction to smile, "cheese" has also sometimes been replaced by other surprising words in order to induce comedic effect and, by extension, the desired and amusing facial contortions.

Seizing on this sort of conceptual confusion was an important strategy for artists in the late 1960s, and an unlimited source of humor. Part of what is funny about William Wegman's endless photographs of weimaraners for example, beyond their chameleon versatility and anthropomorphic flexibility, is their natural *inability* to smile. They have no choice but keep a straight face, even when positioned in the most bizarre of scenarios, including masquerading as bikini models, posing as pumpkins, or imitating a painting by Arcimboldo.

For conceptual artists of the late sixties and early seventies, the German artists Bernd and Hilla Becher posed an important model. Having collaborated on an elaborate international search to document vanishing industrial terrain since the 1950s, the Bechers continued to compile their extensive archive of "anonymous sculptures" until Bernd's death in 2007. Very different from "popular, romanticized Modernist views of early 20th century industrialization that transformed banal industrial sites into gleaming futuristic visions, typified by Charles Sheeler's photographs of the Ford Motor plant in Dearborn, Michigan, in 1927," (Stainback, 1992: 9) the Bechers devoted their life's work to recording "typologies" of disappearing industrial architecture such as blast furnaces, water towers, lime kilns, and cooling towers, each marked by their increasing "uselessness" despite their historical connection to labor and productivity.[2] Taking individual portraits of industrial architecture, their images are notoriously discussed as bearing no trace of emotion, being instead humorless "straight" standardized shots of archetypal structures. Michael Fried, among others, has rightly compared the persistent frontality of the Bechers' architectural photographs to the frontal pose of a subject facing the camera. (Fried, 2005: 569) This analogy however could be stretched further. Viewed through this lens, the details of these industrial structures become anthropomorphic. Pipes, ladders, lattices, scaffolding, and silos, among a multitude of other aspects, transform perceptually into facial features, resulting in a new conception of the Bechers' archive, less as groupings of "anonymous sculptures" and more so as communities of expressive characters in which elusive smiles and frowns abound.

A direct example of the "influential" connection between Huebler and the Bechers, that goes beyond the formal logic that I have discussed and gives insight into Huebler's humorous counter-discourse, is *Variable Piece #101, West Germany, March 1973,* (Fig. 3.2) on the occasion

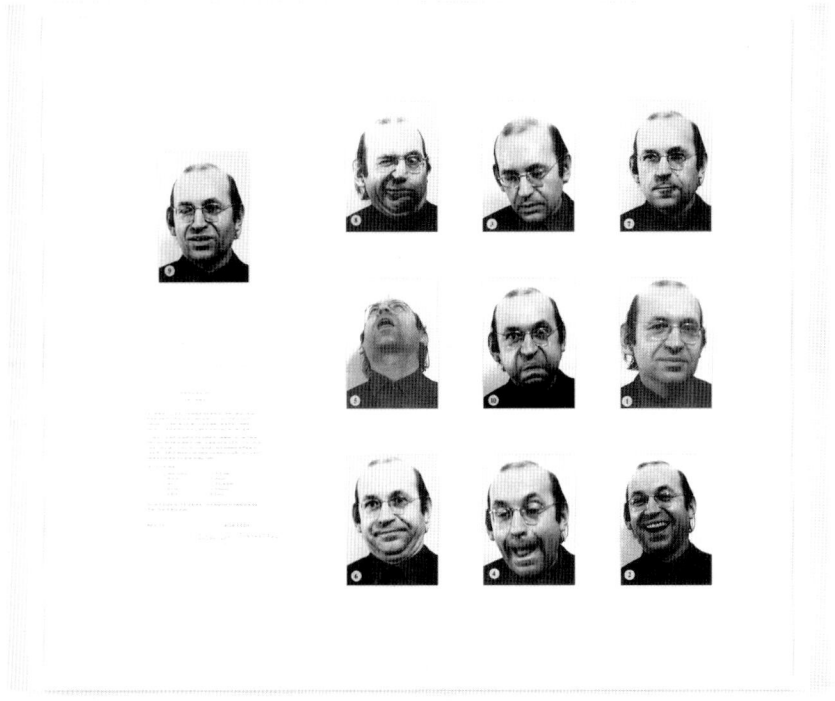

of Huebler taking photographs of Bernd Becher as he asked him to act out stereotypes of various roles, including a "priest," a "criminal," a "spy," an "old man," a "philosopher," a "nice guy" a "police man," and a "lover." In a clever and nearly anachronistic reversal of roles the question becomes: who's under the influence? For it has been suggested that this piece be read as two friends getting drunk together. (Godfrey, 2002: 8) Here, images and concepts are indeed as contorted as Bernd's face. Bernd Becher as an icon of straight-forward seriousness and the advent of early photoconceptualism becomes the embodiment of buffoonery, in a sense performing the overlooked characters possibly disguised within his own serial typologies. His own face repeated over and over, with a twist. Read as an inebriated friend, these images playfully challenge the assumed sobriety of New Objectivity, while exposing objectivity in photographic terms as always compromised, and with one's perceptual subjectivity continuously questioned and contingent. It becomes nearly impossible to trace the stereotypes to their corresponding representations.

Figure 3.2

Douglas Huebler, *Variable Piece #101, West Germany, March 1972* (1972). © 2007 Estate of Douglas Huebler/ Artists Rights Society (ARS), New York.

The portraits are of course shot "straight-on" in a manner similar to the assiduousness of the Bechers' photographs, yet they do so in order to challenge the practice of the Bechers and other photographers who claim that they do "not hide or exaggerate or depict anything in an untrue fashion." (Grauerholz and Ramsden, 1981: 18) Huebler's counter-figurations point instead to an overriding inability to identify any singular identity with, or within, any particular system. These grimaces present themselves as fragments of a greater whole, and mimic the very of idea of a system by pushing the limits of a singular subject's multiplicity of identities. In performing this system, they reveal the absurdity of the system itself, and, moreover, point to the illusory status of the straight face.

These portraits, together with a written statement, constitute the final form of the piece. As Gordon Hughes' thoughtful study of this piece demonstrates, the "laconic, bureaucratic voice of a written statement ... serves as the straight man to Huebler's photographic portraits as Becher's face contorts to fit its impersonations." (Hughes, 2007: 53) Two months after the shoot, Huebler mailed the photographs to Bernd, asking him to order them in relation to the list of verbal terms he had been asked to portray. His acting out for the camera and the word to image correlation are never clearly retraced however. Humorously, they seem only to become increasingly mixed up, as they play provocatively on the viewer's desire to believe the associations based on one's own connotative capacities. Lacking coherence, the chronology of the system is disturbed by chance, interrupted by time, derailed by laughter, and it is hard to sort through which images might be more convincingly natural (e.g. "artist" or "Bernd Becher") and which are more staged (e.g. "spy" or "criminal"). As clichés, repetitions and resemblances are pushed to their limits, and meaning is at once removed, multiplied, and compounded, the grimaces captured by the photograph remain fugitive. They collapse "the structure of the system into an undifferentiated system of indifference;" (Huebler in Van Leeuw and Pontegnie, 1997: 128) pol in other words, despite the orderly grid and the conventional frame, the subject remains on the loose.

Further to the camera's claims to scientific objectivity, it is important to note how the link between photography and physiognomy, particularly in Germany, is being marked and mocked in *Variable piece no. 101*. Physiognomy, the discredited pseudo-science of reading difference across images, implicates photography in a slippery history of surveillance culture and categorization. As a mode of resistance, Huebler consistently destabilizes the photograph's documentary status by pointing to the kinds of information it ultimately cannot convey. (Miller, 2006: 220–227) In refusing to take themselves too seriously, these photographs deliberately provide comic relief from modernism's solipsistic position; they are denial of any concept of "true" knowledge grounded in the self.

Huebler's *Variable Piece #28, Truro, Massachusetts (1971)* may be seen as a foil to the work with Bernd Becher as pliable subject. Using the medium less as a foray to knowledge and rather as a development of productive engagement, "Huebler's Conceptual Art takes Clement Greenberg's literalism to the brink of parody." (Miller in Van Leeuw and Pontegnie, 1997: 177) Presenting the photographs in the form of documentation alongside the text in fact prevents one from mapping out certainty. The format might suggest that rationalism underpins this information; yet the text and the images tell us otherwise. Instead each of Huebler's pieces is playful and open-ended, revealing a profound suspicion of dogmatism, and unfastening the very idea that meaning, let alone photography, can ever be decisive. In this way, the artist's project recalls Karen Pincus's summation of ambivalence. Noting the structure of "ambi-valence," Pincus explains that the concept is "not only a conscious sense of uncertainty, but also, more rigorously, the coexistence of two different and perhaps irreconcilable elements." (Pincus, 2009: 5) In other words, such photoconceptual practices and the attendant humor they produce are deeply connected to the viewer's inevitable inability to keep them straight.

Making Faces

In addition to the deadpan economy of means that characterizes much conceptual art from the late 1960s onwards, the extensive use of puns in perception, visual deconstructions, and slapstick seriality also makes a strong case for how conceptual art's seemingly dry, rote, or emp-tied-out formal qualities—which art historian Benjamin Buchloh fa-mously named the "aesthetics of administration"—were in many cases also used for the administration of absurdity. (Buchloh, 1990: 105–143; Diack, 2012:75–86) Mike Kelley succinctly describes the significance of conceptual art from the late 1960s onwards, and how the restrained aesthetic of "a poorly printed photograph or diagram, accompanied by a caption" typified at once a pathos-inducing parody "of dominant modes of the presentation of 'knowledge'" and a resistance to the rise of psychedelic counter-culture graphics and the fantasies championed as obtainable in commercial advertising. (Kelley, (1997) 2003: 184) As a student of Huebler and John Baldessari, among other now canonical figures of the movement, Kelley's own artistic practice was certainly influenced by the seemingly benign and yet ultimately subversive and humorous possibilities of conceptual art. Regarding Huebler's work in particular, Kelley describes his reaction: "I have an unconscious physical response—I laugh. I am confused, and this is a surprise in that, on the surface, his works often looks so *dumbly straightforward*. There is an image, typically a quite mundane and recognizable one, accompanied by text which one would expect would elaborate on, or explain, the image… You are left with yourself, and the nervous laughter of doubt." (Kelley, (1997) 2003: 180)

The straightness of the piece is a ruse of sorts, sincere but obscure, humorous in its resistance to being settled one way or another. Kelley's phrasing of "dumbly straightforward" indeed captures one of the central paradoxes of the entwinement between conceptual art and photography, namely the ways in which photography as a medium was frequently dismissed as integral to the work of art, and yet the very possibility of the piece arguably rests on the material and esthetic life of the photograph. In what has now become a widely circulated platitude regarding conceptual art, Huebler claimed in 1969: "I use the camera as a 'dumb' copying device that only serves to document whatever phenomenon appears before it through the conditions set by a system." (Huebler. 1969: n.p.) Many conceptual artists similarly used the perceived neutrality, or "dumb" quality, and the ways it enabled what Mel Bochner dubbed "joke art" and cultivated "a cosmic sense of humor" according to Robert Smithson, to their advantage.

Humor in particular forms a critical conceptual tool in part because it is disarming, thus allowing one to take account of the seemingly ordinary in its absurdity, its strictures, in its false presentation of playing it straight. Despite the prevalence of humor in early conceptual art—albeit often couched in a deadpan sensibility—conceptualism has been historicized as one of the driest and most serious artistic movements in the twentieth century. Not coincidentally, the context in which this turn to photography occurs is amidst intense social crisis and instability, including the War in Vietnam, the struggles for Civil Rights, the emergence of the Women's movement, and furthermore the widespread Leftist suspicion of all official information. One need only think of Dada hijinks during the First World War to realize the ripe relevance of such disjunctive socio-political moments for humor. The comic highlights gaps in logic that are falsely sutured in order to carry on with everyday existence despite incomprehensible upheaval.

Series such as Bruce Nauman's *Studies for Holograms* (1968–69; Fig. 3.3) challenge the straight-faced stoicism of conceptual art by involving the artist's own body as material on which and with which to act. These screen-printed duotones, photo-mechanically reproduced from infrared photographs, depict the artist's face contorted physically and distorted representationally. (Pascale, 1999: 40) In this way, an analogy between the mechanical control of the camera and the mechanical control of the body underscores these pieces. Viewed within the context of

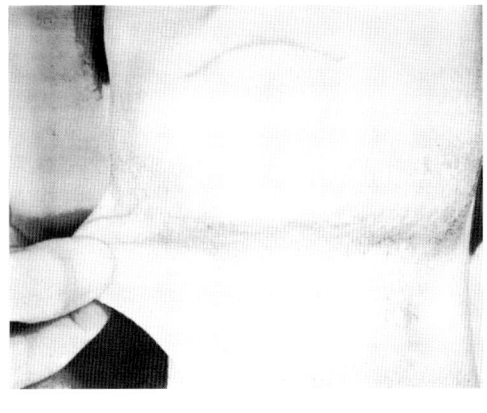
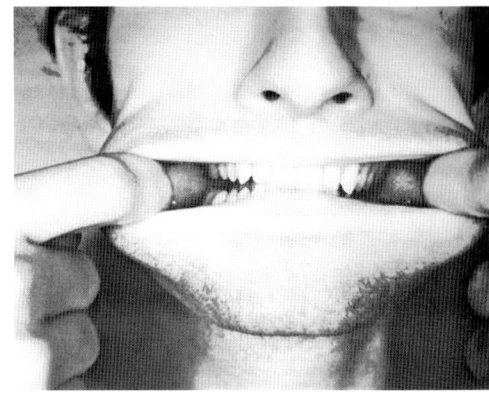
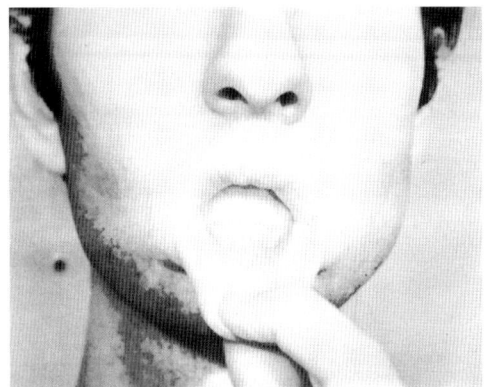
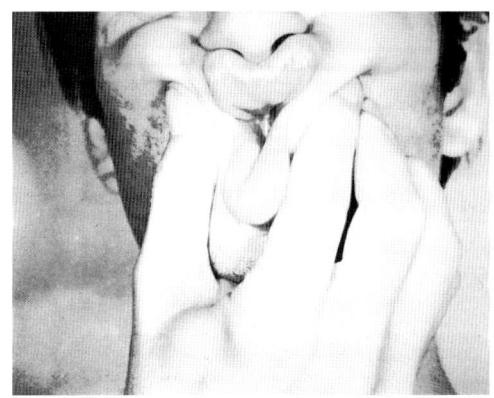
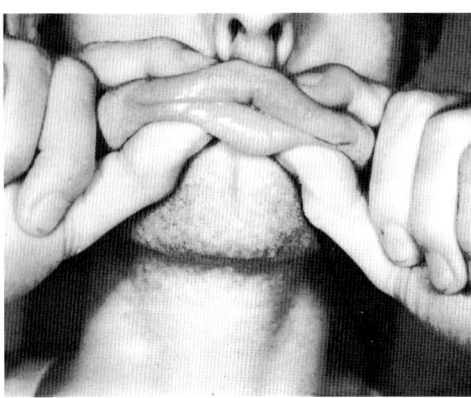

Figure 3.3

Bruce Nauman,
Studies for Holograms
(1970). 26 × 26 in.
(66 × 66 cm), each of 5,
set of five silkscreens,
edition 120 of 150
Collection of Museum
of Contemporary Art
San Diego © 2016 Bruce
Nauman / Artists Rights
Society (ARS), New York.

intense political and social upheaval in the United States (including a crescendo of resistance and civil disobedience in connection with the Civil Rights movement between 1954 and 1968 and rising violence culminating in events such as the Kent State shootings of 1970) and internationally (namely the war in Vietnam), these images must be seen as more than childish insolence. Though their content is ostensibly not political, in their emphasis on discomfort and deformed information, Nauman's intensive play at "making faces" can arguably be read as very much a reaction to and against their time, and a questioning of the possibility of protest not just in art but in the public realm more broadly.

This moment of unrelenting social crises and increasing self-consciousness was in part orchestrated by the infiltration of photographic media into all aspects of life, public and private, at home and abroad, leaving unclear which artistic direction was relevant to the experience of contemporary life. As the various uses of photography became increasingly prevalent, a full gamut of criticism was set in motion. Nauman's expressive contribution to the *Information* exhibition (curated by Kynaston McShine at the Museum of Modern Art in New York as an "international report on art" in 1970), (McShine, 1970: 1) entitled *Grimaces* (1969) (in fact duplicates from his *Studies for Holograms*), visibly mocks not only the clichéd photographic imperative to smile, but demonstrates a painful inability to do so. The tacitly taciturn character of these images derides the very idea of self-expression in an art context as well as within a broader public framework. There is also a tension between the way in which these images look like the artist is trying to force himself to speak versus the possibility that the hands imaged are not his own and rather belong to an external interrogator.

This riddled muteness manifests itself both as a result of the confines of the photograph as a visual medium rather than an auditory one, and alternately by the way the hands pictured in the photographs manipulate the artist's mouth. The photographic prints of this series are cropped intentionally below the artist's eyes, focusing attention exclusively on the lips and neck and their sequential distortions as Nauman fools around with his visage. Including pinched and pulled lips, squeezed cheeks, and strained neck, these images appear simultaneously banal and mischievous. By contrast to this naivety they are further complicated by being reproduced in large format, at a scale larger-than-life and in a shade of nauseating yellow, which accentuates a disturbing undertone and spreads the sensation of unease to the viewer. Speaking on the body and its correlation to emotions, Nauman has explained: "The idea of making faces had to do with thinking of the body as something you can manipulate. I had done some performance pieces — vigorous pieces dealing with standing, leaning, bending — and as they were performed, some of them seemed to carry large emotional impact." (Cordes, 1989: 25) As photographic documents, these images perform humor by amplifying the medium's conceptual and ontological uncertainty.

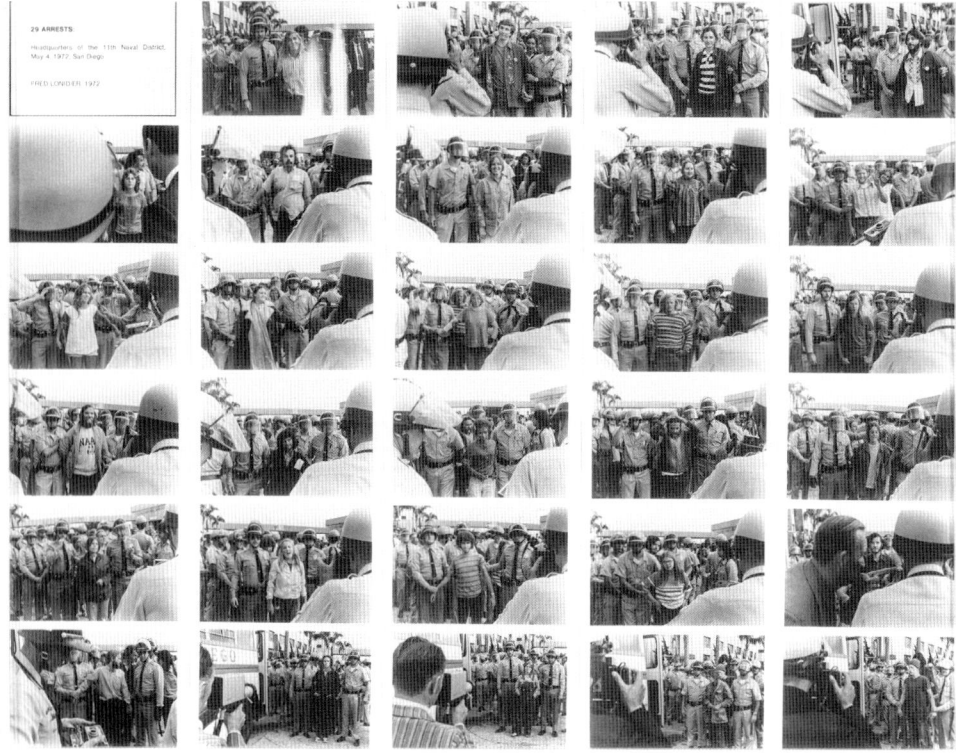

Comedic Camera

The Nixon administration's renewed bombing campaign of North Vietnam in 1972 provoked student protests across the United States. It is in relation to this specific context that Fred Lonidier's *29 Arrests: Headquarters of the 11th Naval District, May 4, 1972, San Diego* (Fig. 3.4) needs to be considered. On site, at a staged sit-in blocking the doorway of the Naval Supply Center in San Diego through which war material was shipped to Southeast Asia, Lonidier candidly captured protesters with his camera as they were systematically arrested by the police for their civil disobedience. Displayed in the quintessential conceptualist grid, the series reveals the varying reactions of both arrestees and ar-resters. One of the most striking elements of these photographs is the large number of individuals held in custody who, in spite of (or perhaps due to) the seriousness of the situation, break into amused smirks and mocking smiles. Some with toothy grins, some with side-cocked heads, others appear struggling to hold back laughter at the moment of their arrest, in face of the camera. In the very instant of the photographic documentation of themselves, they persist in subjectively defying

Figure 3.4

Fred Lonidier, *29 Arrests: Headquarters of the 11th Naval District, May 4, 1972, San Diego* (1972). Thirty photographs with texts on panel. Framed: 30 3/8 × 39 5/16 in. (77.2 × 99.9 cm) Collection Museum of Contemporary Art Chicago, Restricted gift of The Buddy Taub Foundation, 2014.51 Photo: Nathan Keay, © MCA Chicago.

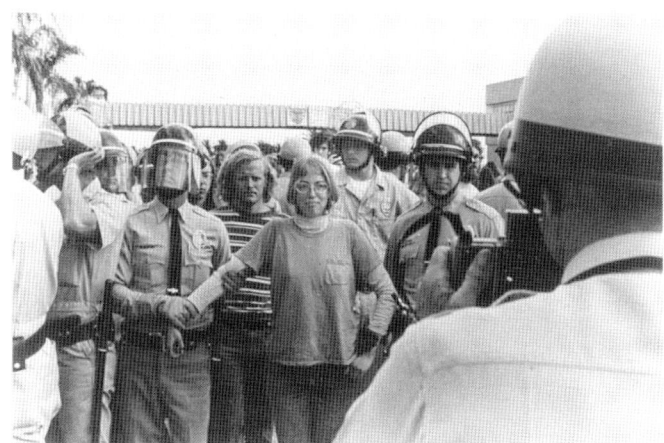

Figure 3.5

Fred Lonidier, *29 Arrests*, 1972 (detail) © MCA Chicago.

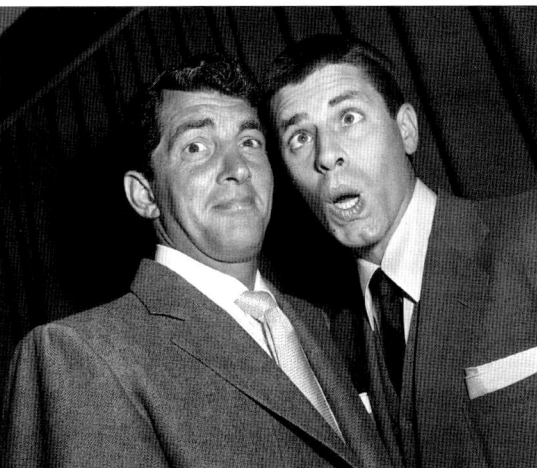

Figure 3.6

Legendary US comedy double-act Dean Martin and Jerry Lewis are pictured larking around, 1953 © Getty images.

authoritarian restraint. The looks on the faces of the policemen flanking the individual arrestees are worth acknowledging as well. Many seem uncertain, and themselves thrown off kilter by the camera's presence and the response of individual protesters. As the officers strain to keep straight faces, they contribute further to the comedic duo, performing the role of Dean Martin to the protesters' Jerry Lewis. Using conceptual art's notorious investigations of language, media, and systems, *29 Arrests* puns on the logic of "arrest" within both law enforcement and photography, while engaging in a critique of police practices more broadly. (Fig. 3.5–3.6)

There are in fact two cameras involved in this set-up, which intensifies the contentious dynamic of opposing forces on display. Shooting over the shoulder of an officer bearing a Polaroid camera and making booking photos of each arrestee, the domed helmet of the police photographer recurs in Lonidier's images. (Young, 2016: 130) Other traces of this mise-en-scene are detectable in shots where we see the police photographer reloading his film. Standing to the side of the police officer, Lonidier humorously intervenes in the police process and its "enforced visibility," (Young, 2016: 131) by documenting the subjects' insolent resistance to be either straight-faced or straight-laced in confrontation with the law. (Fig. 3.7)

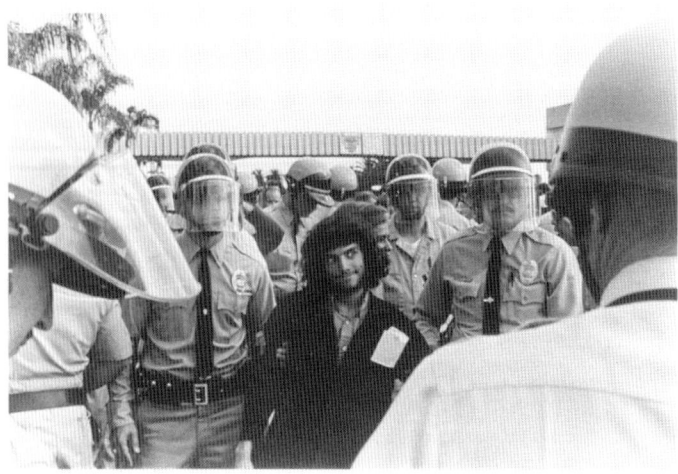

Figure 3.7

Fred Lonidier, *29 Arrests*, 1972 (detail) © MCA Chicago.

29 Arrests can further be understood as both a reference to and a critique of Ed Ruscha's deadpan embrace of photographic banality as a conceptual strategy. In Buchloh's estimation, "*29 Arrests* substitutes an image of interested political struggle for the indifferent transcription of banal swimming pools and parking lots familiar from Southern Californian photo-conceptualism, specifically Ed Ruscha's photo-books such as *Twentysix Gasoline Stations* (1963)." (Young, 2016: 130) Fred Lonidier's *29 Arrests* is thus "situated not only explicitly in an oppositional citationality to Ruscha's oeuvre of books enumerating photographic readymades," but also an act of "reclaiming a space of political agency and agitation at a moment when that discursive space had become both aesthetically more accessible and politically more urgent." (Buchloh, 2014: 123) In this case, Lonidier points to the insufficiency of the straight face, and the inability of his subjects to behave in a restrained manner despite being arrested, which at once ironizes and politicizes the uses of photography in conceptual art. Referring the "democratic agitation" inherent in Lonidier's piece by contrast to Ruscha, Pamela Lee nevertheless notes that "Lonidier's work is deadpan in its own way, lacking the wrenching expressionism one might associate with his charged subject matter." (Lee, 2016: 86) In this way, the collective civil disobedience performed by and for the camera in 29 *Arrests* might be conceived as an uproarious form of resistance that further marks the unruly possibilities of humor and laughter in conceptual art.

Conceptualism's Click

In an oft-quoted passage from "The Author as Producer" (1934), Walter Benjamin states: "There is no better starting point for thought than laughter." I argue such logic is absolutely formative to understanding conceptual art. A direct link to photography is embedded here as well. Specifically in the French translation the passage reads "Notons juste en passant qu'il n'y a pas de meilleur déclic pour la pensée que le rire." Note the declic—or the "click"—the recognizable onomatopoeia of the camera, the triggering mechanism, both premeditated and spontaneous, which is evoked here to mark the eruption of thought precisely as coincident with laughter. On the one hand, photography, like humor, allows human vision to access phenomena that would otherwise be invisible to the naked eye. On the other hand, it withholds the possibility of ever truly mastering the subject. Humor, like photography, exceeds ordinary expectations of both comprehension and tangibility, so that even when you have it suspended before you, you still might not entirely *get it*. Through this lens, even the sobriety and clarity of minimalism starts to be seen as stumbling blocks for pratfalls. (Heiser, 2008: 37) Ultimately conceptual artists using photography employed the photograph as a prosaic yet multi-dimensional material; it is at once object and subject of inquiry. Indulging in its anonymity and in its surfeit of detail, these artists repeatedly manifest an interest in photography's vulnerability, in other words, its inability to keep a straight face.

Notes

1. For an in-depth discussion of deadpan in this regard, see John C. Welchman, "'Don't Play It For Laughs': John Baldessari and Conceptual Comedy," *Black Sphinx: On the Comedic in Modern Art* (Zurich: JPR Ringier, 2010), 245–268.

2. See Blake Stimson, "The Photographic Comportment of Bernd and Hilla Becher," *The Pivot of the World: Photography and Its Nation*, (Cambridge, Mass.: MIT Press, 2006: 137–175), for an insightful analysis of the Becher's use of photographic uniformity in relation to standardization, sequential experience, and the critique of humanism.

Bibliography

Benjamin H. D. Buchloh, "Conceptual Art 1962–1969: From an Aesthetic of Administration to the Critique of Institutions," *October*, 55 (Winter 1990): 105–43.

Benjamin H. D. Buchloh, "Allan Sekula, Or What Is Photography?" *Grey Room*, 55 (Spring 2014): 116–129.

Christopher Cordes, *Bruce Nauman: Prints, 1970–1989* (New York: Castelli Graphics, 1989).

Tim Davis, "Photogeliophobia: Fear of Funny Photography – A Diagnosis," *Aperture*, 212 (2013): 40–45.

Heather Diack, "The Gravity of Levity: Humour as Conceptual Critique," *RACAR: revue d'art canadienne / Canadian Art Review*, 37, 1 (2012): 75–86.

Michael Fried, "Barthes's *Punctum*," *Critical Inquiry*, 31 (Spring 2005): 539–574.

Mark Godfrey, *Douglas Huebler* (London: Camden Arts Centre, 2002).

Angela Grauerholz and Anne Ramsden, "Photographing Industrial Architecture: An Interview with Hilla and Bernd Becher,' *Parachute*, 22 (1981): 14–19.

Jorg Heiser, "Pathos Versus Ridiculousness: Art With Slapstick," in *All of A Sudden: Things That Matter in Contemporary Art* (Berlin: Sternberg Press, 2008), 15–94.

Douglas Huebler, statement accompanying the 1969 group show *Prospect '69* at Kunsthalle Dusseldorf, curated by Konrad Fischer and Hans Strelow, n.p.

Douglas Huebler, "The Art of Following Bird Calls," *Harvard Crimson*, November 1, 1972, http://www.thecrimson.com/article/1972/11/1/the-art-of-following-bird-calls/ (Accessed August 15, 2017).

Gordon Hughes, "Game Face: Douglas Huebler and the Voiding of Photographic Portraiture," *Art Journal*, 66, 4 (Winter 2007): 52–69.

Pamela M. Lee, "'There was no radicalization…. It was *normal* for us': Teaching and Learning in the UCSD Department of Visual Arts, 1967–76," in *The Uses of Photography: Art, Politics, and the Reinvention of a Medium*, ed. Jill Dawsey (Oakland, CA: University of California Press and Museum of Contemporary Art, San Diego, 2016), 80–93.

Mike Kelley, "Shall We Kill Daddy (1997)," in *Foul Perfection: Essays and Criticism*, ed. John C. Welchman (Cambridge, Mass.: MIT Press, 2003), 178–193.

Kynaston McShine, *Information* (New York: Museum of Modern Art, 1970).

John Miller, "Double or Nothing: The Art of Douglas Huebler," *Artforum*, April 2006: 220–227.

Marianne Van Leeuw and Anne Pontegnie (Eds), *Origin and Destination: Alighiero e Boetti and Douglas Huebler* (Brussels: Société des Expositions des Beaux-Arts de Bruxelles, 1997).

Mark Pascale, "Studies for Holograms, 1970 by Bruce Nauman," *Art Institute of Chicago Museum Studies*, 25, 1 (1999): 40–41.

Karen Pincus, *Alchemical Mercury: A Theory of Ambivalence* (Redwood City, CA: Stanford University Press, 2009)

Charles Stainback, *Special Collections: The Photographic Order from Pop to Now* (New York: International Center for Photography, 1992).

Jeff Wall, "'Marks of Indifference,' Aspects of Photography in, or as, Conceptual Art," in *Reconsidering the Object of Art 1965— 1975*, eds Ann Goldstein and Anne Rorimer, exh. cat. (Los Angeles CA: Los Angeles Museum of Contemporary Art, 1995), 247–267.

Benjamin J. Young, "Documents and Documentary: San Diego, c. 1973," in *The Uses of Photography: Art, Politics, and the Reinvention of a Medium*, ed. Jill Dawsey (Oakland, CA: University of California Press, Museum of Contemporary Art San Diego, 2016), 112–161.

"No Photographs Allowed": Conceptual Wit in Some Belgian Photo-based Artists' Books[1]

Johan Pas

Conceptual Wit

Early in 1975, Belgian artist Marcel Broodthaers had a solo exhibition at the Museum of Modern Art in Oxford, *The Privilege of Art* (Le privilège de l'art).[2] As usual, Broodthaers designed the layout for the catalog, which came out as a small booklet in black and white. The first page showed a photograph of a card with the sentence "No photographs allowed" printed on it. Under the picture was the name of Marcel Broodthaers in large capitals. The following four pages of the catalog showed a sequence of black and white photographic images of naked trees, each of them with the captions "No photographs allowed," two of them in English, the others in French and German. These sentences were repeated on most of the following pages that showed works and texts of Broodthaers. Even the blank back cover of the booklet bore the prohibiting words, this time in French. Broodthaers' ironical (or for some even cynical) position towards art (and its reproduction) was expressed in his statement in the catalog:

> I choose to consider Art as a useless labour, apolitical and of little moral significance. Urged on by some base inspiration, I will not conceal that if the errors are mine I will derive a kind of pleasure from that fact: a guilty pleasure because it would depend on victims — those people who have believed me to be right. (Broodthaers, 1975: n.p.)[3]

Broodthaers' ironical exposure of his "guilty pleasure" affected his use of the photograph and the book and catalog medium. In a rather contradictory and tautological way, the artist represented the photographic medium as frustrated, mockingly juxtaposing it with its traditional function as a vehicle for the reproduction of art works. Photographing a sign (probably in an exhibition) forbidding photographing, reproducing it in an exhibition catalog full of photographic reproductions that, according to the caption on the back cover, is not to be photographed, can be considered a teasing and even disruptive gesture. What to do with such a prohibition, especially if one considers reproducing this catalog to accompany an essay on "conceptual wit" in artists' books? Its linguistic and tautological nature indeed brings it into the sphere of high conceptual art as we know it. But what's in a name? Whereas 1960s and 1970s conceptual art is commonly perceived (and presented) as deadly serious and intellectualist, in a lot of works and publications wit, irony, and persiflage are involved. Because the humor involved in conceptual art is never very explicit and often comes in a disguise of administrative or academic language, I suggest referring to it as "conceptual wit." If, as so many argue, Marcel Duchamp is the grandfather of conceptual art, it seems logical that Duchampian wit (word games, role play, contextual humor, vernacular appropriation, ironical distantiation, tautology, deconstruction of the artistic identity, etc.) left its traces in 1960s and 1970s conceptual art.[4] On top of that, Duchamp was one of the first artists to explore and exploit the medium of photography. Last but not least, together with Stéphane Mallarmé and René Magritte he was — at least from the early 1970s on — a main figure of reference for Broodthaers.[5]

Conceptual wit in 1960s and 1970s art happens on the level of verbal language, verbo-visual semantics and linguistics, but also in the exploration of alternative uses of mass media and communication technologies. More specifically, the alternative, investigative role of photography in relationship to its more pedestrian functions is being both explored and deconstructed by artists as diverse as Ed Ruscha, John Baldessari, Bruce Nauman, Douglas Huebler, Mel Bochner, William Wegman, Allen Ruppersberg, Martha Rosler, Eleanor Antin, and Adrian Piper in the United States, and Jan Dibbets, Ger Van Elk, Giulio Paolini, Victor Burgin, Sigmar Polke, Giovanni Anselmo, Christian Boltanski, Gilbert & George, Hans-Peter Feldmann, Braco Dimitrijevic, Valie Export, Sanja Ivekovic and Annette Messager in Europe. (Fogle, 2003; Witkovsky, 2011)

Partly following in the footsteps of Pop art, these and other conceptualist artists, apart from using the photograph as mere documentation of projects and events, started to make use of photography in an ironical, critical, subversive, or deconstructive way. In their installations and multi-media pieces photography acted as an antidote for painting: it radiated a no nonsense feeling of objectivity, it was straightforward, mechanical, quick, and easily multiplied. As a consequence, photographic conceptualism was ideally suited for print. So the use of photography by conceptualist artists in the 1960s can be associated with the emerging conceptualist artists' book. Most of these are also rooted in humor and irony: think of Ed Ruscha's pioneering deadpan photobooks of the 1960s and John Baldessari's witty photobooks of the 1970s in the United States. In Europe, Christian Boltanski, Gilbert & George, Hans-Peter Feldmann, and of course Marcel Broodthaers all created artists' books that employed humor and wit in order to challenge the conventional, serious notions of both the photographic and the book medium. (Maffei, De Donno, 2008; Dickel, 2008)

Moreover, both conceptualist photography and the artists' book responded to the growing popularity of performative art. As a suited vehicle for "intermedia" practices (as described in the early 1960s by Fluxus performer and publisher Dick Higgins) the artists' book offered the possibility to combine written language, graphic and photographic imagery and even musical and performative scores. But apart from hosting documentation on ephemeral acts and intermedia events like environments, happenings, body works, or multi-media performances, the book medium itself has some typical performative characteristics. Finding, purchasing, keeping, holding and shelving the book, browsing its pages, reading and reflecting its content, and activating the interactions between its physical and conceptual components all are part of the activities performed by the user of the book. Already by opening the book and activating its contents, the reader becomes a co-author of the work. The photographic-performative aspect in these small artists' publications is that the reader / looker is invited to reflect upon the act of seeing a photograph, whereas the artist articulates his critical position towards the mass medium, employing it in a deliberate unserious, amateurish, anti-esthetic, or deadpan way. In quite a few cases the artist himself performs the role as a model or an actor, injecting the fiction factor into the seemingly documentary narrative of the photobook.

In Belgium, conceptualist art grew out of Post-Surrealism and the Pop art and happening related activities of artists as diverse as Broodthaers, Jef Geys, Panamarenko, Hugo Heyrman, and Jacques Charlier. (Pas, 2014; Decan, 2016; Pas, 2017) All of them made use of printed matter to document and communicate their ephemeral or conceptual projects. The photocopied magazine *Happening News*, published by Panamarenko, Hugo Heyrman, Yoshio Nakajima, and Wout Vercammen in 1965, was the first Belgian artists' initiative in print to explore the possibilities of photocopy and photography. The cover of the first issue showed a sequence of performative and distorted self-portraits by Heyrman and Nakajima made by abusing a public photo-booth. (Fig. 3.8) Appropriated commercial slogans such as 'NOW', 'FREE! BEST SELLER' and 'ORIGINAL' promote the artists and

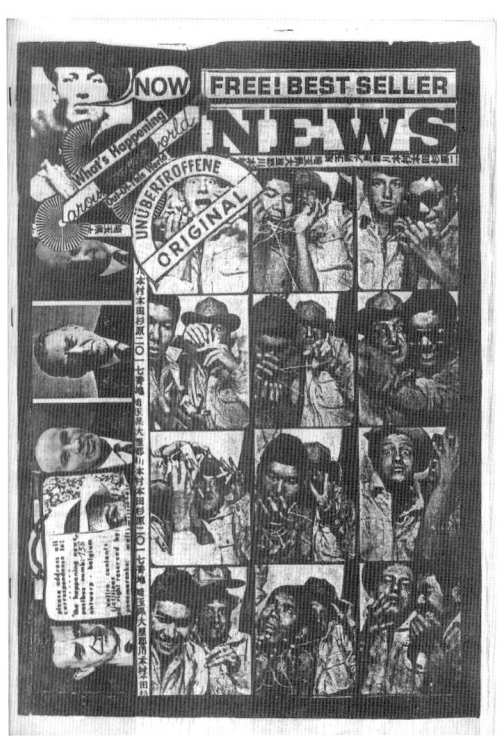

Figure 3.8

Panamarenko, Hugo
Heyrman, Yoshio
Nakajima and Wout
Vercammen (eds),
Happening News (cover),
1, Antwerp: published by
the artists, 1965.

their magazine but also ironically reflect postwar consumer society and its rhetorics. The magazine contained many collage-like compositions with appropriated textual material from advertising, newspapers, and even Van Ostaijens' dadaist book *Bezette Stad* from 1921, clashing with the readymade and self-made photographs. (Pas, 2017: 77–82) In 1972 Jef Geys appropriated a commercial tabloid and turned it into his personal communication channel, the *Kempish Information Bulletin* [Kempens Informatieblad], using it for documenting his art projects but for advertising commercial services as well. (89–90) Duchampian parody is performed here by the displacement of a mainstream medium (the commercial tabloid) and inserting it into an artistic context.

These pioneering artists were followed by a younger generation of conceptualists, some of these associated with formalist neo-constructivism or deadpan relational research: Leo Copers, Werner Cuvelier, Filip Francis, Yves De Smet, Daniël Dewaele, Philippe Van Snick, Danny Matthys, Maurice Roquet, and the group CAP (*Cercle d'Art Prospectif*: Jacques Lennep, Jacques Lizène, Jean-Pierre Ransonnet, and Jacques-Louis Nyst). Despite the efforts of the Belgian pilot galleries Whide White Space, MTL, Yellow Now, Plus-Kern, and New Reform it took some time before conceptualist art was accepted and appreciated.

Publications by artists, notwithstanding their confusing effect produced by conceptual wit, played a role in the process of dissemination.

Until recently, the Belgian contribution to the field of conceptualist photography and artists' publications has been largely neglected, the oeuvre of Broodthaers being a significant exception to this. (Pas, 2001; Decan, 2016; Pas, 2017) In order to reveal this rather unknown territory to the reader, this essay focuses on Belgian artists' publications and their use of irony, parody, and wit. In the course of the 1960s and 1970s Belgian artists, like their international peers, made use of performative parody, often in a deliberate dialog with photography and book print. The Belgian books discussed in this paper demonstrate different strategies of conceptual wit like parody, persiflage, irony, appropriation and anachronism in the way the photographic images interact with the written text and the performative, interactive medium of the book. In that sense, the publications in the presentation can be seen as challenging the conventional photobook and paving the way for Postmodern art strategies of the 1980s, commonly associated with explicit irony, persiflage, anachronism, and appropriation.

In other words: Postmodern parody is not an invention of the cynical 1980s but is deeply rooted in the conceptual wit of late and post-conceptual practices of the 1970s, as the examples in this essay will demonstrate clearly. Often mimicking the representative strategies of documentary photography, these radical conceptualist publications were already blurring the borders between photographic fact and photographic fiction and in doing so also questioning the borders between photography as creative presentation or as documentary representation. A second bottom line is the "de-skilled" use of art photography, liberating the medium from its own conventional esthetics and opening it for new conceptual and visual possibilities. This "liberated" photography even turned out to become a major stakeholder in the Postmodern art world of the late l980s. For the following discussion of some remarkable publications I used a trifold structure, focusing on the offbeat treatment of "semantics," "research" and "portraiture."

Subversive Semantics

In Belgium, the former poet, photographer and filmmaker Marcel Broodthaers was the first to explore this new territory in depth. His roots in Belgian Surrealism and his enthusiasm for the emerging Anglo-Saxon Pop art triggered him to treat photography as a powerful poetical tool, transgressing conventional poetry and bringing it into the realms of verbo-visual parody. The catalog for his first show in the Antwerp Wide White Space Gallery, *Mussels Eggs Fries Pots Charcoal*

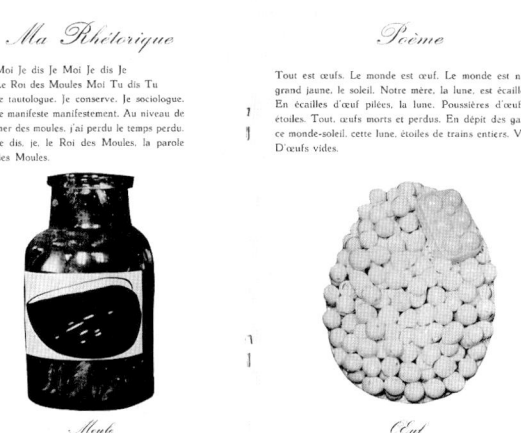

Ma Rhétorique

Moi Je dis Je Moi Je dis Je
Le Roi des Moules Moi Tu dis Tu
Je tautologue. Je conserve. Je sociologue.
Je manifeste manifestement. Au niveau de
mer des moules, j'ai perdu le temps perdu.
Je dis. je. le Roi des Moules, la parole
des Moules.

Moule

Poème

Tout est œufs. Le monde est œuf. Le monde est né du
grand jaune, le soleil. Notre mère, la lune, est écailleuse.
En écailles d'œuf pilées, la lune. Poussières d'œuf, les
étoiles. Tout, œufs morts et perdus. En dépit des gardes,
ce monde-soleil, cette lune, étoiles de trains entiers. Vides.
D'œufs vides.

Œuf

Figure 3.9

Marcel Broodthaers, *Moules Œufs Frites Pots Charbon* (detail), exh. cat., Antwerp: Wide White Space Gallery, 1966.

[Moules Oeufs Frites Pots Charbon] in 1966 was crucial in this development. The random-like title already played with non-artistic vernacular references. The publication elaborated on the same principles as Broodthaers' earlier drawn contributions to *Happening News* and his transformation of the magazine *Phantomas* into a conceptual sketchbook in the same year, but the big difference was that the artist made use of photographic images here.

Three cut out black-and-white reproductions of the assemblages *Mussels, Egg,* and *Fries* [Moule, Oeuf and Frites] accompanied the short, poem-like statements *My Rethoric, Poem,* and *Theoremes* [Ma Rhétorique, Poème, and Théorèmes]. (Fig. 3.9) However, the photographic images were not to be considered reproductions, nor were the texts to be read as captions. On top of that, all the texts appeared in an awkwardly old-fashioned typography. Both the form and the content of this small publication made it completely useless as a conventional catalog with an introduction and a list of the exhibited works. Instead, this frustrating anti-catalog turned out a printed extension of the exhibition.

Broodthaers, always in for some "guilty pleasure," seemed to be pleased with the result of the experiment. For his show *Don't say I didn't tell you – The Parrot* [Ne dites pas que je ne l'ai dit – Le Perroquet] in the same gallery, much later in 1974, he decided to reproduce the original brochure of 1966 but with some subtle alterations. The word *Perroquets* was added in red on the cover and the *Théorèmes* were repeated next to the original ones under the title *Le Perroquet*, literally doubling the page and playing with the connotations of echo and repetition. In the gallery installation, which featured two palm trees, a tape recorder, and a living parrot, the doubling was repeated: two copies of each of the two booklets were presented together in a simple glass case. This play with tautology mimicked the imitation of sound by a parrot; it also questioned the traditional status of the exhibition catalog as an authentic form of documentation and brought it into the sphere of artistic creation.

From then on, the outlines of Broodthaers' publishing practice would become even blurrier, an aspect of his work that the artist was quite aware of:

> What it [the catalog] is: all in all, a strange object: it belongs as much to advertising as to art in the sense that, although it is an artistic object, it does its own advertising as much through the words as through the images depicting all the objects I have made and which have featured in various exhibitions. It would be a catalogue of the very conception if the oeuvre did not refute the catalogue form; this is not a catalogue. The *Ceci n'est pas une pipe* by R. Magritte is not far away. (Broodthaers, 1971: n.p.)

Other converted or expanded "catalogs" in which Broodthaers played sophisticated and ironical games with the notions of exhibiting, documenting, reproducing, and self-representing were *Marcel Broodthaers. MTL* (MTL Gallery, Brussels, 1970), *Fig.1, Fig.2, Fig.0, Fig.12* (Städtisches Museum Mönchengladbach, 1971), *The Eagle from the Oligocene until Now* (Der Adler vom Oligozän bis heute) (Städtische Kunsthalle, Düsseldorf, 1972), *Catalogue* (Palace of Fine Arts, Brussels, 1974), *The Angelus by Daumier* (L'angelus de Daumier) (Musée National d'Art Moderne, Paris, 1975) and the catalog that was described at the beginning of this essay.

Broodthaers' autonomous artists' books that he produced since 1969 on the other hand draw from the tradition of the poetry book and share an elegant, almost classic style. In reaction against the reductive esthetics of minimalist and conceptualist practices, he preferred conventional forms of typography. This resulted in a sophisticated, archaic effect, not unlike the contemporary tongue-in-cheek publications by the British artists Gilbert & George. Despite his ironical elegance and sophistication, Broodthaers could also be overtly critical. In *Magic: Art and Politics* [Magie: Art et Politique] (1973) he poetically investigated the tensions between vanity and activism he observed in the practice of Joseph Beuys. He did this in a subtle way by reproducing an open letter from himself to the German artist, and adding a fake letter by the French composer Jacques Offenbach to Richard Wagner. Both of them had appeared in the newspaper *Rheinische Post* before and a photographic reproduction of the newspaper page was included as a proof. The second part of the book contains poetical statements concerning "being Narcissus" and "being an artist," illustrated with the photographic sequence of a writing slate with Broodthaers' printed signature that disappears in the end, the photographic signature making room for a real hand-made signature in ink on the last page of the book, a "real" echo of the signatures reproduced on the earlier pages.

Whereas *Magic*...demonstrates multilayered word-and-image games, the book *A Voyage on the North Sea* (1974) functions like a meta-media project without any text. Announced as "a book suggesting image as function / a book suggesting the text as function," Broodthaers described it as "more than a theory, the subject of this proposition reflects a simple image of the frustration that rules the social condition of today, for example this year." (Broodthaers, 1974: n.p.) In a special 1976 issue of the American magazine *Art Rite*, dedicated to artists' books, it is (as the only Belgian publication in the issue) reviewed:

> Two pictures of ships: a photo of a week-end sailboat, and an oil painting of a frigate. The voyage is really through the painting, cinematically, through scale variations, repetitions, successions of different details and enlargements, and hue variations of reproductions. The book stands for the voyage art makes through the media as well as evoking travel. A must if only for its exotic uncut pages. (*Art Rite*, 1976: 22)

These uncut pages, containing the invisible page numbers in the fold, indeed give the book its teasing physical quality, because it suggests the possibility of cutting the pages, an aspect Broodthaers explicitly forbids in the note for the reader, ending with "It is up to the attentive reader to find out what devilish motive inspired the book's publication. To that end he may make use, if need be, of select readings from today's prolific output. See catalogues, papers, revues." (Broodthaers 1974b: n.p.) Once again, Broodthaers teases the reader who is looking for an artistic message or a fixed meaning. Instead of providing useful information on the artist and his work, Broodthaers' use of the book and of photography only offers a kind of pleasing frustration. The limited edition was accompanied by a 4'15" film constructed like the pages of a book. The interactions among the found (kitsch) painting, the color/ black and white photography and the static film contained within in a single edition makes *A Voyage on the North Sea* a fascinating exercise in ironic iconoclasm, stretching the relationships between the (photographic) book and its pedestrian functions.

But Broodthaers was not the only Belgian artist interested in an offbeat and witty use of photographs and books. In 1972 the artist Jacques Lennep invited a dozen young artists to participate in an innovative artistic program. They were quite different in their artistic approaches, but shared an interest in new media and artistic research. One year later the so-called Group CAP (*Cercle d'Art Prospectif*) held its first exhibition. (Van Lennep, 2002) Lennep coined the term "relational art" to describe their artistic vision. When the more "realist" artists decided to go their own way, the relational approach of CAP became central. The new group consisted of Lennep, Jacques Lizène, Pierre Courtois, and Jacques-Louis Nyst. Later on, Jacques Evrard and Jean-Pierre Ransonnet joined their ranks. They all investigated social relationships and new ways of communicating their work and ideas, such as installation, photography, video, multiples, and artists' books. In doing so, they established a manner of working not unlike conceptualist art made at that time in France by Bernar Venet, Christian Boltanski, Didier Bay, Jean Le Gac, Paul-Armand Gette, and the *Collective d'Art Sociologique*. At the same time, and probably because of their Belgian background rooted in Surrealism, the use of humor and parody was more outspoken than in the work of their French peers.

Lennep and Nyst used the book medium more extensively than the other CAP members: both created an autonomous artists' booklet with photographs for a 1974 CAP group catalog. While Courtois provided a dry file with photographs and data about a mysterious car accident, Evrard contributed a folded poster with deadpan photographs of people looking at artworks (*Museum*), and Lizène even produced a small hilarious record on which he orally imitated the sound of a Honda moped (represented with a photograph on the sleeve), *Attempt at Imitation* [Tentative d'imitation].[6] Lennep's contribution, *Art tells Stories* [L'art raconte des histoires] was his first artists' book, whereas Nyst's *Dialogue between a photograph of leaves and three black spots* [Dialogue entre une photographie de feuillage et 3 taches noires] was preceded by the similar but more elaborate *We are no Cybernauts* [Nous ne sommes pas des cybernautes]. (Nyst, 1973) Despite its title, this "livre de lecture" (book for reading) contained almost no text. It was a playful exercise in deconstructing photographic images, using the text captions and page sequences as a research tool. By juxtaposing photographs and linear drawings, highlighting their visual relationships, and using a subtle form of visual humor, Nyst invited the reader/viewer to reread and reconsider the images, and compare the qualities of both photographic and graphic representation. The poetical-pedagogical book would make the reader/viewer aware of the unconscious processes involved in reading, looking, and browsing.

In the title of a photowork of 1974, Nyst even went as far as defining the book medium as "a machine to animate the mechanisms of thinking." This artists' book came only a year after his solo exhibition in the gallery Yellow Now, the first in a series of exhibitions explicitly announced as demonstrations of artistic research in the field of photography and its claims to reality. (Decan, 2016: 252–253) Like Broodthaers, Nyst was interested in the relationships between text, photography, film, and print. As a pioneer in video art, he explored the potential of mass media in a poetical manner, showing some influences of Surrealist humor and parody. His most coherent book came out of a video with the same title: *The Object* [L'Objet]. (Fig. 3.10) (Nyst, 1976) Both in the book and in the film, the object, a tiny metal kettle, is painstakingly described, explored, commented on, and represented from many angles and in different situations, but without a proper definition, making the whole enterprise a rather frustrating experience for the reader. It also ironically commented upon the use of "objective" textual and visual language as used in science, a way of working that can also be seen in the publications of his conceptualist peers.

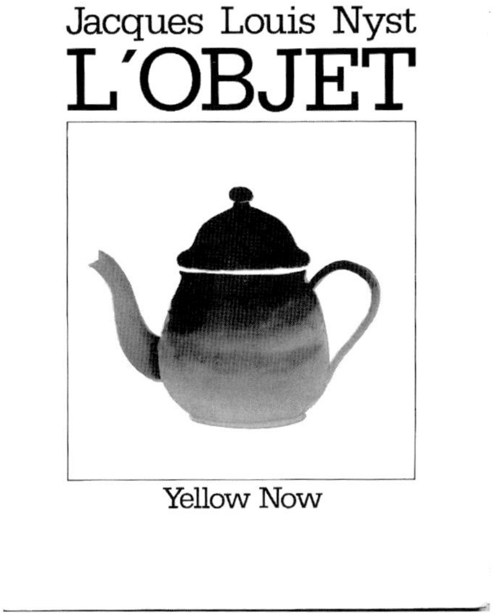

Jacques Louis Nyst
L'OBJET

Yellow Now

Figure 3.10

Jacques Louis Nyst, *The Object* [L'Objet] (cover), Liège: Editions Yellow Now, 1976.

Deadpan Research

Indeed, in the course of the late 1960s, quite a few Belgian artists turned to the realm of scientific research to open up the range of their artistic practice. Methods and processes derived from science proved a source of inspiration, as were the "neutral" use of language and the "objective" photographic representation of documentary material. Documentary photography was employed for presenting non-spectacular situations, mimicking scientific research and presenting irrelevant data as objective facts, with a touch of Dada and Surrealism. Jacques Charlier is one of the Belgian artists seriously involved with humor, irony and parody. He was (and still is) a multimedia artist, constantly trying to bridge the gap between high and low art, between artist and audience, between playfulness and criticality. In an "autobiography" published in 1983, the artist described his media as follows: "painting, sculpture, photography, film, video, texts, humorous drawings, caricature, comics, advertising, photo novel, guitar, song, reportage, diverse jokes." (Charlier, 1983: 144, our underlining)

Indeed, in Charlier's oeuvre the joke is a medium as good as another. In the early 1960s Charlier became intrigued by the American Pop art paintings he saw at the Ileana Sonnabend gallery in Paris. He became part of a band of young happening artists and pranksters in Liège and he co-edited their mimeographed periodical *Total's*. (Pas, 2017: 82)

He also worked as an employee at the Provincial Technical Services in Liège. Bridging the gap between the adventurous world of avant-garde art and the daily routine of bureaucratic life, Charlier created a unique brand of proto-conceptual post-pop art by appropriating events, persons, images, and materials from the technical services and transplanting them into the art world. Because for his work as a technical draftsman — preparing the works of public infrastructures — he had access to administrative tools such as technical photography, a professional typewriter, a photocopier, a stencil machine, and a lot of paper. Charlier also managed to find assistants among his colleagues in the administration. From about 1963, the period he learned about Pop art, Charlier began to collect (and later to show) "professional documents" — found photographs of roads, canals, pipelines, and public works as deadpan readymade images. His early books demonstrate how Charlier created an ambiguous *terrain vague* between the worlds of advanced art and of public services. Print enabled him to compile readymade imagery from the office and translate it into an artistic medium. Here the artists' book functioned as an in-between, connecting the daily professional context and the art world.

In 1966 or 1967 Charlier distributed a small tract with a photocollage of hands handling machines and printouts, and a short ironical statement: "In a world of super-machine(s) what else is there to do than to activate the machine, to disassemble, to sabotage. I prefer to activate the machine, to thwart its functions. *Nothing* is more perfect than the product of the machine, *nothing* is faster, *nothing* is more anonymous." (Charlier, n.d.) The book *Pressure* [Pression] released in one copy at the end of 1967 seems to echo the ironical stance of the pamphlet. It contained fifty pages with sequences based on only four photographs; two showing high-pressure compressors, two with details of them. Charlier enriched these images with written (e.g. the word "pression" gradually being compressed until it disappears) and drawn additions by hand, suggesting simplistic and impossible ways of connecting the machines or details. By such recycling of vernacular imagery, Charlier showed his affinity with the 1950s Situationist strategy of *détournement*. By applying standard office tools like mimeograph, markers, archival cardboard, tape for the spine, and presenting the result in a dry, business-like publication, Charlier also playfully announced the so-called "bureaucratic esthetics" of conceptual art.

In an untitled book of the same year, Charlier created thirty pages with different sequences, by using six deadpan photographs of excavation works from the technical services. The grainy images are repeated over and over again, a process during which they first appear bleached so that they are barely readable to become sharper and with more detail, not unlike the grainy images that Andy Warhol had shown at the

Sonnabend gallery a few years earlier. On the following pages, Charlier simply added handwritten codes and indications in different colors such as crosses, arrows, perspective and dotted lines, confusingly suggesting different perceptions of the generic scenery by the projected viewers A, B, and C. Here Charlier's contrarian, anti-esthetic use of the landscape genre anticipated the photographs and magazine works of the American artist Robert Smithson, whose work became known in Belgium only much later.

Both *Pressure* and *Untitled* can be regarded as proto-conceptual experiments with ironic image appropriation and the conventional book form. Unfortunately their unique character reduced their impact. Although the books seem perfectly publishable, it is not completely clear whether Charlier at that time intended them to be multiplied at all. Maybe the whole process to have them published appeared too cumbersome. But they had paved the way: a bit later Charlier released smaller, stapled brochures that echoed the look and feel of the first books. *Bye Bye Beat* and *Blocs* (both 1968?) made use of mimeography, adhesive letters for the cover, and mimeographed pages. The same happened in *Canalisations* (1968 or 1969). Here Charlier combined typed texts in green and grainy black and white photographs to document a site-specific project using tubing, pipes, water faucets, and ventilators for a confusing air and water happening in a newly build house.

The Flemish artist Leo Copers had a comparable post-Surrealist and post-Pop investigative attitude, be it in a different area. In 1967 the young artist made a pilgrimage to René Magritte's funeral, but he arrived too late. With its uncanny poetry and use of poor, natural elements, Copers' early work seemed to combine Belgian Surrealism, Anglo-Saxon Pop art and Italian Arte Povera. Triggered by the absurd sight of a light bulb floating in a polluted Ghent canal, the artists' ambitious motto was "Every day a new idea." In 1969 Copers began to experiment with burning lights and fire in water. This led to his first self-made edition *Still Lives-Interiors-Landscapes-Marines with* PHILIPS TL *40W/33* [Stillevens-interieurs-landschappen-zeestukken met PHILIPS TL 40W/33] (1971). (Fig. 3.11) Apart from the humorous title that combines traditional genres of painting with the vernacular contemporary object of a fluorescent light tube, the look and feel of the publication must have been utterly confusing.

The cardboard folder contained ten straightforward photographs by the artist's wife Martine Kint showing a burning fluorescent light tube floating in a bathtub, a shower, a canal, a swimming pool, a lake, and the sea. The laborious work of enlarging, printing, and making the folders limited the first edition. Much later, in 2008, a remake with large color prints in a box was published in a larger edition. Copers' obsession with impossible or unnatural situations also became apparent

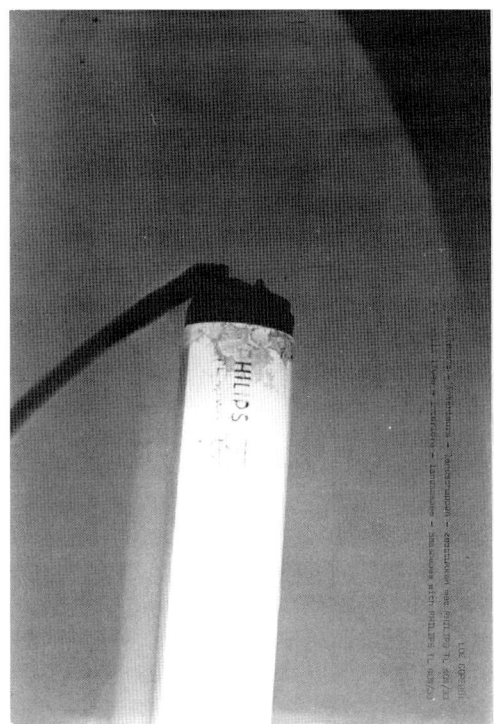

Figure 3.11

Leo Copers, *Still Lives-Interiors-Landscapes-Marines with PHILIPS TL 40W/33* [Stillevens-interieurs-landschappen-zeestukken met PHILIPS TL 40W/33], Wetteren: published by the artist, 1971, (photographs by Martine Kint).

in *A different Day* [Een andere dag]. (Copers, 1973) Employing photography in an unorthodox manner, the folder with three black and white photographs and explanatory text by the artist documented a photographic experiment. In order to demonstrate that "every photograph is real and therefore can prove anything," Copers asked a professional photographer to falsify his landscape photographs so that the sun would appear as an uncanny black star. This kind of absurd research, sometimes leading to visual falsifications, is typical for this generation of Belgian conceptualists. It gives their printed output a characteristic look and feel that differs from the more austere publications of their Anglo-Saxon peers. Mixing subjective, autobiographical elements and objective visual facts can be associated with the use of the staged portraiture and self-portraiture.

Staged Selves

As early as 1971, the constructivist conceptualist Mark Verstockt included a full frontal, life-size photographic self-portrait (folded as a large poster) in his experimental book-object *This is not A BOOK*. Eying the looker straight in the face, it echoed his tautological and witty use of research for the creation of an interactive meta-book that playfully invited the reader to reflect on the medium of the book and his own reading and looking habits. (Verstockt, 1971: Pas, 2017: 19–20) Jacques Lennep, the founder of the CAP group, on the other hand opted for a sociological approach. "Part-time artist, part-time art historian," Lennep worked in the Royal Museum of Fine Arts in Brussels. Bridging the gap between art and life, he set out to combine artistic and scientific research. Documentary photography was employed here for presenting a non-spectacular sociology in which ordinary daily life functioned as a research subject. Lennep ironically adopted scientific methods to make an inventory of acts and routines of daily behavior. For this purpose, video, photography, and the book medium proved adequate tools. Lennep's first booklet was, as already mentioned, *Art tells Stories* [L'art raconte des histoires] (1974). It playfully combined elements from art history, referring to his job at the museum, with a sociological curiosity and an awareness of recent artistic developments such as Land art, Performance art and Narrative art. He even appropriated a sequence of street photographs of the 1920s by attributing it to an "anonymous conceptual artist."

A bit later Lennep produced a funny booklet showing photographs of tourists typically posing in front of the tower of Pisa, *The Tower of Pisa* [La Tour de Pise] (1976). From that year on, he embarked upon his ambitious *Musée de l'homme* [Museum of Mankind] for which he developed a series of exhibitions with publications. (Lennep, 2010) Each exhibition was dedicated to a specific living person: the old Monsieur Bonvoisin, who carved sculptures out of chestnuts (1976); the flamboyant Ezio Bucci, a supporter of sporting club Charleroi (1977); Paul Van Bosstraeten, a dedicated orchid grower (1977); Alfred Laoureux, a fanatic collector (1978); Madame Paul Six, who collected dedications of famous people (1978); Tania, a professional nude photo model (1979; Fig. 3.12); and the young Yves Somville, who played the role of Christ in a local passion play (1980). Seemingly randomly selected, these authentic persons were elaborately filmed, photographed, interviewed, their activities described, all of it compiled in accompanying publications designed in an appropriate style. In the case of Yves Somville, Lennep even staged a live performance based upon the activity of his subject.

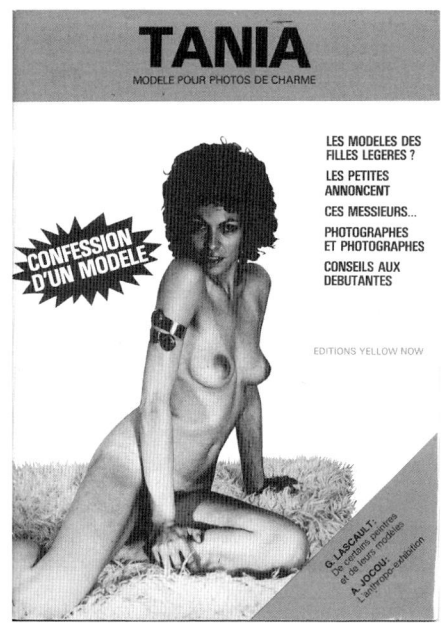

Figure 3.12

Jacques Lennep, *Tania, Modèle pour photos de charme* (cover), 1979, (Liège: Editions Yellow Now – Brussels: Galerie Isy Brachot).

The Brussels artist Maurice Roquet, who was also a graphic designer, developed a comparable fascination for the theatrical and absurd aspects of daily life. He saw common movements and daily rituals as performative situations or readymade happenings. Concluding that the interactive art of the 1960s had failed, he began to send out works by mail, inviting the recipient to experience a mini-happening. In the line of Fluxus, he called these missives "*théâtre intérieur*" or "*théâtre mental*" (interior or mental theater). The first, sent out early in 1971, was *Three movements for five photographs, a bottle of beer, a transistor radio, and diverse*. The box provided a sequence of black and white amateur photographs from the 1930s, a fragment from the Brussels city map, a folded white sheet, a crumpled letter with the words crossed out, a sheet with a stroke of orange, three colored leaves describing the movements, an instruction leaflet, and an introductory text. (Fig. 3.13) The beer bottle and the radio had to be provided by the recipient. Following the set of dry instructions, the reader became both an actor and a co-author of the theatrical play, performing, imagining, and experiencing it at the same time.

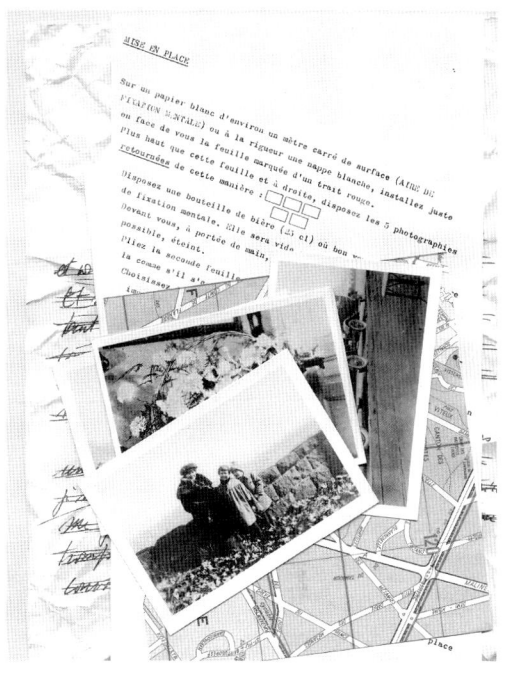

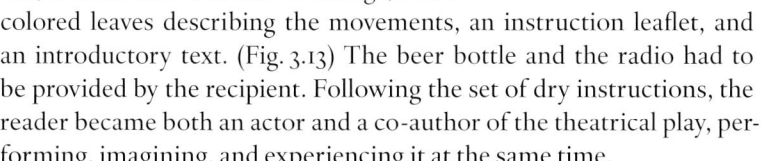

Figure 3.13

Maurice Roquet, *Three movements for five photographs, a bottle of beer, a transistor radio, and diverse*, 1971, box with photographs, map, letters, Brussels: published by the artist.

Other boxes contained tactile and audio exercises with instructions and ingredients. Later Roquet's sendings became more conceptual, taking the forms of official-looking but rather absurd contracts (*Contract of Identification*) or questionnaires (*Inventory nr.1*). In 1973 he started to observe the small gestures of people in public space, like persons touching or holding each other while strolling. Using documentary photographs and neutral descriptive language, Roquet represented this "public theatre" in a sociological fashion, inserting his deadpan observations in exhibition catalogs. Elaborations of these small "events" were the slide projection and the booklet *Making an entrance/Making an exit*. (Roquet, 1974) Showing snapshot, candid camera photographs of anonymous people leaving or entering their doorway, and describing the conditions in which the events took place, Roquet represented the coming up or leaving of the "stage" of public space as tiny theatrical situations. At the same time he made the reader a voyeur.

From the mid-1970s Charlier created publications to question artistic positions and art world systems. *Fabulous Monsters Story* was a limited edition with graphic and textual documents, original photographs,

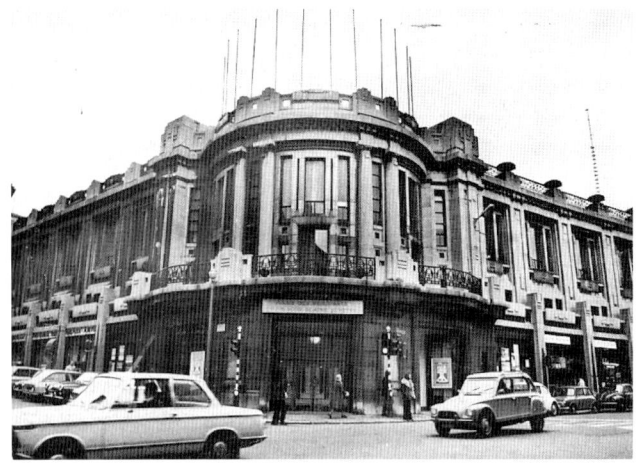

Figure 3.14

Jacques Charlier, *Opening of the exhibitions J. Charlier, On Kawara, 7-1-1975* [Vernissage des expositions J. Charlier, On Kawara/ Vernissage van de tentoonstellingen J. Charlier, On Kawara, 7-1-1975] (cover), Brussels: Société des expositions du Palais des Beaux-Arts a.s.b.l./Vereniging voor tentoonstellingen van het Paleis voor Schone Kunsten v.z.w., 1975.

and even a music cassette contained in a plain brown archival folder. (Charlier, 1975) It contained information about the absurd roleplays Charlier and his colleagues of the Technical Services performed under the direction of the artist during their lunch breaks. The result is absurdist and even Surrealist in spirit. In other books Charlier more explicitly addressed art world issues. For these, he applied visual strategies from photojournalism, comics, or caricature. In January 1975, during the opening night of the exhibitions at the Brussels Palace of Fine Arts with his work (photographs of exhibition openings) and that of the Japanese conceptual artist On Kawara, Charlier had pictures taken of the assembled art crowd. The journalistic photographs, not unlike the ones used by Jacques Evrard in the CAP catalog of 1974, were compiled in a small photo album that was presented after the exhibition. (Fig. 3.14) It offered a sociological view on art world rituals and behavior, but also a who's who of the Belgian and international art scene. The book has a witty tautological effect: on some pictures one can observe people staring at Charlier's photographs depicting artsy people at exhibition openings. (Charlier, 1975b)

In the same period Charlier created photographic self-portraits challenging portrait conventions and undermining the seriousness of the conceptual artist. These can be seen as photographic performances, playing with notions of integrity, authenticity, and self-representation. Combining elements from popular photo novels and comics, Charlier enacted cliché roles such as the contemporary artist, the rock star, and the art expert. *Portrait of an Expert* [Portrait d'un connoisseur] features Charlier wearing a suit and a fake nose with glasses. (Charlier, 1978) The sequence of twenty-four photographs was made in 1975 and represents an arrogant art expert contemplating a work of art that is invisible to the reader of the booklet, who finds himself in the position of the art object scrutinized by the critic. Charlier's staged self-portraits echo Christian Boltanski's highly theatrical and explicit, and therefore rather unfunny *Comic Sketches* [Saynètes Comiques] (1975). In using the photographic sequence as a narrative device and in employing themselves as role players, these artists prefigured the post-conceptual move to staged photography and narrativity that would become key elements of Post-modernist art practice.

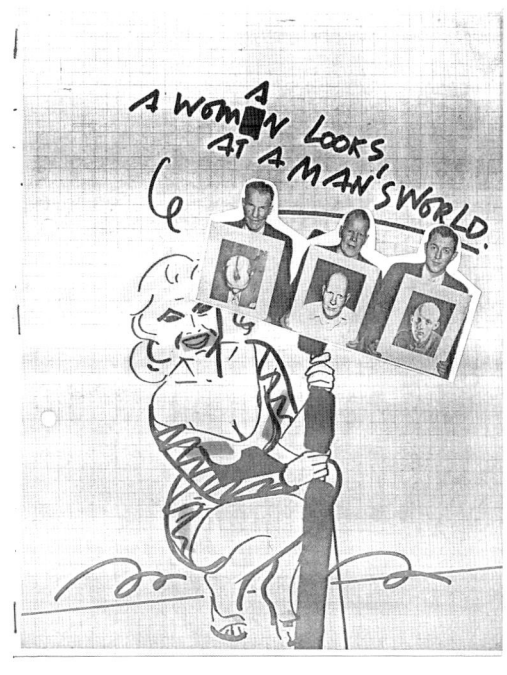

In the second half of the 1970s photoconceptualism became like another mainstream art movement, triggering reactions from the younger generation, among them female artists challenging male and mainstream paradigms. Towards the end of the 1970s, in the slipstream of Performance art and Punk rock, the Flemish artist Anne-Mie Van Kerckhoven employed the photographic self-portrait in combination with textual statements. Her early photocopied (sometimes hand-colored) and stapled, self-made booklets released in the context of her exhibitions, radiate the atmosphere of the New Wave DIY scene. Examples are the untitled booklet for Art Something (Amsterdam) of 1979 and *A Woman Looks at a Man's World* (1980; Fig. 3.15). A few months after this last booklet, Van Kerckhoven released the first issue of *Public Annemy*, her personal zine of which five issues appeared in the early 1980s. Already in the title the artist playfully suggests and undermines the subversion of her position. Adopting and adapting the clinical idiom of modern social science and cybernetics, and juxtaposing these collage-like statements with photographic sequences of self-portraits and graphic interventions, she challenged the conventions of objective truth and the monolithic self, revealing in more than one way "the truth about reality." (Van Kerckhoven, 1980: 4) Due to the breakthrough of revivalist Postmodern painting, the photographic artists' book would become a marginal phenomenon in the 1980s, only to pop up again at the end of the decade. By that time, conceptual art had become art history, ready to be rediscovered by a new generation of artists-publishers. But like printed traces of conceptual wit and its subversive semantics, deadpan research and staged selves, the grainy and simple artists' booklets of the 1960s and 1970s continue to fascinate and function as poetic booby traps until this day.

Figure 3.15

Anne-Mie Van Kerckhoven, *A Woman Looks at a Man's World*, Antwerp: published by the artist, 1980.

Notes

1. This essay draws heavily upon the chapter *Primary Information: Conceptualist Strategies, 1969-1979* in my book *Artists' Publications: The Belgian Contribution* (2017).

2. Marcel Broodthaers, *Le Privilège de l'Art*, Museum of Modern Art, Oxford, 26 April 26-1 June 1975. The catalog was based upon the one made for his exhibition *Invitation pour une exposition bourgeoise* at the Nationalgalerie in Berlin, that took place shortly before.

3. English translations of quotes from Broodthaers are taken from Moure, 2013.

4. On the relationship between Duchamp and neo-avant-garde and conceptual art, see *Ubrigens sterben immer die anderen. Marcel Duchamp und die Avantgarde seit 1950*, Museum Ludwig, Köln, 1988, and Benjamin Buchloh et al (eds), *The Duchamp Effect, October 70*, Fall 1994.

5. In a statement in the catalog of *Der Adler vom Oligozän bis Heute* Broodthaers explicitly refers to Duchamp, the readymade and its effect on contemporary (conceptual) art, see Broodthaers, 1972: vol.1, 13-14. See also Haidu, 2010: 182-183.

6. *CAP: Pierre Courtois, Jacques Evrard, Jacques Lennep, Jacques Lizène, Jacques Louis Nyst*, Belgisches Haus, Köln, 10 October-9 November 1974

Bibliography

Art Rite, #14, New York, 1976.

Marcel Broodthaers, Unpublished note, 1971, in *Marcel Broodthaers. Collected Writings*, ed. Gloria Moure, (Barcelona: Ediciones Poligrafa, 2013), 304.

Marcel Broodthaers, *Der Adler vom Oligozän bis Heute. Marcel Broodthaers zeigt eine experimentelle Ausstellung seines Musé d'Art Moderne, Département des Aigles, Section des Figures*, exh.cat. (Düsseldorf: Städtische Kunsthalle, 1972).

Marcel Broodthaers, Announcement for the book and the film *A Voyage on the North Sea*, 1974, in *Marcel Broodthaers. Collected Writings*, ed. Gloria Moure, (Barcelona: Ediciones Poligrafa, 2013), 392.

Marcel Broodthaers, *A Voyage on the North Sea. November 1973* (London: Petersburg Press, 1974).

Marcel Broodthaers, "To be a straight thinker or not te be | To be blind," in Marcel Broodthaers, *Le privilège de l'art*, exh.cat. (Oxford: Museum of Modern Art, 1975), n.p.

Jacques Charlier, *Dans un monde de super-machine...*, self-published, n.d. (1966 or 1967).

Jacques Charlier, *Fabulous Monsters Story* (Brussels: Editions Lebeer Hossmann, 1975).

Jacques Charlier, *Vernissage van de tentoonstellingen J. Charlier, On Kawara 7–1–1975* (Brussels: Vereniging voor Tentoonstellingen van het Paleis voor Schone Kunsten, 1975).

Jacques Charlier, *Portrait d'un connoisseur* (Liège: Musée St.Georges/Yellow Now, 1978).

Jacques Charlier, *Dans les règles de l'art* (Brussels: Editions Lebeer-Hossmann, 1983).

Leo Copers, *Een andere dag* (Ghent: VMHK, Jeugd en Plastische Kunst, 1973).

Liesbeth Decan, *Conceptual, Surrealist, Pictorial: Photo-based Art in Belgium (1960s-early 1990s)* (Leuven: Leuven University Press, 2016).

Hans Dickel, *Künstlerbücher mit Photographie seit 1960* (Hamburg: Maximilian-Gesellschaft, 2008).

Douglas Fogle (ed.), *The Last Picture Show: Artists using Photography 1960–1982*, exh.cat. (Minneapolis: Walker Art Center, 2003).

Rachel Haidu, *The Absence of Work. Marcel Broodthaers, 1964–1976* (Cambridge, Mas.: The MIT Press, 2010).

Jacques Lennep, *Un musée de l'homme | A Museum of Mankind* (Liège: Yellow Now, 2010).

Giorgio Maffei, Emanuele De Donno (eds), *Libro Sensibile: la fotografia nel libro d'artista dagli anni '60 ad oggi* (Spoleto: Edizioni Viaindustriae, 2008).

Gloria Moure (ed.), *Marcel Broodthaers. Collected Writings* (Barcelona: Ediciones Poligrafa, 2013).

Jacques-Louis Nyst, *Nous ne sommes pas des cybernautes. Livre de lecture* (Brussels: André De Rache, 1973).

Jacques-Louis Nyst, *L'objet* (Liège: Yellow Now, 1976).

Johan Pas, "De soep van Daguèrre: Het fotografische beeld in de Belgische kunst sinds 1975," in Flor Bex (ed.), *Kunst in België na 1975* (Antwerpen: Mercatorfonds, 2001), 136–147.

Johan Pas, *Beroepsdocumenten aan hun samenhang onttrokken: Een aspect van het Belgisch conceptualisme belicht via drukwerk uit de verzameling van Johan Pas*, exh.cat. (Antwerpen: Galerie S&S, 2014).

Johan Pas, *Artists' Publications: The Belgian Contribution* (London: Koenig Books, 2017).

Maurice Roquet, *Making an entrance|Making an exit* (Brussels: Yves Gevaert, 1974).

Anne-Mie Van Kerckhoven, *Komfort über alles!, Public Annemy nr.2* (Antwerp: published by the artist, 1980).

Jacques Van Lennep (ed.), *CAP | Art relationnel: Un aspect de l'art contemporain en Belgique* (Tournai: La Renaissance du Livre, 2002).

Mark Verstockt, *This is not A BOOK* (Antwerpen: Mercatorfonds, 1971).

Matthew S. Witkovsky (ed.), *Light Years: Conceptual Art and the Photograph 1964–1977*, exh.cat. (Chicago, New Haven and London: The Art Institute of Chicago, Yale University Press, 2011).

Laughter Protocol: Elements of Humor in Proto- and Conceptual Photography in Croatia

Sandra Križić Roban

Innovative artistic practices in the former Yugoslavia, and consequently in Croatia, marked, in particular, the 1970s. Many important developments in this field are characterized by the use of new media, a change in the understanding of the notion of an artwork, and the specific social engagement that artists displayed. (Matičević, 1982: 8) Although the examples singled out in this paper at first glance appear serious, uninteresting, or even boring, many of them in a humoristic way comment on the social-political reality and the circumstances in which the artists developed their strategies.

In order to better understand this period, we need to briefly examine the crucial changes—on both a political and artistic level—that occurred in Yugoslavia after World War II. Socio-politically, this period was marked by the rapid emergence of industrial modernization, fueled by the advent of new technologies and the rise of the general educational level. The modernist reconstruction of the state also found its translation in the official cultural policy with its willingness to accept, among other things, new forms of art. Hence the official doctrine of socialist realism, dominant in a relatively short period (1945–1953), was gradually left behind. Instead, connections were re-established with interwar avant-garde experiences through, for instance, an interest in the esthetics of the New Objectivity and reverberations of Russian and German avant-garde tendencies. These tendencies, which we could label as post-war modernism, were dominant in the 1950s and 1960s.

In its early phase, post-war modernism retained certain characteristics of a particular derivate of *socialist modernism.* (Denegri, 2003: 173) It was a peculiar blend of influences: despite the independent development of the urban centers of the former Yugoslav Republics, it is possible to trace their development within a wider, common context, situated at the crossroads between the East and the West. In the Yugoslav context, the period from the end of World War II through to the beginning of the 1970s is considered one of the most dynamic, not only in terms of politics but also in terms of culture. (Kolešnik, 2012: 128) Thanks to modernization and a belief in science and technology, rural areas were abandoned in favour of the building of a modern urban society. The idea of modernization is particularly noticeable in the field of architecture and urbanism, which saw the development of the symbolic and ideological presentation of socialist content. In the field of art, the phenomenon of abstract art followed these developments in architecture and urbanism; it was a phenomenon tied to the idea of individual freedom. Likewise, a critical discourse developed at the same time, and to a large extent contributed to the definition of autonomous art. Let us mention, too, touring exhibitions and the participation of Yugoslav artists at various international art manifestations, which together influenced the development of all artistic media.

In the first post-war period the influence of the Communist party on art and the development of criticism was significant, but at the beginning of the 1950s, the Party's interference generally started to decrease. That still did not imply that its policies could be subjected to any kind of criticism. For Yugoslavian citizens, humor was one of the rare available ways to blow off steam – nevertheless it should be noted that various jokes on the account of state officials could have resulted in imprisonment, dismissal from one's job or some other form of repression. Freedom of expression was limited and it was perhaps due to this controlled *impossibility* or *half-possibility* that humor was often draped in irony, mockery and sarcasm. Humor was also used to mock people from other nationalities as well as those who were different in some way (too feminine men, or masculine women, for instance); darkly humorous comments were not rare either. Yet such "humoristic outbursts" happened mainly in the private sphere, far from the threat of repercussion. As for the artists, they seldom engaged in humor. Although detailed research into humor in this period has not yet been undertaken, judging by the artistic works that are available to us, we can surmise that most artists took their profession and status seriously. We should not forget the existing laws and rules in which we can find information about the Party's control in the period, and despite the supposedly guaranteed freedom of expression, the list of forbidden items encouraged self-censorship and the avoidance of any, including humorous, comments on the socio-political order.

From the 1950s onwards, the Croatian art scene was also marked by a few innovations in photography, in terms of both its form and content, which opened the complex question of the role of photography in the context of contemporary art. The extent to which these innovations were important for the gradual development of the medium is demonstrated, among other things, by the fact that in the 1950s numerous photoclubs, which had been active even during the interwar period and in the majority of Croatian cities, were omnipresent. Members of these photoclubs mainly exhibited landscapes and intimate views, pictures of monumental modernist achievements and individual artistic motifs, alongside the inevitable humanistic approach close to the esthetics of the exhibition *The Family of Man*. In the earlier period, experiments were rare: most photographers adopted a documentary approach. However, gradually, many significant photographers began altering their artistic expressions, mostly in accordance with their individual interests and concerns. (Matičević, 1997: 12) Therefore, the development of contemporary photography in Croatia can and should also be traced through articulated individual, subjective strategies. Some authors took an interest in representing architectural structures, which can partially be linked to the period of intensive industrial and technological renewal and scientific discoveries. But above all else, it is important to note that a segment of these works depicts alienation and poses questions about the meaning of human and technical existence. In the line of experiences which can be linked to abstract expressionism, works of certain authors depict complex psychological processes. The extended effects of the devastations of war and the distorted existential context were also the reasons why these authors took an interest in what often remained invisible to the human eye. In the field of photography, we come across experiments similar to those in painting, based on post-war abstraction, Art Informel and Surrealism. They all, in a certain way—especially if we interpret them within the national context of that time—attest to "the radical" artistic points of view which cannot be explained outside their socio-political framework.

Proto-conceptual Tendencies – The Gorgona Case

Early proto-conceptual developments allow us to reflect on how the camera was used as a tool. Thanks to this "tool" photography could, among other things, function as a medium through which information was communicated. It functioned as an instrument through which various artistic strategies were created, whose origins did not necessarily lie in the medium of photography. In the context of Croatian art, the notion of proto-conceptual practice refers exclusively to the art group Gorgona. Gorgona was active in the period between 1959 and 1966 and was very early on characterized as an alternative spiritual phenomenon, contributing to the spread of art to existential spheres, with whom only a small circle of individuals have been familiarized up until recently. "Maybe Gorgona deserved to stay in the shadows. If we start to talk about these things, they die."[1]

Gorgona was a hermetic group, inclined to irony, nihilism, absurdity and privacy, which resulted in almost inconspicuous artistic actions and scarcely available information on the group itself. These actions consisted, among other things, of mailing cards and personal correspondence, writing instructions, creating work-sketches and filling out questionnaires with absurd questions that the Gorgona members posed to each other, such as: "Do you consider Gorgona as a result, an attempt or a failure?," "Is Gorgona boring?," "What is the name of your medical doctor?." It is possible to link their specific actions to the surrealist tradition. More than anything else, however, we associate Josip Vaništa, as the "ideologist" of the group and the initiator of many of their activities, and the other members of the group with existential philosophy. Through the French *Nouveau Roman*, fundamental meaninglessness becomes one of the characteristics of many of their works. In addition, Vaništa studied Zen Buddhism and eastern philosophy, as well as the manner in which individual artists interpreted empty space in their works. The members of the Group often went on joint strolls in order to conduct "a committee inspection of the beginning of spring."[2] Members of the group gave each other titles and functions amongst themselves, a fact we learn from the correspondence exchanged between the members, describing the activities they undertook. The individual comments, as well as the titles of the roles that they held, reveal their witty commentary on the bureaucratic language used in the cultural domain at the time. In September 1962 they printed invitations to an exhibition that never took place, which read "You are obliged to attend." This invitation was sent to fifty addresses, without any additional explanation. In the socialist period which favored simple communication in the spirit of "comradery" over stuffy civic etiquette, the highly pompous style used to emphasize the importance of attending an exhibition ascribes a new level of meaning. The tone of the message is actually a sarcastic comment and critique of the social norms that had been preserved, even insisted upon, despite the claims that they had been surmounted due to the new socio-political system.

Over time, the group had become known for its anti-magazine *Gorgona*. Alongside its members, the authors who entirely devised some of the magazine's issues were Victor Vasarely, Harold Pinter and Dieter Roth, while Piero Manzoni, Enzo Mari and Robert Rauchenberg expressed the wish to develop their concepts for future editions. The magazine was established during the profoundly ideologized 1960s. It was dubbed an anti-magazine in order to emphasize its difference from the standard concept of a magazine, and it was imagined and created as an artist's book or a book as a work of art, by a

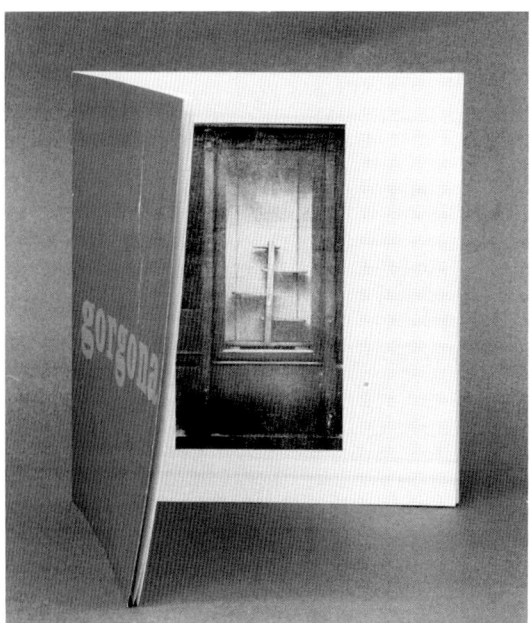

Figure 3.16

Josip Vaništa, Magazine
Gorgona, 1st issue,
1961. Photo by Boris
Cvjetanović. Courtesy of
Museum of Contemporay
Art, Zagreb.

group of authors who were "absorbed by a magazine on the margins, in which [they] introduced some dark ingredients, absurdity and emptiness."[3] (Fig. 3.16) The magazine's first issue, published in 1961, today holds an almost mythical status. The issue featured nine identical photographs, taken upon the instructions that Josip Vaništa had given to the photojournalist Pavao Cajzek. The photograph was taken after Vaništa, during a stroll, noted an empty shelf in the display of a Zagreb store. Thanks to the writings of the author himself, it is possible to reconstruct what caught his attention: "A spatial construction without function, which was offered for sale."[4] The textual description and the integral documentary footage testify to a small second-hand shop, mediating the atmosphere that dominated the city of Zagreb at that time. (Gattin: 2002, 29) The photograph can also be interpreted as a witty comment on the growing consumerist craze which started to spread in Yugoslavia in the early 1960s.

   In the documentary footage displaying the shop, we can notice a number of details which contribute to gaining deeper insight into the circumstances which captured Vaništa's attention. In addition to the empty shelves, there is a vase with three flowers and a lamp haphazardly placed in the other part of the shop window, thus creating a surreal and completely unappealing composition. The composition is "rounded out" by the inscription "Unusual America." The peculiar mixture of rural and urban clothing and the body language of the woman filmed from the back upon entering the shop, as well as the unkempt, almost dilapidated awning, give the final finish to the ironic commentary of the entire scene from which the abovementioned detail is isolated and reduplicated.

"The dissonance and the obvious intelligibility of the whole, as well as its foolishness, serve as irrefutable proof that its impossibility has been overcome in the only way possible, by preserving its main best feature." (Gattin, 2002: 10)

Gorgona is an intellectual whole to which we cannot attribute a certain artistic activity or medium. The group cannot be described by a single definition, since "definitions are but the simplest descriptions of facts… they describe only one thing." (Knifer, 1983: 28) Gorgona anticipated typical artistic practices of the 1970s, among other things, through the use of the book as an artististic work, art as behavior, the use of language as a medium and art as an idea. (Gattin, 2009: 21) Predisposition towards irony is frequently found in their works. (Dimitrijević, 1977: n. p.) It is possible to relate it to metaphysical emptiness and a realism in which elements of astonishment, "interventions from the side of secure and lasting material artistic objects" dominate. (Denegri, 2012: n. p.) The members of the group were brought together by a tendency towards spaces of isolation and silence, and the intellectual contemplation of "nothingness." Their activities through the years have developed an almost mythical status, yet it is important to emphasize that they were themselves responsible for the establishment and preservation of their "marginal" position outside the hierarchy of the local artistic scene. Its work was not forbidden and its members' occasional exhibitions were held in the Šira picture-framing workshop, located in Zagreb city centre.

In a few of their actions and works, dating from the early 1960s, it is possible to recognize the visual translation of the meaningless and the absurd as oft-mentioned strategies in the context of conceptual art. The collage *Thought for April* depicts a photograph of a headless man, taken from a newspaper; the space is minimally marked by a line on the lawn, in the background. Nothing is happening; "The word replaces the image," as I was once told by Vaništa. The work's title suggests contemplation, yet the man in the suit is headless and the *marche à pied* is literally reduced to a mechanical "step by step." Vaništa revealed that this image is reminiscent of Henri Troyat, the French writer, historian and academic, and his "headless" 10 kilometer-long daily running sessions while on vacation. As a well-versed connoisseur of the French cultural scene, in the *Thoughts for Months* Vaništa also refers to Yves Klein and his thesis on the connection between life and art, and to the void as the basic preoccupation shared by both artists within the zone of immaterial sensibility. (Stipančić, 2007: 155)

Adoration is an intimate work, a performance act photographed by Branko Balić, a photographer who was close to Gorgona and documented several of their actions and portraits. (Fig. 3.17) His photographs preserved the atmosphere of one of Gorgona's "delusive" actions, performed in 1966. This action was a homage to the painter Julije Knifer whose exhibition was taking place at the Gallery of Contemporary Art in Zagreb. It consisted of a play with a hat, kissing Knifer's hands, lifting a top hat into the air, and the group's members posing for photographs. All of the actions listed above are in fact humoristic comments on the formal ceremo-

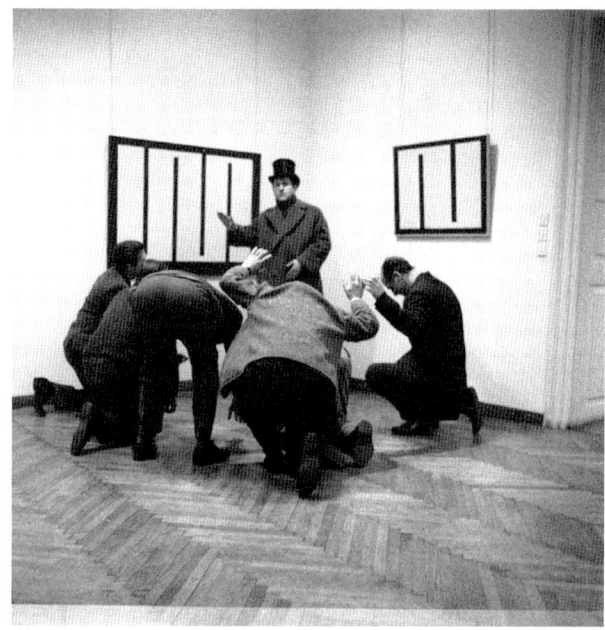

nies that usually accompany exhibitions. When directed by Gorgona, however, the "ceremony" was held without an audience and only for the camera. In this way, they poked fun at the social ritual of the exhibition, as well as the position of the artist himself. The top hat, and the kissing of hands, speak of the status that many artists desired, and which the members of the group always refused to accept. It was their way of achieving pleasure in life through humor, thereby momentarily triumphing over the rest of society. Such playfulness and mockery reflect the spirit of the Neo-Dada. The photograph was taken immediately after the New Year's festivities: Vanista recalls his fellow members and himself mocking the programed merriment which everyone is expected to express during those days. (Stipančić, 2007: 159) As Đuro Seder, one of Gorgona's members, also observed, "*Adoration* did not address reality and made no political comments; the jokes and the absurdity resulted from the artists' individual preferences."[5]

Gorgona adopted the strategies of expanding the space of the non-material art and of art as behavior. Their statements refer to nihilism and the questioning of social norms from which the group members distance themselves in different ways, for instance by engaging in "headless strolls." They felt isolated in their artistic practice, and as such it is no surprise that these several likeminded individuals aimed to try out a collective "experiment of living." (Stipančić: 2007, 149) Their artistic strategy can be perceived as a constructive aspect of "self-organisation and the self-institutionalising action." (Bago, Majača: 2009, 120)

Some of their experiments have been recorded through *staged photographs*, as Gattin called them. One such photograph was also taken by Branko Balić in the courtyard of the Contemporary Art Gallery—it depicted Ivo Steiner (a sociologist who worked for the Ministry of Culture at the time, a distinguished connoisseur of culture and art, educated in Frankfurt and Paris) sitting between two trash bins. (Fig. 3.18) We should also not neglect the humorous tone in this photograph, which offers a funny and even ironic critique of the cultural and art scene.

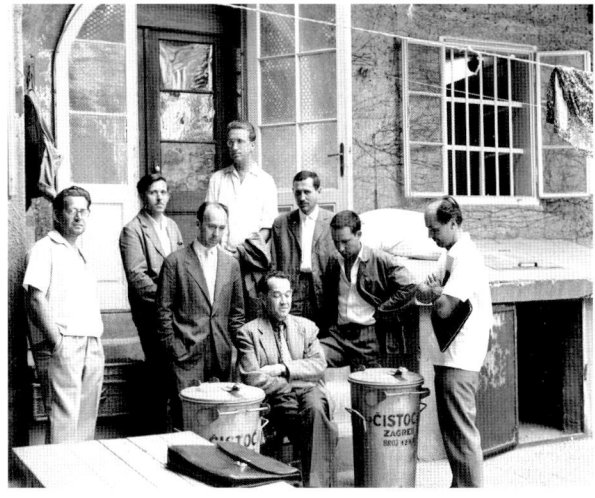

Figure 3.18

Branko Balić, Members of *Gorgona* in the courtyard of the Gallery of Contemporary Art, Zagreb, early 1960s. Courtesy of Institute of Art History, Zagreb.

Their several collective identities are not preserved in group recordings, but are, as is the case with *Collective legitimacy (Photo-compensation)*, the result of a different kind of intervention. This series of appropriated and "revised" photographs was created in 1961. Josip Vaništa reworked his portrait to resemble the composer Milan Horvat and combined it with the retouched portraits of his fellow Gorgona members. He noticed how strongly they resembled other artists (Jean Marais and Ivan Kožarić, Paul Gauguin and Julije Knifer, Matko Meštrović and Gertrude Stein, Đuro Seder and Delacroix, Radoslav Putar and the actor who rested his head on Marina Vlady's bosom). Vaništa's game with non-existent situations could be understood as a reaction to a social identity that was shaped through interaction with others, at a time when it seemed as though nothing was happening and when art was being created in pursuit of a normal life. Because of the accidental discovery of similarities between historical figures and the members of the group, the subconscious association, the non-dismissible humor as well as the willingness to play, the work can be linked to Surrealism, which appeared simultaneously in Zagreb and Belgrade at the beginning of the 1930s. In addition, this work, and the practices of the Gorgona members in general, reveal links with the specific humor of the New York Neo Dada movement, as well as the influence of Marcel Duchamp, because of the priority given to the personality of the artist's subject, and not his object.

The aforementioned works treat photography as a transformative medium. Yet the medium itself was not able to convey complex mental processes, and as such the structure of the work itself required the addition of language. Language was a method of wider communication, which was necessary for the creation of the anti-magazine, for example, and was inescapable in the intellectual formation that their whole practice depended on. Language is food for the soul, a medium that helped them to exchange stories amongst themselves and to elaborate them, or to write out absurd commentaries. Although today the individual members of the group insist on the seriousness with which they approached their collective practice, it is impossible to ignore Gorgona's humor and irony. Their jokes were never banal; they were the result of a concept based on the collective contemplation of art, the focus of which is not the material object but rather its maker, and an absurd behavior which could never be entirely decoded.

The Goran Trbuljak Case – A Critique of the Art System (and an Occasional Manipulation)

The new social role of artists and new means of expression began to resonate strongly in the public sphere from the 1960s onward. In Croatia, an innovative period in contemporary art began in the second half of the 1960s, which was to a large extent characterized by the so-called New Art Practice (1966–1978). This included a variety of developments which bore witness to the use of new media, a changed artistic practice and understanding of the very notion of the artistic work, and the specific social engagement of the artist. (Susovski, 1978: 3) During this period artists analyzed and questioned reality, and approached several parts of society, as well as cultural institutions, critically.

Although the artists who adhered to the New Art Practice did not constitute a formal group, Goran Trbuljak can be considered as a "practitioner" as he critically questioned the role of art in society and its deep-rooted systems. At the very beginning of his career, in the late 1960s and early 1970s, Trbuljak explored the existential questions of (being) an artist. He scrutinized the conditions of artistic production, exhibiting only a few artefacts, which attested to his authorial intentions. For instance, a piece of canvas and paint were sufficient to inform the viewer about his intention to paint. Trbuljak's concepts were almost always formed from words, which he perceived as a kind of "material" from which he derived meaning in his art practice.

Insightful, intelligent and inclined to self-irony, Trbuljak has, from very early on, demonstrated his analytical skills, scepticism and a sense of humor, which we still notice in his practice today. In the national context, Trbuljak's artistic contribution is also important because he is perceived as a direct successor of Gorgona's poetics. Trbuljak is sensitive to the non-representative depictions that he encounters in everyday life: he combines motifs, freely explores different media and changes the context in order to transform their meaning. Squatting in a vacant apartment and temporally transforming it into an art studio was a part of his complex conceptual strategy of questioning the meaning of the exhibition space, the artist's role and position, as well as his social relevance. (Trbuljak, 1978: 31–33) The photographs recorded in the medieval Lotrščak Tower in Zagreb, which he broke into and used as an art studio for several days, reveal the unusual and occasionally absurd vistas, and reflect the author's skepticism and analytical approach, softened through humor and irony.

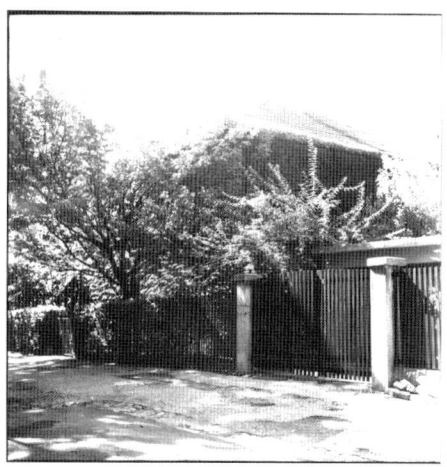

In the photo-series called *Four Houses at Rokov perivoj and One Nearby* (1976–1977), Trbuljak dealt with the working conditions of artists, as well as with the problem of their working space. (Fig. 3.19) Even though in the 1970s there was a system of assigning rooms in municipal and state ownership for art studios, the artists of the New Art Practice, who critically questioned the role of art in society and dethroned the modernist artist by refusing to produce pretty pictures to decorate the apartments of the red *bourgeoisie*, were usually ignored. Within the context of practice that contemporary art history termed "critique of the art system," Trbuljak photographed urban villas, the homes of distinguished artists in Rokov perivoj, a high-class district of Zagreb. He thereby tackled the structural issue of artistic production in the time of socialism, doing this with an inevitable humoristic approach. Beneath each of the five black-and-white photographs that show these houses, the artist wrote an explanation:

> In this house lives my peer and namesake. His mother, a painter, has had a large number of independent exhibitions all over the world. Her works have mostly been presented in our diplomatic missions, consulates and embassies.

Or:

> I remember the period between 1955 and 1964, when my class went to visit a house that had just been built by a famous sculptor. I was not familiar with his sculptures back then and for a long time afterwards the house lingered in my memory as the only sculpture that he had ever made. Even years later, having become acquainted with his work, my perception remained the same – for me that house really appeared to be the only sculpture he ever made.

Trbuljak's works from this period, at a time when artists went out into and worked in the public space, are frequently recorded through photography, through which the photograph affirms its role as a document. Nevertheless, the artist himself also highlights the existence of the *spaces in between*; such as when, on a photograph that is a document, he adds a text written by hand or with a typewriter. His work is characterized by processuality, concealing and maintaining distance (with respect to the work and the audience), as well as by his inclination to doubt and to question the meanings of his personal artistic practice. He focuses on objective reality, on prosaic details from which he then distances himself with the help of ironic statements. The photograph thus confirms the word, while the word confirms the photograph, highlighting the double nature of reality. One statement reads, for example, "From time to time I stuck my finger through a hole in the door of the Modern Gallery without the management's knowledge." (Fig. 3.20) This light-hearted and provocative action was directed at the passers-by, although we do not know how many of them really noticed Trbuljak's finger inviting them to enter the Gallery. The artist's relaxed and unbinding gesture is in contrast to the serious and untouchable institution. Trbuljak's approach is witty and

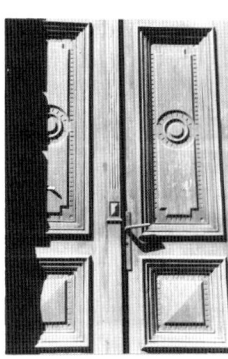

Kroz rupu na vratima Galerije moderne umjetnosti povremeno sam provlačio prst bez znanja uprave galerije

Figure 3.20

Goran Trbuljak, "From time to time I stuck my finger through a hole in the door of the Modern Gallery without the management's knowledge.", 1969. Courtesy of the artist.

somewhat impudent; it mocks the institution of culture while, at the same time, being liberating for the artist himself who, through such actions, gains space for his artistic practice.

A number of his works are marked by a specific humor, utilizing self-conscious irony to examine his position and perception of himself as an artist. The cycle *Ant* (1970) is a procedural game, which explores the relationship to a living being through a self-reflexive confessional form. (Fig. 3.21) The photographs show the uneven surface of a wall and a marked space where he killed an ant, with a typed inscription underneath: "I killed an ant." "I killed another ant." … "I killed an ant because of art." "I killed an ant without a reason." "I killed an ant because it gave me a dirty look."

In his installations and "invisible" performances in public spaces, he uses strategies of recognition, evaluation and appropriation, creating witty urban mimicries counting on a sensitized audience. In a certain way, his work appears to be destabilizing within the system itself, leaving individuals feeling insecure in an artistic ambiance, which is neither descriptive nor pictorial.

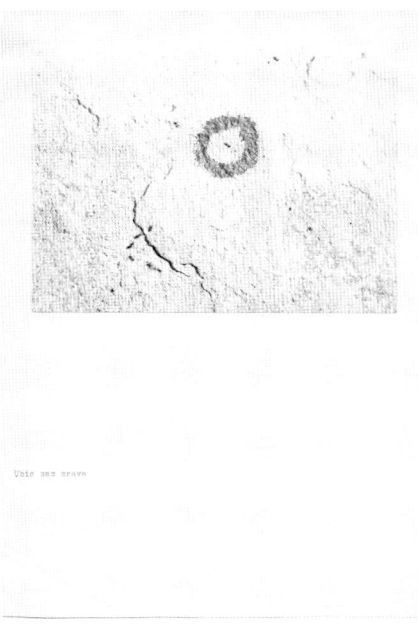

Figure 3.21

Goran Trbuljak, from the series *Ant*, 1970. Courtesy of the artist.

Mladen Stilinović's Linguistic Discussion

Mladen Stilinović approached art beyond the ontological questions of the medium. Moreover, his artworks have an aura of poverty and are often made out of modest materials, including various ordinary objects for everyday use, such as textiles, dishes, notebooks, cardboard pieces and plain sheets of paper. He often appropriated photographs from mass media or obtained them from the flea market. He took some pictures himself, while the rest were taken by others following his instructions. Photographs are elements which help him to build specific compositions, adding to them with lingual declarations, drawings and subjects. In this way he explores the main themes in his opus, such as political ideology, the ideology of art, manipulation of language, positions of power, and economy and money.

Stilinović was an attentive observer and referred directly to the perceived and intellectually-processed reality. In his surroundings, he noticed traces of social divisions, inequality and political action. An infantile slogan "Ado loves Stipa" [Ado voli Stipu] was placed between

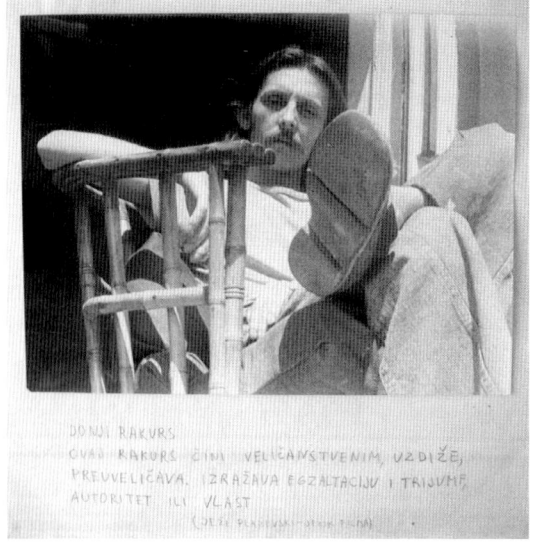
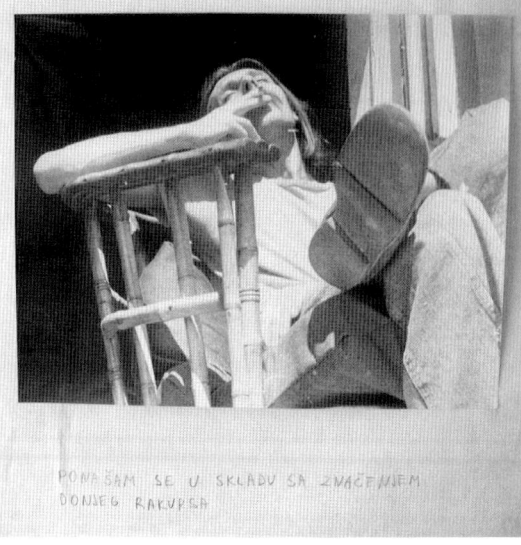

official banners during Labor Day celebrations (*1st May 1975*, 1975).
(Fig. 3.22) It referred to the pathetic proclamations of the collective
program which, at the time, functioned on the principles of the so-
called *red bourgeoisie*. Such a program was not based on the concept
of equality, but rather operated as a capitalist society under the mask
of socialism. Within such a socio-political context, the proclaimed celebration of the aforementioned holiday was just theoretical. Stilinović

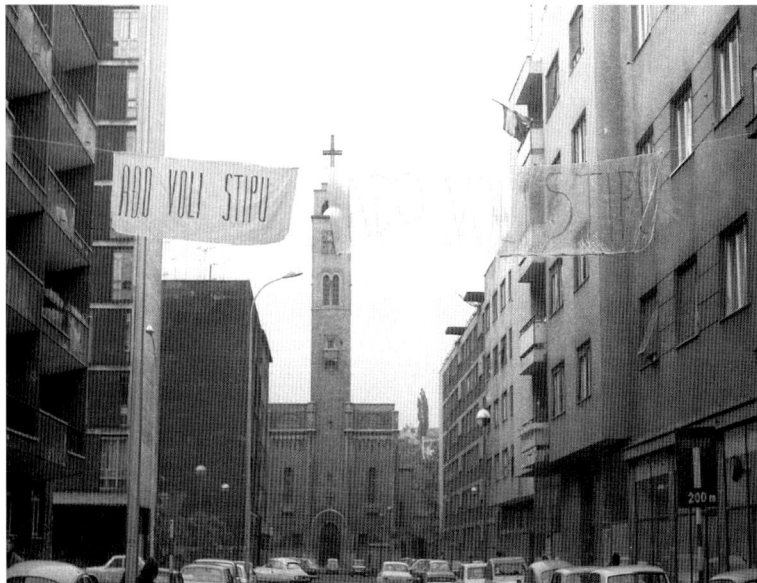

Figure 3.22

Mladen Stilinović, *Ađo
Loves Stipa* (from *1st May
1975*), 1975. Courtesy of
Artist's Estate, Zagreb.

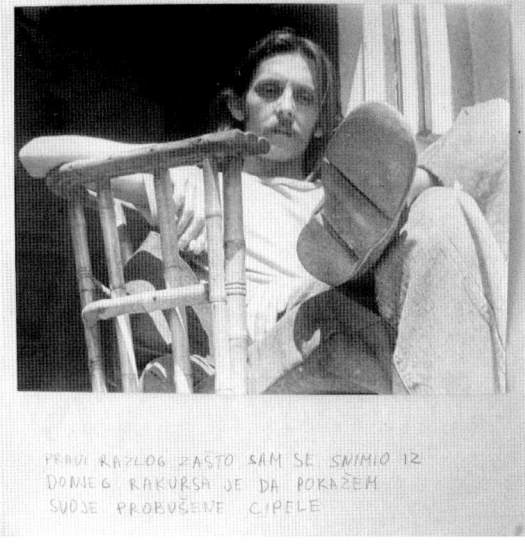

PRAVI RAZLOG ZAŠTO SAM SE SNIMIO IZ
DONJEG RAKURSA JE DA POKAŽEM
SVOJE PROBUŠENE CIPELE

PORIJEKLO ZNAČENJA DONJEG RAKURSA

supplemented its fragmented and reduced meaning with an intimate message addressed to his wife, expressed by a witty comment which spoke about the invisibility of official proclamations in public discourse.

Stilinović confronted social limitations and society's lack of understanding, to which he reacted through knowledge, research and humor. Over the years, he developed a personal strategy of documenting social reality, which helped him to define his artistic position in society, as well as to outline the position of the individual. In the course of his complex and long-standing artistic practice, Stilinović produced photographs that indirectly speak of the author who does not describe the visible, but rather focuses his work on making what is *seen* to become once again *visible*. For instance, in *Low Camera Angle* (1978; Fig. 3.23), Stilinović followed the rules of the low camera angle while actually photographing a hole in the sole of his shoe. In his wish to give it a pathetic ending, Stilinović ends the sequence with a view of the sky, which—as the artist once told me—is a reference to Jerzy Płażewski's film theory and the symbolic relation of the camera angle and the sky.

Stilinović simultaneously used humor as the only available strategy of survival and freedom. The titles of his works often play a key role and function as humorous teasers, supplying the work with its full meaning. In the cycle *Artist at Work* (1978; Fig. 3.24), the artist is photographed as he changes positions while sleeping on a couch. The ironic message that trivializes the position of the artist ("slacker") during the socialist period—when the principal norm was labour—can be seen as a part of the artist's deliberations on idleness. In his *Praise of Idleness* from 1993, he stated that it is "a privileged category of artists from the East,"

Figure 3.23

Mladen Stilinović, *Low Angle*, 1978. Courtesy of Artist's Estate, Zagreb.

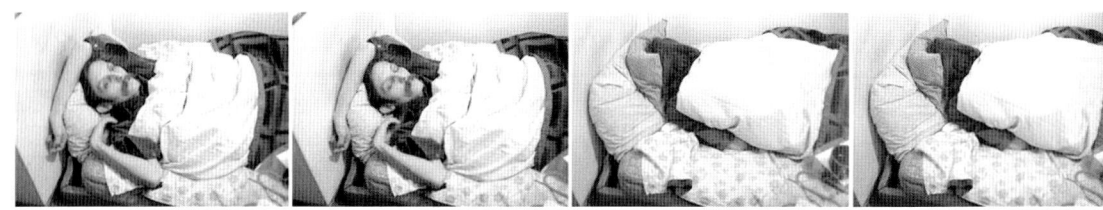

who — unless they speak English — cannot even be considered as being artists. (Stilinović, 1993: 1003)

In the 1970s, Stilinović was exploring the philosophy of language and reading the pioneers of modern semiotics, such as Bakhtin, with whom he agreed that "speech is a sensitive indicator of the socio-political systems and of social and political changes." (Stipančić, 2013: 38) Stilinović used words — witty and ironic combinations of images and text — to critically question everyday life. The media at that time described daily life as a celebration of production and progress. They employed empty words, metaphors and symbols celebrating socialist achievements, while at the same time entirely different processes were taking place in the background.

There are two pivotal colors in his work — red and pink. Red is the color of revolution, communism and socialism, to which the artist "gives" its freedom by ridiculing the standard symbolism. Pink is a diluted version of red, a color of rococo, pleasure and the *petit bourgeoisie*. Its meaning is opposite to the color red which had an almost sacrosanct status in the former Yugoslavia. Stilinović gives a humorous tone to the meaning of red through his statements about it being washed-out. He puts the color to an auction, appropriates it and blanches it, as a sign of his cynical rebellion against the social symbolism and the ruling ideology. In his photography, he "circumvented" the routine assumptions about the medium and its role; it is draped in humor, testifying to its depletion. By becoming a part of his unique expression, photography enabled him to act "outside the crowd," to rebel.

Conclusion

The Croatian segment of conceptual art can undoubtedly be considered as a part of concurrent international tendencies. Since it was formed in an urban surrounding and marked by certain aspects of social and cultural reality, it represents "an alternative to the crisis of modernist art." (Šuvaković, 2005: 313) The examples considered above

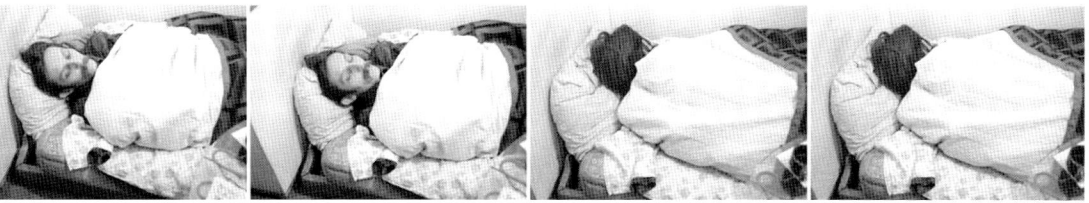

illustrate the specific cultural, social and political atmosphere that has dominated Croatia since the 1960s.

The proto-conceptual strategies that started to emerge in the early 1960s and conceptual art practices in the 1970s prioritized freedom of creation and behavior, autonomy from the state, and intellectual resistance to the forces that deprived the individual of a life lived in accordance with his personal needs. These artists used humor, irony and absurdity as secondary means to somewhat alleviate the conditions of artistic production, without diminishing the subversive aspects of their works. They responded to social divisions, disparities, limitations and lack of understanding with knowledge and, often enough, humor. This was how they created an important *oeuvre* of analytical, critical and self-reflexive works, making almost invisible interventions in public or certain exhibition spaces. The experiments in language, critiques and parodies of political and social norms, as well as of artistic ones, attest to the emergence of a new generation of artists who — with varied intensity — were active within social and artistic fields.

Figure 3.24

Mladen Stilinović, *Artist at Work*, 1978. Courtesy of Artist's Estate, Zagreb.

Notes

1. Josip Vaništa in his letter addressed to me, written on January 8, 2013.

2. The words of Radoslav Putar, as quoted in Vaništa's letter.

3. From the text "What is Gorgona?", written by Vaništa in his letter addressed to me, January 8, 2013.

4. Ješa Denegri, "Gorgona – Nekad i Danas" ("Gorgona – Then and Today"), http://post.at.moma.org/content_items/261-gorgona-nekad-i-danas (accessed on December 12, 2014)

5. From an interview with the author, Autumn 2014.

Bibliography

Ivana Bago, Antonia Majača, "Pljuni istini u oči (a zatim brzo zatvori oči pred istinom)" ["Spit in the Eye of Truth (Then Quickly Close Your Eyes Before It"], Život umjetnosti, 83 (Winter 2008): 108–141.

Ješa Denegri, "Problemi umjetničke prakse posljednjeg decenija", in Nova umjetnička praksa 1966 – 1978., ed. Marijan Susovski (Zagreb: Galerija suvremene umjetnosti, 1978), 5–13.

Ješa Denegri, "Inside or Outside 'Socialist Modernism'? Radical Views on the Yugoslav Art Scene, 1950–1970", in Impossible Histories. Historical Avant-gardes, Neo-avant-gardes, and Post-avant-gardes in Yugoslavia, 1918–1991, eds Dubravka Djurić, Miško Šuvaković (Cambridge: MIT, 2003), 170–208.

Marija Gattin, Protokol dostavljanja misli (Zagreb: Muzej suvremene umjetnosti, 2002).

M. Ga [Marija Gattin]/Nada Beroš, "Gorgona", Akcenti – Zbirke u pokretu, exh. cat. (Zagreb: Muzej suvremene umjetnosti, 2009), 20–21.

Julije Knifer, "Zapisi", Život umjetnosti, 35 (1983): 28–34.

Ljiljana Kolešnik, "Konfliktne vizije moderniteta i poslijeratna moderna umjetnost [Conflicting Visions of Modernity and the Post-war Modern Art]", in Socijalizam i modernost: Umjetnost, kultura, politika 1950-1974 [Socialism and Modernity. Art, Culutre, Politics 1950-1974] (Zagreb: Institut za povijest umjetnosti & Muzej suvremene umjetnosti, 2012), 107–179.

Davor Matičević, Fotografija u Hrvatskoj od tisuću devetsto pedesete do danas, exh. cat. (Zagreb: Muzej suvremene umjetnosti, 1997), 9–18.

Mladen Stilinović, "Pohvala lijenosti", Kolo, 11–12 (1993): 1003–1004.

Branka Stipančić, Josip Vaništa. Vrijeme Gorgone i Postgorgone [The Time of Gorgona and Post-Gorgona] (Zagreb: Kratis, 2007).

Branka Stipančić, Mladen Stilinović. Nula iz vladanja [Mladen Stilinović. Zero for Conduct], exh. cat. (Zagreb, Muzej suvremene umjetnosti & Mladen Stilinović, 2013), 34–41.

Miško Šuvaković, Pojmovnik suvremene umjetnosti (Zagreb, Ghent: Horetzky, Vlees&Beton, 2005).

Goran Trbuljak, "Izložba u Galeriji Nova", SPOT, 11 (1978): 31–33.

About the Authors

Kevin Atherton (PhD) is a Manx artist born in the Isle of Man in 1950 who has been based since 1999 in Ireland, where until recently he was the "Head of Post Graduate Pathways" in the Faculty of Fine Art at the National College of Art and Design (NCAD) Dublin. Prior to moving to Ireland in 1999 he had been the Head of Fine Art Media at Chelsea College of Art (University of the Arts London). As a part of the generation of artists who pioneered video and performance art in the UK in the 1970s Atherton has performed and presented work throughout the world including at Tate Britain, The San Francisco Museum of Modern Art (SFMOMA), and at the Museum of Modern Art Vienna (MUMOK).

Mieke Bleyen is a postdoctoral researcher at the Lieven Gevaert Research Centre for Photography and the Institute for Cultural Studies at the KU Leuven. Her fields of interest are photography theory, contemporary art, (post-) Surrealism, and visual culture. For her PhD research she developed the concept of "minor photography" in the context of the photographic work of Belgian surrealist Marcel Mariën. This resulted in two publications: *Minor Photography. Connecting Deleuze and Guattari to Photography Theory* (2012) and *Minor Aesthetics. The Work of Marcel Mariën* (2014) both published within the Lieven Gevaert Series, Leuven University Press.

Anna Corrigan is a translator and editor living in Berlin. She holds a BA in Comparative Literature from Cornell University and an MA from St. Andrews University, Universidade Nova de Lisboa, and Universidade Santiago de Compostela (Erasmus Mundus Crossways in Cultural Narratives). She is currently applying for a PhD to continue her research on visual culture and the avant-garde in Argentina.

Liesbeth Decan teaches theory and history of photography at LUCA School of Arts – Campus Sint-Lukas Brussels, where she is also the co-ordinator of the research group Photography Expanded. Her research is focused on the use of photography by artists, especially in Belgium, between the 1960s and early 1990s. She is a fellow professor of the Lieven Gevaert Research Centre for Photography, Art and Visual Culture. In 2016 she published the book, *Conceptual, Surrealist, Pictorial. Photo-Based Art in Belgium (1960s – early 1990s)* (Leuven University Press, Lieven Gevaert Series).

Hilde D'haeyere is a photographer and film historian who investigates photographic aspects of silent cinema. Much of her work is on slapstick comedy, with a focus on film style, movie technology and the mechanisms of humor. Recent publications include "Slapstick on Slapstick" in *Film History* 26:2 (2014), "Mack Sennett" in *Oxford Bibliographies in Cinema and Media Studies* (Oxford University Press, 2015), and "Frankfurter Slapstick: Benjamin, Kracauer and Adorno on American Screen Comedy," in *October* 160 (2017), co-authored with Steven Jacobs. Currently she holds a post-doctoral research fellowship at the KASK School of Arts at the University College Ghent in Belgium, where she heads the master's program Film.

Heather Diack is Assistant Professor of Contemporary Art at the University of Miami. Diack holds a PhD from the University of Toronto, and is a graduate of the art history program of McGill University and the Independent Study Program of the Whitney Museum of American Art. Her recent writing has appeared in *Bruce Nauman: A Contemporary* (Laurenz, 2018), *The "Public" Life of Photographs* (M.I.T. Press and Ryerson Image Centre, 2016), *Photography and Doubt* (Routledge, 2016), and journals including *Visual Studies* and *photographies*. Diack's scholarship has received numerous awards and fellowships including a Terra Foundation for American Art Visiting Professorship at the Freie Universität Berlin and an Ansel Adams Research Fellowship at the Center for Creative Photography.

David Helbich has been living and working in Brussels since 2002. He studied composition in Amsterdam and Freiburg. His works take place on stages, on paper, online and in the public space. His trajectory moves between representative and interactive works, pieces and interventions, between conceptual work and actions. They have recently been presented at Martin-Gropius-Bau (Berlin), Palais de Tokyo (Paris), Oude Kerk (Amsterdam), Queens Museum and UnionDocs (New York). Apart from being a teacher, as for example at the International Summer Courses for New Music Darmstadt, he is the author of the bestselling photo books *Belgian solutions – volume 1* and *volume 2* (Luster, Antwerp). Many of his works address concrete physical and social experiences. A recurrent interest is the direct work with a self-performing audience. His concepts are often presented in print, such as photo and score books as well as in live performances and audio guides.

Louis Kaplan is Professor of History and Theory of Photography and New Media at the University of Toronto. His most recent book on *Photography and Humour* (2016) was published by Reaktion Books in London as part of their Exposures series. His previous books include *Laszlo Moholy-Nagy: Biographical Writings* (Duke, 1995), *American Exposures: Photography and Community in the Twentieth Century* (Minnesota, 2005), and *The Strange Case of William Mumler, Spirit Photographer* (Minnesota, 2008). Kaplan has published widely in the areas of photography studies, art history, and visual culture and he has an abiding research interest related to the role of humor in modern and contemporary art and culture. Professor Kaplan is a contributing editor to *History of Photography* and a member of the international board of advisors for *C/R: The New Centennial Review* and the *Journal of Photography and Culture.*

Ann Kristin Krahn is a doctoral candidate at Braunschweig University of Art. As of October 2013, she holds a scholarship in the PhD program "The Photographic Dispositif" founded by the German Research Foundation. Her dissertation project "CHRONOTATION. Zeit und Prozess im Werk Dieter Appelts" focusses on the sculptural, performative and photographic work of German artist Dieter Appelt and deals with questions of processuality and temporality in photography. Between 2005 and 2012 she studied German Literature and Philology at the Technical University Braunschweig as well as Art History and Aesthetics at Braunschweig University of Art. Recently, she co-edited the conference proceedings *Fotografisches Handeln* (Weimar: Jonas Verlag, 2016), which expanded the view of photography as image towards the notion of distributed agencies in the photographic act.

Sandra Križić Roban received an MA and PhD in art history from the University of Zagreb. Active as a critic, curator, lecturer and writer, Križić Roban is a senior research advisor at the Institute of Art History in Zagreb, where she also served as the editor-in-chief of the art journal *Život umjetnosti* (2000–2017). She is the author of the only two comprehensive studies on contemporary photography and painting in Croatia: *At Second Glance: The Positions of Contemporary Croatian Photography* (2010), and *Croatian Painting from 1945 to Today* (2013). In 2013 she co-founded *Office for Photography*, a not-for-profit association dedicated to researching and promoting contemporary photography. Her main research topics include contemporary art, history and theory of photography, post-war architecture, public space discourse and contemporary war memorials.

Esther Leslie is Professor of Political Aesthetics at Birkbeck, University of London. She is author of a number of books including *Walter Benjamin: Overpowering Conformism* (Pluto, 2000), *Hollywood Flatlands: Animation, Critical Theory and the Avant Garde* (Verso, 2002); *Synthetic Worlds: Nature, Art and the Chemical Industry* (Reaktion, 2005); *Derelicts: Thought Worms from the Wreckage* (Unkant, 2014) and *Liquid Crystals: The Science and Art of a Fluid Form* (Reaktion, 2016). She runs a website with Ben Watson: www.militantesthetix.co.uk.

Katarzyna Ruchel-Stockmans teaches contemporary art, photography and new media at the Free University of Brussels (VUB) and at KASK School of Arts, Ghent. Her research interests include photography and art theory, media archeology, documentary practices, postcolonial theories, East European cultures, history and representations. She is member of the Network for Research on Drones and Aesthetics. Her book *Images Performing History* appeared in 2015 with Leuven University Press.

Susana S. Martins is an FCT research fellow both at the Institute of Art History, Universidade NOVA de Lisboa (PT) and at the Institute of Cultural Studies, Katholieke Universiteit Leuven (BE). She holds a doctorate in photography and cultural studies from the KU Leuven. In her research on the history and theory of photography, she has been working on the intersection of photography, national identities, exhibitions, and print culture. Author of several journal articles on these topics, and involved in a project on printed photography and propaganda, she co-edited, with Anne Reverseau, the book *Paper Cities. Urban Portraits in Photographic Books* (2016). Martins has also been lecturing in the fields of photography, 19th-century visual culture and contemporary art history. She is currently Visiting Assistant Professor at Universidade NOVA de Lisboa.

Paulien Oltheten studied at the Rijksakademie, Amsterdam, and was in 2013 a resident artist at ISCP, New York. In 2017 she was working at Cité des Arts in Paris. She has given performances in cultural institutions such as PAC Milan (2018), Jeu de Paume, Paris (2017), De Buren, Brussels (2016); Fondatione Ratti, Como (2015); KW, Berlin (2015); NCCA Moscow (2015) and Helmhaus Zurich (2015). Recent exhibitions of her work include *Nouveau Prix Decouverte,* Les Rencontres de la Photography, Arles (2018); *Where do we go from here*, Annet Gelink/Ellen de Bruijne gallery, Amsterdam (2017); *The measure of our travelling feet*, Marres (2016); *Paulien Oltheten & Anouk Kruithof*, Stedelijk Museum Amsterdam (2014); *Off Walking*, MoCP Chicago (2013); *Desire Lines*, ACCA Melbourne (2013); *It's my imagination you know*, gallery

Fons Welters Amsterdam (2012) and *Walk on a line...* Nederlands Fotomuseum, Rotterdam (2011).

Johan Pas holds a PhD in art history. His field of research is the exhibition and publication histories of the 20th-century avant-gardes and neo-avant-gardes. He has talked, curated and published extensively on these subjects, his most recent book being *Artists' Publications: The Belgian Contribution* (Koenig Books, 2017). In 2015 he founded CRAP (Collection for Research on Artists' Publications) that holds a representative library of avant-garde and artists' publications released between 1888 and 2018. Pas teaches at the Royal Academy of Fine Art Antwerp and since October 2017 has been the dean of that institute. He is currently preparing, with David Vermeiren, a book on the editions and multiples of Guillaume Bijl. Johan Pas lives and works in Antwerp.

Lieven Segers holds a PhD in the Arts (on humor in arts) and teaches at the PXL-MAD (Hasselt) and LUCA School of Arts (Genk). He lives and works in Antwerp. Recent solo exhibitions of his include *Niets aan de hand, niets in de mouw en nog steeds niets tegen de muur* (Intersections, Art Rotterdam, 2018), *Niets aan de hand, niets in de mouw, niets tegen de muur* (Base Alpha Gallery, Antwerp, 2017), *Er Is Altijd Wel Iets Anders Te Doen* (Van Goghhuis, Zundert, 2017), *When The Mona Lisa Was Stolen In 1911, People Queued For Hours To See The Vacant Wall* (Box, Cc Maasmechelen, 2017), *Le Petit Maitre Liègois Meets Bassie Lebon* (duo-show with Jacques Lizène, Sint-Lukasgalerie, Brussels, 2015) and *The Joke Is On Me* (Base Alpha Gallery, Antwerp, 2015). As a guest curator he has also curated multiple exhibitions, such as *Pom Po Pon Po Pon Pon Pom Pon* for Middelheimmuseum Antwerp (2015), *11 kunstenaars tegen de muur* (Antwerp 2016), and *Un voyage autour de ma chambre* (Het Bos, Antwerp 2015).

Lieven Segers

Niets aan de hand, niets in de mouw, niets tegen de muur

2017

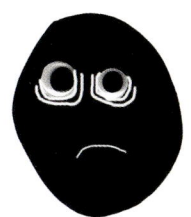
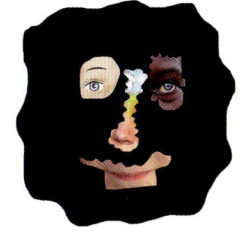
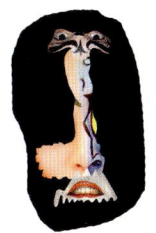
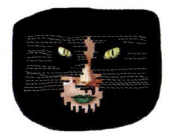
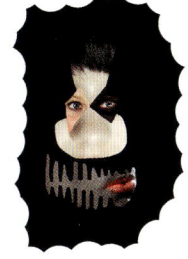
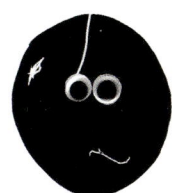
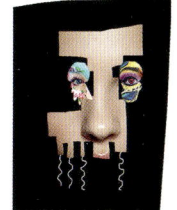
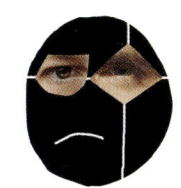
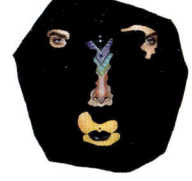
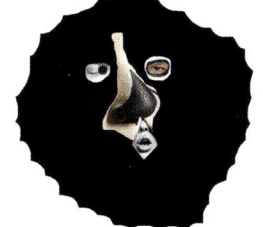
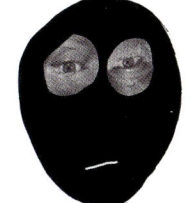
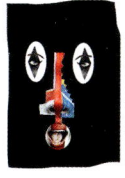
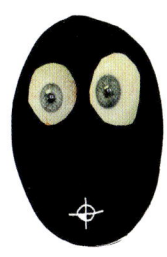
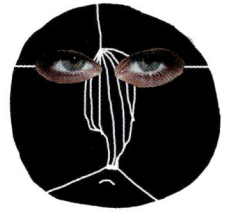
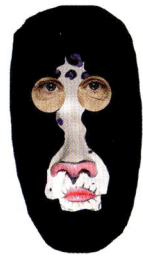

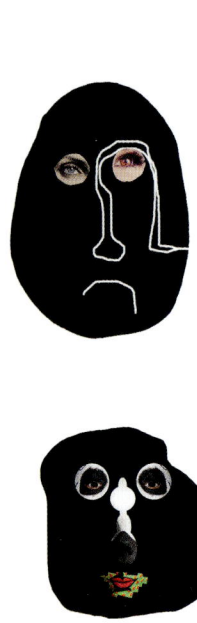
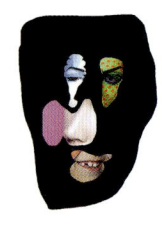
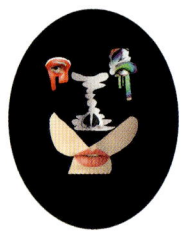
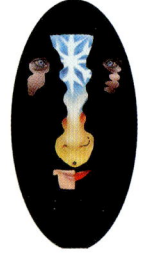
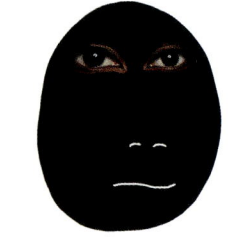
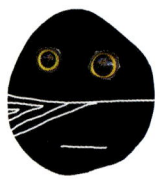
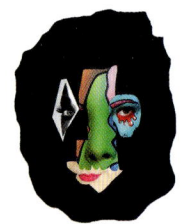
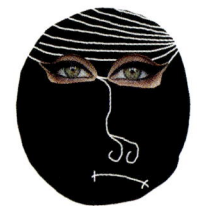
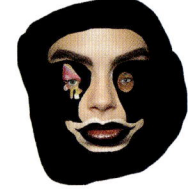
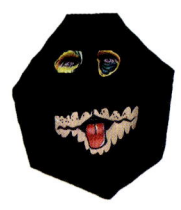
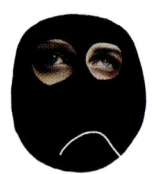
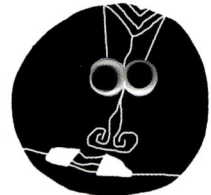

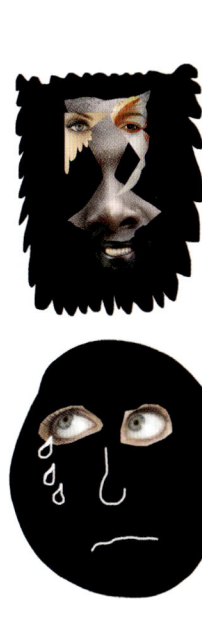
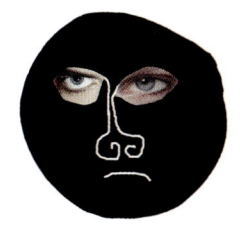
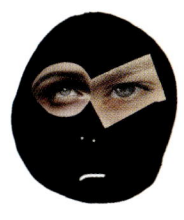
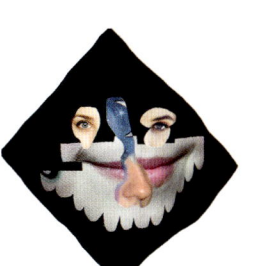
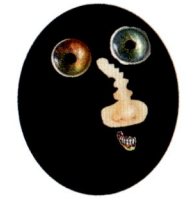
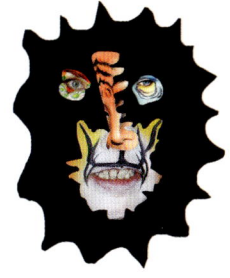
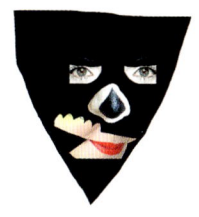
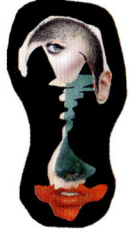
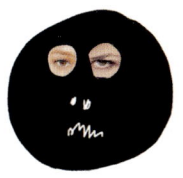
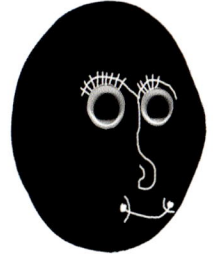
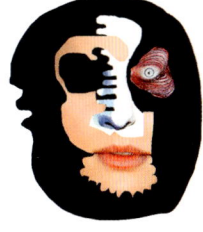
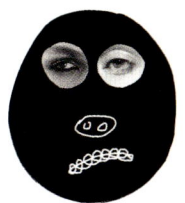
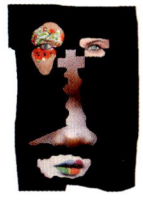
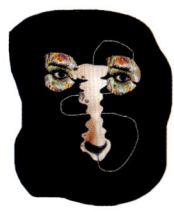

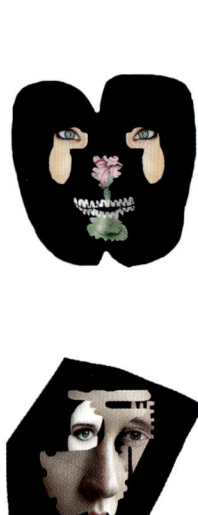 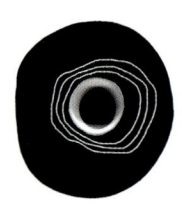 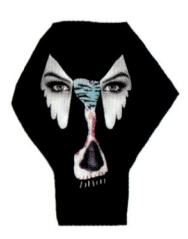
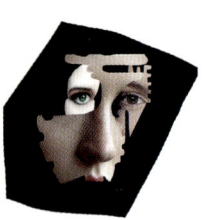 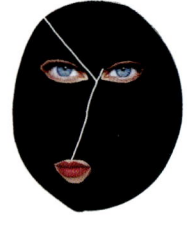 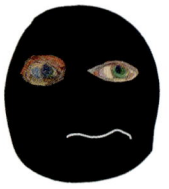
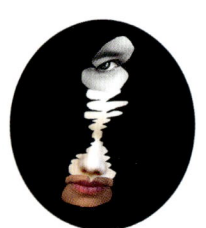 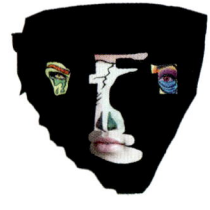 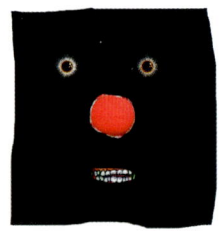
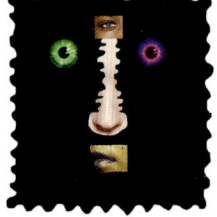 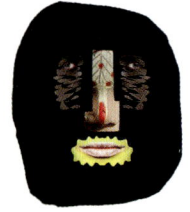 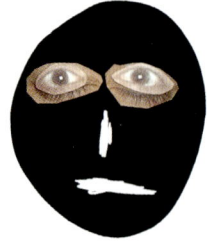
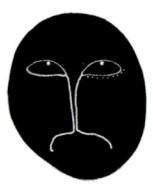 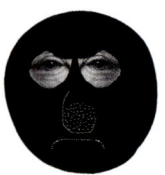 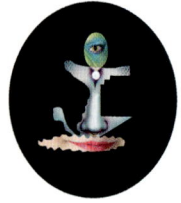

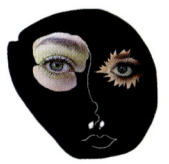
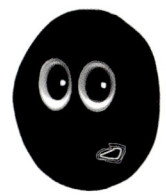
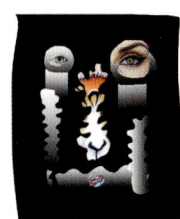
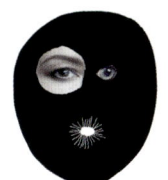
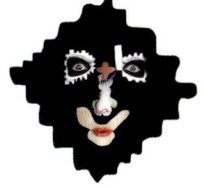
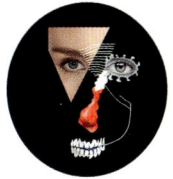
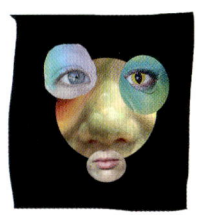
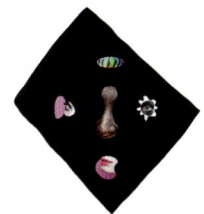
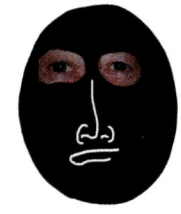
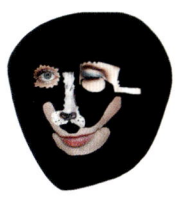
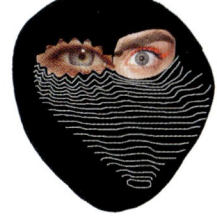
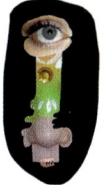
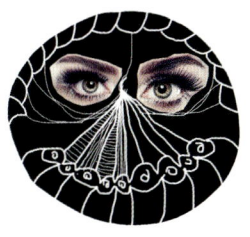
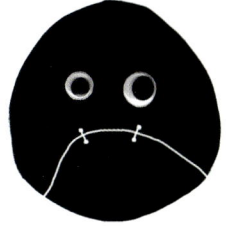
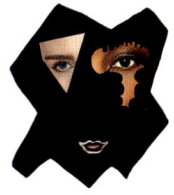

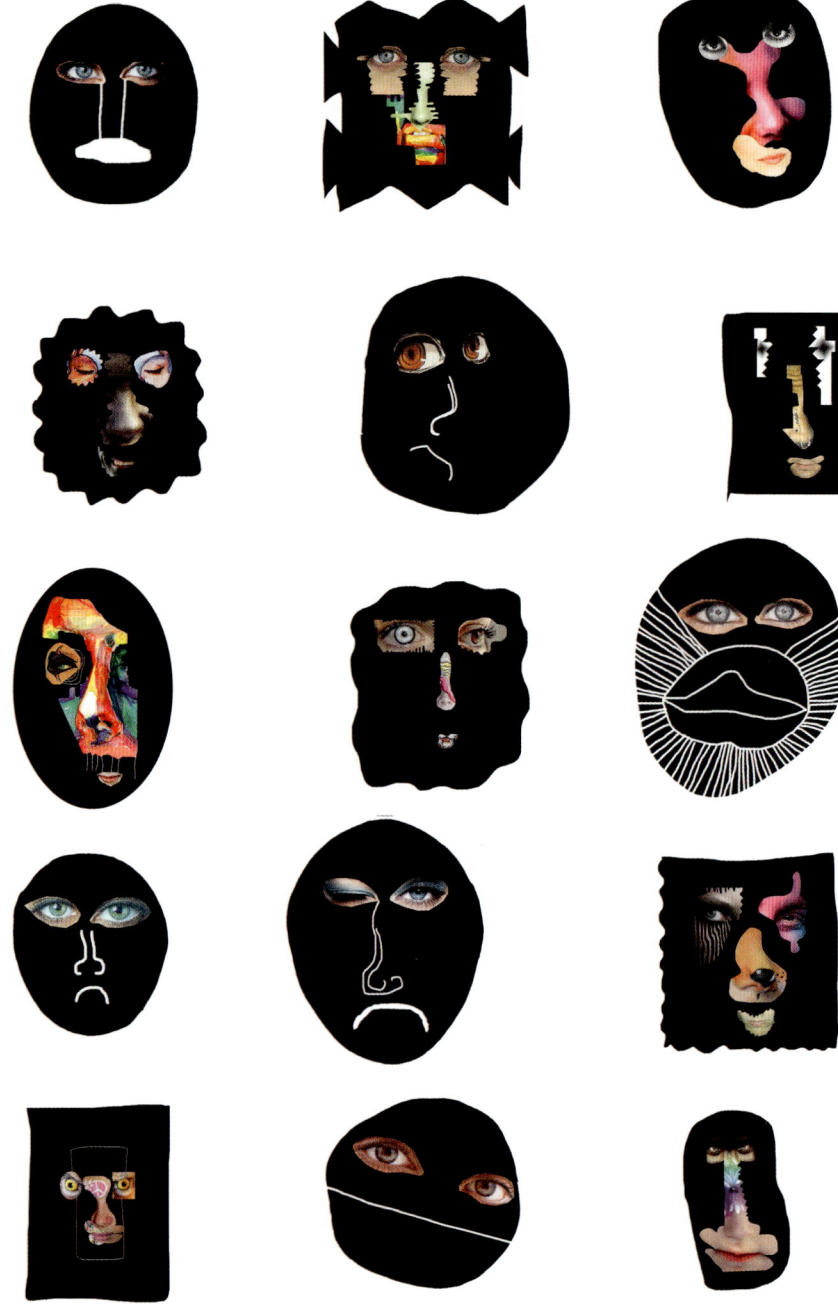

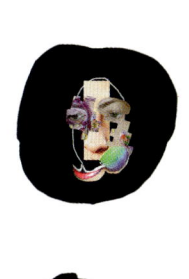
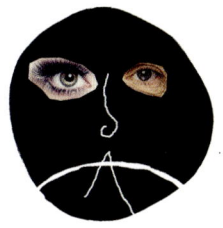
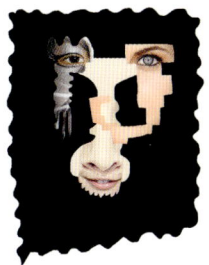
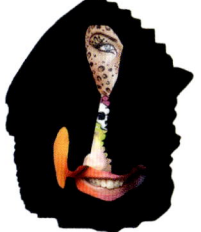
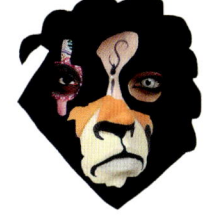
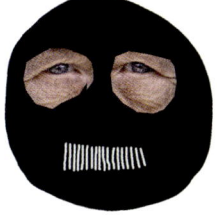
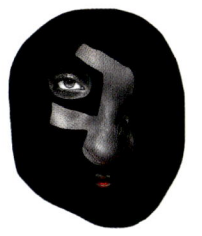
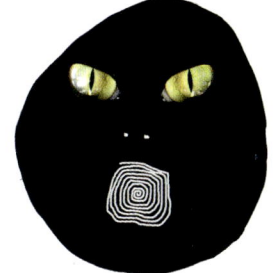
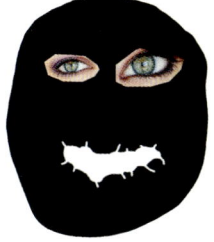
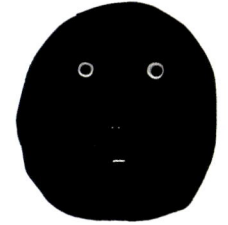
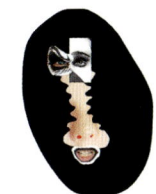
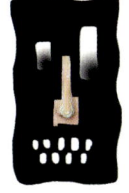
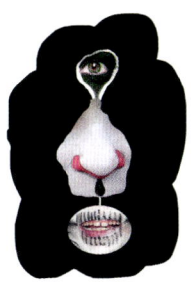
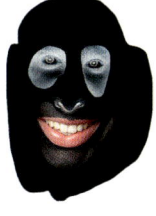
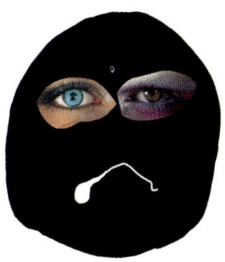

David Helbich

Trying to look like a building
Instagram + print
2015 – ongoing

1. Guggenheim Museum, New York

2. The New Museum, New York

3. Cathedral of St. Peter, Cologne

4. Tate Modern, London

5. Carnegie Hall, New York

6. St. Peter's Cathedral, Bremen

7. Atomium, Brussels

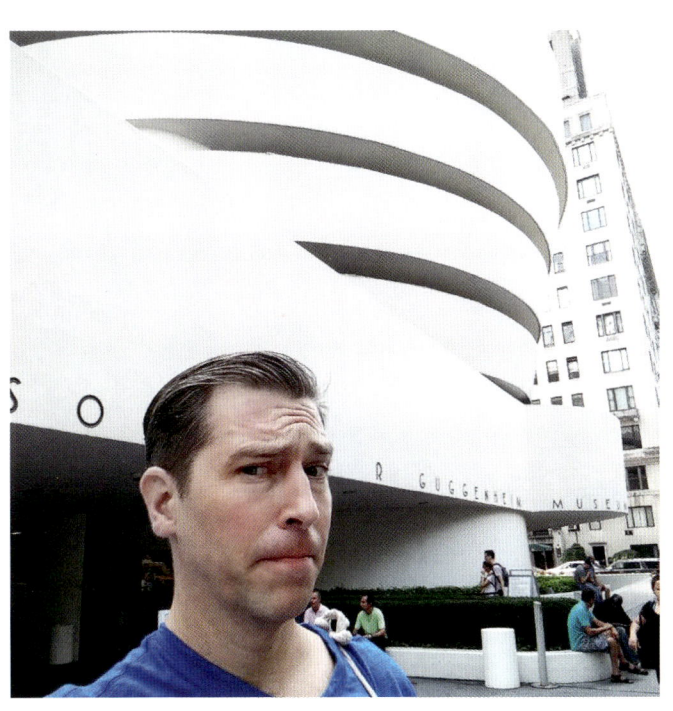

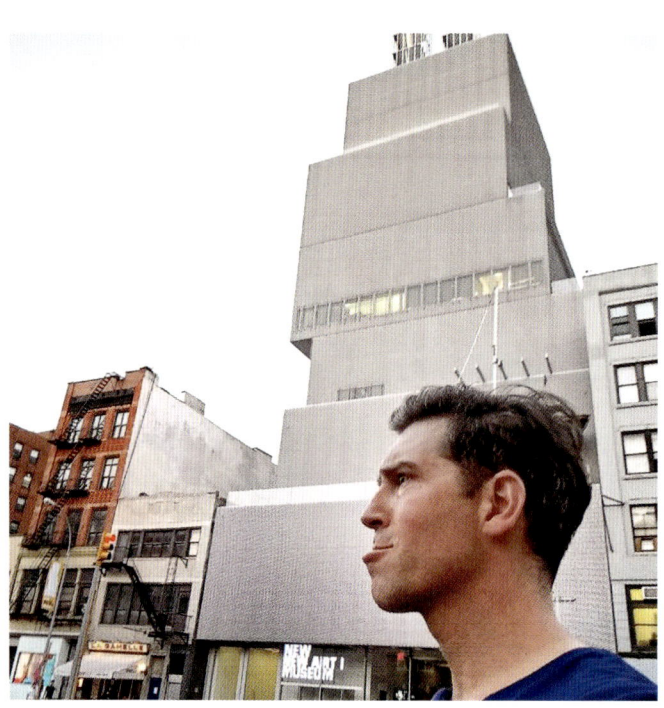

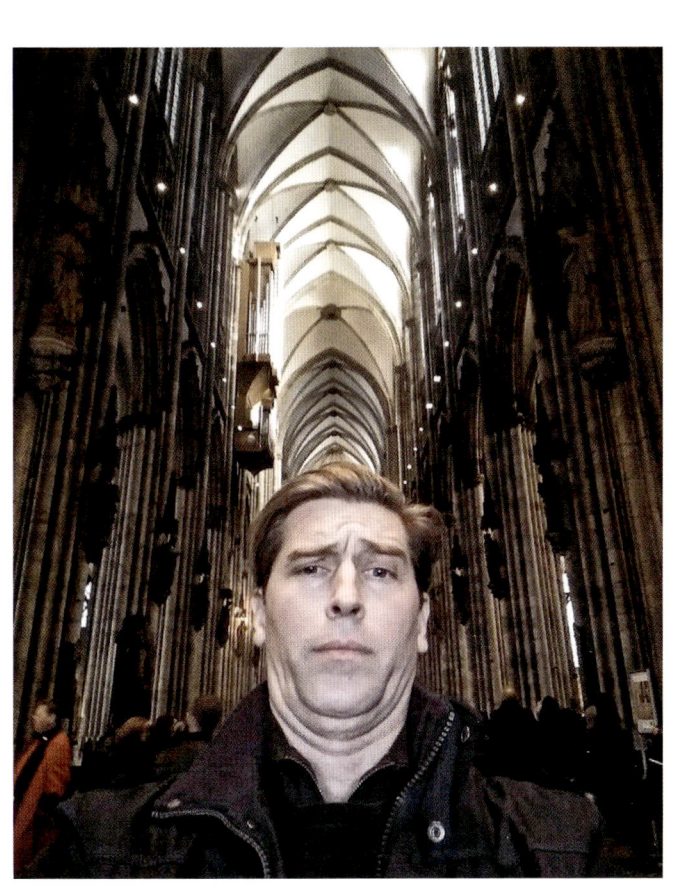

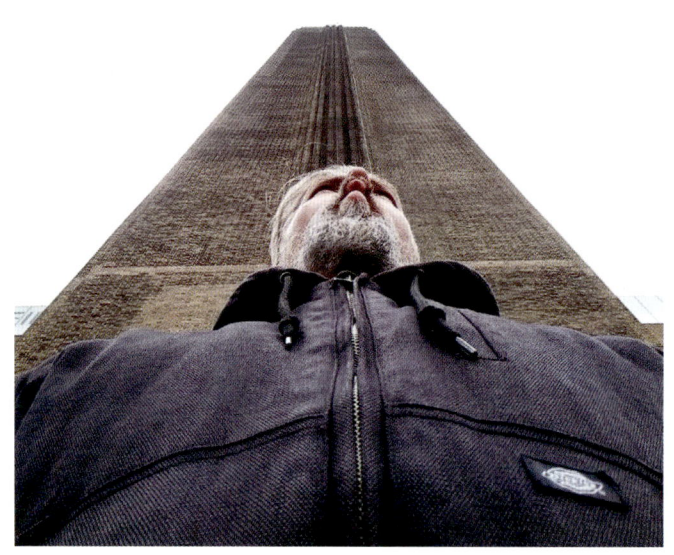

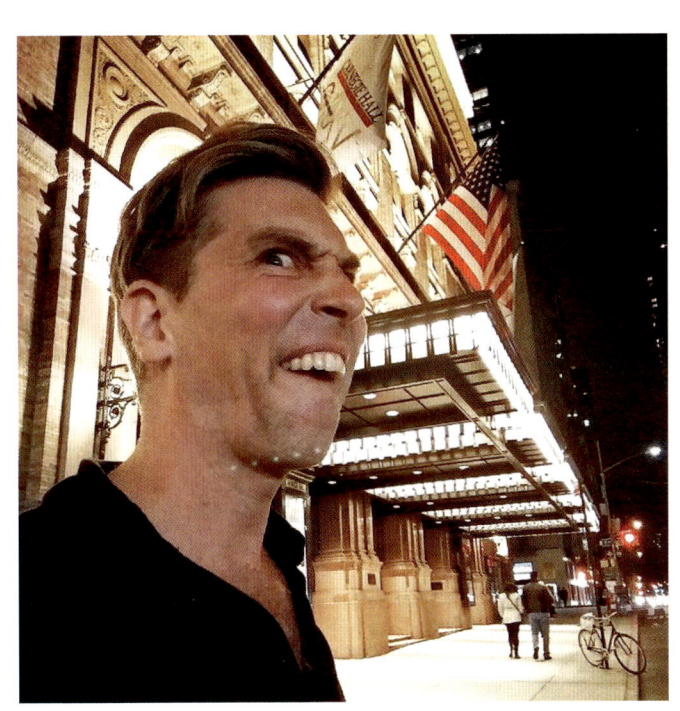

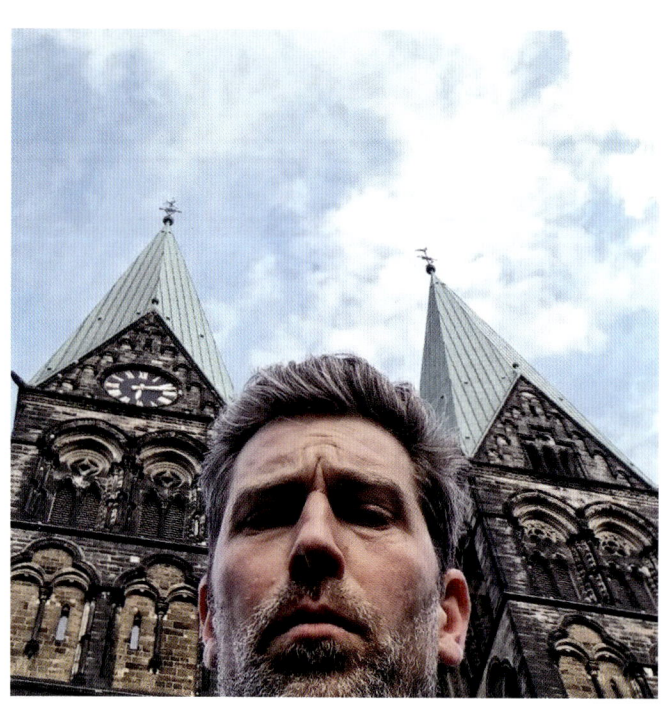

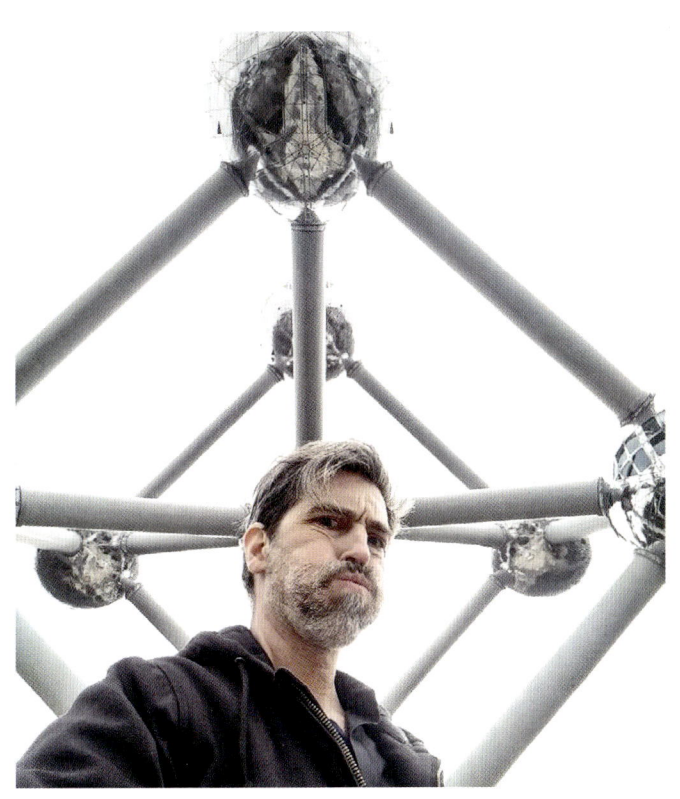

Colophon

Every effort has been made to contact all holders of the copyright to the visual material contained in this publication. Any copyright-holders who believe that illustrations have been reproduced without their knowledge are asked to contact the Lieven Gevaert Research Centre for Photography, Art and Visual Culture.

Lieven Gevaert Research Centre for Photography, Art and Visual Culture
Arts Faculty KU Leuven
Blijde-Inkomststraat 21 box 3313
B-3000 Leuven
Belgium

Editors: Mieke Bleyen and Liesbeth Decan
Lay-out and cover design: DOGMA

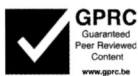

© 2019 by Leuven University Press / Universitaire Pers Leuven / Presses Universitaires de Louvain. Minderbroedersstraat 4, B-3000 Leuven (Belgium).

ISBN 978 94 6270 165 6
D/2019/1869/3
NUR: 652

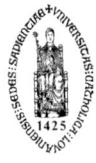 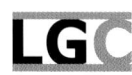 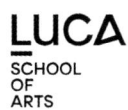 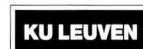 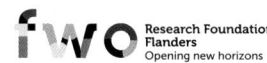